Power, Resistance and L
Therapy with Survivors of Trauma

This book offers reflections on how liberation might be experienced by clients as a result of the therapeutic relationship. It explores how power and resistance might be most effectively and ethically understood and utilised in clinical practice with survivors of trauma.

Power, Resistance and Liberation in Therapy with Survivors of Trauma draws together narrative therapy, coordinated management of meaning (CMM) and liberation psychology approaches. It critically reviews each approach and demonstrates what each contributes to the others as well as how to draw them together in a coherent way. The book presents:

- an original take on CMM through the lenses of power and resistance
- a new way of thinking about resistance in life and therapy, using the metaphor of creativity
- numerous case examples to support strong theory–practice links.

Through the exploration of power, resistance and liberation in therapy, this book presents innovative ways of conceptualising these issues. As such it will be of interest to anyone in the mental health fields of therapy, counselling, social work or critical psychology, regardless of their preferred model. It will also appeal to those interested in a socio-political contextual analysis of complex human experience.

Taiwo Afuape is a Principal Clinical Psychologist and Systemic Psychotherapist working in South Camden Community CAMHS for the Tavistock and Portman NHS Foundation Trust and Principal Systemic Psychotherapist in an adult psychology and psychotherapy service in CNWL NHS Foundation Trust.

Power, Resistance and Liberation in Therapy with Survivors of Trauma

To have our hearts broken

Taiwo Afuape

Routledge
Taylor & Francis Group
LONDON AND NEW YORK

First published 2011
by Routledge
2 Park Square, Milton Park, Abingdon, Oxon, OX14 4RN

Simultaneously published in the USA and Canada
by Routledge
711 Third Avenue, New York NY 10017

Routledge is an imprint of the Taylor & Francis Group, an Informa business

British Library Cataloguing in Publication Data
A catalogue record for this book is available from the British Library

Library of Congress Cataloging in Publication Data
Afuape, Taiwo, 1975- Power, resistance and liberation in therapy with
survivors of trauma : to have our hearts broken / Taiwo Afuape.
    p. cm.
  ISBN 978-0-415-61188-6 (hardback) – ISBN 978-0-415-61189-3
(paperback)
   1. Psychic trauma–Treatment. 2. Post-traumatic stressdisorder–
Treatment. 3. Psychotherapy. 4. Counseling. I. Title.
  RC552.P67A35 2011
  616.85'210651–dc22

                        2011005143

ISBN: 978-0-415-61188-6 (hbk)
ISBN: 978-0-415-61189-3 (pbk)
ISBN: 978-0-203-80640-1 (ebk)

Typeset in Times by Garfield Morgan, Swansea, West Glamorgan
Paperback cover design by Andrew Ward

Printed and bound by CPI Group (UK) Ltd, Croydon, CR0 4YY

Dedication

Dedicated to my twin sister Kehinde who does not know that I think she is amazing (and that I have a picture of her when we were kids on my wall at work). Special thanks to Mr Akanni Afuape (a deeply special and wonderful man and the only person whose love I have never questioned) and Mrs Bunmi Afuape (I am extremely grateful for our closeness and my inheritance as feisty, committed and passionate).

Contents

Acknowledgements

I would like to thank my loving siblings and gorgeous nephew; you are my heart and my strength (Tayo – intensely wise, deep and thoughtful; Dele – the kindest most generous gentle man I know; Funke/Sola – a thoroughly compassionate woman and sister; Kehinde – funny, sensitive, beautiful and committed; Lanre – vibrant, kind and warm). Thank you for making laughter, togetherness and affection such a fundamental part of my experience of family. Thank you father for your integrity, warmth and gentleness; for emotional sensitivity and intense wisdom. Thank you mother for showing me how to love; for telling me your stories and enabling me to have a richer understanding of you.

Thank you to all my friends, but in particular by best friends:

- Cristian Peña – for being a fantastic friend, always supporting and encouraging me and understanding my need to have a voice.
- Fausat Abioye – for understanding me, making me feel hopeful and alive, and leaving me in a mess of wet pants and split sides.
- Funké Baffour-Awah – I am a better, happier person for knowing you and being your friend. You are a wonderful person.
- Tracy Millar – for being the only person who can get me to do what I fear doing and laugh as I am doing it. Gorgeous person with gorgeous energy.
- Miriam Fornells-Ambrojo – for being the only person who can get me to wear heels! Thinking about you makes me smile instantly.
- Sejal Patel – the only person who gets me moshing and knee-sliding across dance floors! This deep-hearted woman will hold your hand as you struggle with life and death.
- Shampa Hussein and Rebecca Brown – my oldest close friends who love me just as much as they did when we were children.
- Shahid Gani – for never failing to be a ray of sunshine in my life and always being available, especially when I am at my lowest.

- Riz, Wayne, Rob S. and Rob G. – for gorgeous food, gorgeous conversation and gorgeous laughter; for holding my hand and letting me hold yours.

I would also like to thank:

- All the people who have come to me for support as clients. You have taught me many things, among them how to keep my heart open.
- David Lee, Sarah Amoss, David Harper, Zanele Nxumalo, Simon Platts and all the practitioners whom I have worked with and learnt from within the systemic consultation service.
- Glenda Fredman, Sharon Bond, Karen Partridge and Nimisha Patel. I would not be the person or therapist I am today if I had not met you amazing women. Your passion, commitment and abilities never cease to amaze me.
- Clinical supervisors past and present for the influences you have had on me and my thinking, in particular Aruna Mahtani, Bernadette Wren, Ellie Kavner and Gwyn Daniels.
- Adriana Peñalosa-Clarke for invaluable emotional support.
- Barnett Pearce, who moved me deeply when I met him.
- Thank you Tod Sloan for suggesting I write this book.
- Jnanavaca, Dhammadassin, Maitreyabandhu and Subhadramati for inspirational and loving kindness.

As Audre Lorde once said, I am truly grateful to you all for 'protecting me from throwing any part of myself away'. In helping me stay whole you have all helped me write this book.

Thank you Glenda Fredman, Sharon Bond, Cristian Peña and Tom Barlow for reading a draft of this book and giving me invaluable feedback.

Thanks also go to Elsevier Ltd publishing for permission to reproduce the CMM levels of context, Barnett Pearce for permission to reproduce the daisy model and Dulwich Centre for permission to refer to and reference Michael White's ideas from his workshop notes *Attending to the consequences of trauma* published on www.dulwichcentre.com.au on 21 September 2005.

All royalties from this book go to the Medical Foundation for the Care of Victims of Torture and the Afiya Trust – two London-based UK charities.

Introducing the introduction

Can life be captured by measuring it?

Despite the title, the first draft of this book had much less heart in it. Notwithstanding moments where I was present in the text, I tended to veer off into academic language, listing concepts and immersing the reader in unnecessary facts and figures. Interspersing my text with reams of statistics seemed to mirror a preoccupation in today's society with technique and evidence. In the minority world (the West), those who are not scientific and logical (not dominated by the head) are often described as sentimental (dominated by the heart), with an assumption that an orientation towards the head is superior.

Because science is considered in the minority world to be more rational, critical and intellectual than non-science – the highest state of mind, capable of grasping the 'truth' – it often dictates the best approach to take to experience. Scientific language, such as statistics, is a language of power because it can give legitimacy to ideas in ways that subjective experience cannot.[1] Despite challenges to the accuracy of this perspective, we still seem governed by the idea that it is by disconnecting from our hearts that we can see the world as it really is, rather than how we think it is or want it to be. Statistics seem to tell us that something is true, whereas describing personal experience can be easily dismissed, met with disbelief or viewed as self-indulgent. Yet it is personal stories and narratives that move us; that touch our hearts. Reducing human beings and human experience to facts and figures disconnects us, by keeping us in the realm of our heads and away from our hearts.

I felt relieved when Glenda Fredman, one of the people who kindly reviewed a draft of my manuscript, pointed out that I moved her in the parts where I was present and left her cold when I disappeared off the page to replace my voice with apparently superior language. This gave me permission to write more fully from the heart.

In 1998 Jan Fabre, a Belgian artist (sculptor, playwright, stage director, choreographer and designer) created a life-sized sculpture in bronze of a man on a ladder with a ruler in his hands measuring the clouds. In a 2004 interview with Michaël Amy for *Sculpture* magazine, Fabre said that the sculpture 'pays homage to my late brother, who was a dreamer. It expresses the feeling of planning the impossible, which is actually what the artist does. That figure symbolises my trade. Artists attempt to get a grip on things, but it never quite works out as planned. Life is so fluid and flexible: today, we are no longer where we stood yesterday . . . As an artist, I constantly measure the clouds . . . with the full understanding that it is an impossible mission' (Amy, 2004, p. 43).

Although Jan Fabre argues that artists try to measure the clouds, there is an explicit understanding that this task is impossible. It is this impossibility that makes art beautiful: a beauty-based awe in the face of nature's limitless possibility and complexity; not a belief in the ability to outsmart the universe by defining, controlling and quantifying it. In contrast, science has often tried to measure the immeasurable in ways that are intrinsically oppressive to diverse existence, such as the 'wondrously complex, multi-faceted, fluid set of human capabilities' that we call 'intelligence' (Gould, 1997, p. 56).

Ani (1994) makes a distinction between the 'madness of the head'[2] and what I refer to as the madness of the heart, arguing that Europeans both revere and fear the power of science. This fear can be seen in horror movies that depict the 'mad scientist' (for example Dr Frankenstein and Dr Jekyll). This is not 'the emotional confusion of an overly sensitive human being who refuses to accommodate to the inhumanity of contemporary life' (Ani, 1994, p. 245) – what we might call a form of resistance or a madness of the heart – but the madness that comes from giving power to 'the very absence of humanity' (Ani, 1994, p. 245) in the name of obtaining superior knowledge; that is, a madness of the head. Ani (1994) argues that we fear this head madness because we sense that in the cold rationalism that utilises the complete power of the head we risk losing connection with our heart.

Creative resistance from an engaged heart

Growing up in my household, the mystical, the emotional, the logical and the illogical reigned. As a result, I always felt deeply connected in my relationships and to the world around me. Life in the UK was not easy for my parents, who between them experienced bullying at work[3] and numerous intimate bereavements – of babies and parents – as well as racism and hostility. Yet they demonstrated creative resistance to these experiences by telling us about connection, loyalty and community. They told us about the development of The Progressive Circle, a group of Nigerian people who supported each other, formed after one of my parents' friends killed himself because he was lonely and depressed in racist Britain.

The summer holidays were also a time of creative resistance. My father encouraged us to play outside to be with our friends and to be with nature. Although we lived in a council flat in the inner city, we were encouraged to notice the trees and value the park nearby. When we came home he would ask us (including our friends) to write him a story or draw him a picture. My twin sister Kehinde and I would help my brother Dele make flapjacks, to distribute among our friends and neighbours. Whereas my father loves giving and receiving flowers as a sign of love, my mother is far more practical and shows love through her food. My mother loved cooking and singing and always sang as she cooked, about faith and freedom. To this day I love food cooked with love and can literally taste the love in it.

All these examples played an important part in shaping my belief that it is through engaging our hearts that we can be most creative and most liberated. I argue throughout this book that creativity is a useful metaphor for understanding and promoting resistance. I bring together narrative therapy, coordinated management of meaning (CMM) and liberation psychology approaches with clinical case examples[4] to reflect on the dynamics of power, resistance and liberation in counselling and therapy with people who have experienced what is often called trauma.

All therapies have a system of values and beliefs that direct what we are invited to critique, and what we are likely to take for granted as inherent in the approach. I have focused on exploring systemic approaches to therapy given that some systemic therapists have implied that the issue of power in therapy has been resolved. Despite this focus, this book is intended to be of interest to any clinician in the social work, counselling, therapy and psychology fields, and argues that all therapies should continuously reflect on themselves and actively involve clients in the process of working with power, resistance and liberation within and outside the relationship.

Introduction

To set the context for this book it feels important to explain who I am so that the reader can understand the influences on my approach to power, resistance, liberation and therapy. In doing so, I challenge the dichotomy between the subjective and objective by merging the personal, professional and political. It has been argued that artificial separations between private and public, psychological and social, mirror strategies of domination that bifurcate the world in simplistic ways and lessen our options for being whole (hooks, 1994). We cannot be objective narrators of fact; nor is it possible to write without an implicit or explicit desire to convince the reader of a particular point of view. Ultimately though, I do not imagine readers to be passive recipients of my reflections but to be an active audience reflecting on their own experiences as they read mine. Knowledge is not universal or static and readers are not empty. As Freire (1973) pointed out, to read (critically) is to rewrite, rather than to memorise or fully buy into the contents of the reading.

About me

I am a Nigerian British-born 35-year-old feminist, socialist/anarchist, 'heterosexual'[5] woman and I am motivated by a deep sense of social justice for all. I believe that the human 'male' and 'female' are social constructs (see Stoltenberg, 2000 for a fuller description of this view). Rather than being tolerant, I am actively pro-Gay,[6] and challenge homophobia and heterosexism.[7] Being a socialist/anarchist makes me lean towards trans-formatist politics, based on the importance of changing existing social structures to ensure equality and fairness for everybody.

I have worked in the NHS as a Clinical Psychologist and Systemic Psychotherapist for a number of years in adult, child and adolescent mental health services. I have helped set up community psychological services for transitional populations (women escaping domestic violence, refugee and asylum-seeking people, homeless people, the travelling community and substance misusers). I have worked in a human rights charity for survivors of torture (the Medical Foundation for the Care of Victims of Torture). I have managed a systemic consultation service. Currently I work in a Community Child and Adolescent Mental Health Service (CAMHS) for the Tavistock, Child and Family Department, as a dual-trained Principal Clinical Psychologist and Systemic Psychotherapist, as well as for Central and North West London NHS Trust with Karen Partridge in a psychology and psychotherapy mental health service training mental health practitioners in systemic psychotherapy. I do not see forms of mental and emotional distress as indications of individual pathology, deficit or disorder, but believe they are manifestations of people's experiences of abuse, oppression and violence.

As a Black African working-class woman, power, resistance and liberation are issues that are close to my heart. I grew up in a political, pro-woman, Afrocentric[8] household and saw everyday acts of community and kindness from my parents. I read about revolutionaries such as Huey Newton, Angela Y. Davis and Assata Shakur[9] as well as activist artists such as Ngugi Wa Thiong'o, Fela Kuti and his cousin Wole Soyinka, and watched films that challenged me to link compassion with activism (such as *In the Name of the Father, Cry Freedom, Biko, Gandhi*).

I regularly endure other people's overt and covert prejudices about Africa and African people, with the richness of these cultures being overlooked, misunderstood and misrepresented (even by those who themselves are targets for racism). I am also aware of my privilege as someone who is able-bodied, a professional earner, identified as heterosexual and free from organised violence and poverty. I became interested in Buddhism at a young age largely as a result of my father, who is a Rosicrucian (a non-religious philosophy based on ancient mysticism and a reverence for nature and the sacred feminine).[10] My father taught me to meditate and my sister Funke introduced me to yoga at a young age. As an adult I officially class myself as a Buddhist. A Buddhist value I connect deeply with is the idea of compassion, not as an individual virtue but as a true 'openness to otherness' (Diprose, 2002, p. 2; quoted in Jenkins, 2009).

One of my earliest memories is of my father gently stopping me from killing an insect I was about to step on, because, as he told me, all living things are sacred. In the same vein, my father would tell me that all human beings are equal and that if I treated people well they would treat me well. As a result I felt unprepared when I realised as a teenager that most of the White people I came across – even those I considered my friends – saw me as inferior to them. At college some of my peers could not hide their surprise and outrage that I had achieved better GCSE results than them. I could not understand why people talked to me about African culture, despite knowing I was African, as though it were backward and base. I noticed how as an African I was portrayed in the media as ignorant and primitive and in need of rescuing. Despite being pushed within my family to work hard, I sabotaged my efforts, hid my talents and found it difficult to talk with any confidence, and sometimes to talk at all.

Though I have firsthand experience, the primary scars I bear from racism are as a witness. When I was a child, as a treat my father would let me accompany him every night when he drove my mother to work. When I asked him why he was so frequently stopped by the police for increasingly ridiculous reasons (on one occasion the police officer told us he thought my father was under-age, despite my father being in his 50s at the time!) he would tell me 'they're just doing their job'. It did not make sense to me that my father had lied to us about human beings while also encouraging us to be political. It was much later that my father told me that he was bullied every day at work for 30 years and my mother told me that a dog was set on her by a racist gang when she was pregnant. It made sense to me on hearing these stories why my parents seemed to be somewhere else during my childhood; deeply connected to us *and* visibly disconnected; why their community and friendships were so important to them and why going home to Nigeria on holiday gave them a new lease of life. My parents and other relatives had been wounded more directly by an overt racism I had otherwise escaped. It made sense to me that my parents loved us enough to survive, and why it took me moving into adulthood to fully appreciate that love.

In 2005, while at a narrative therapy conference, I was talking to Jenny Miah, a clinical psychologist of Bangladeshi origin, about these experiences and she suggested that my father had done something very creative. By telling me we are all equal my father had given me a vision of what should be, what could be and what we should strive to create. He did not lie – he after all helped to shape us into activists deeply concerned about social justice. I realised talking to Jenny that my parents were not passive recipients of racism, but had been, and remain today, creative resisters. They had kept hope and the revolutionary power of possibilities alive. Jenny suggested that this was the greatest gift they could have given me. My mother resisted oppression by creating and valuing community more than herself. My father resisted oppression by passing down to his children the ethical imperative to strive for the liberation of everyone, as though it were already a living breathing reality. I was learning that hope, resistance and liberation are intricately linked; that to live life as though the limits imposed on us do not exist was a type of creativity, a type of liberation.

What we cannot or will not imagine is rarely able to come to fruition and it remains important for me to imagine possibilities of personal, interpersonal, collective and political transformation and to believe in the inherent capacity of all people to be compassionate. For Diprose (2002) hope is intimately linked to social justice whereby generosity 'grounds a passionate politics that aims for a justice that is not here yet' (Diprose,

2002, p. 14). We do this by getting to know people in ways that humanise them, in 'a world in which there is room for many worlds' (Subcommander Marcos, Zapatista Army of Liberation (EZLN), Mexico, 2000; quoted in Sandoval, 2000).

From my mother I learnt about community. Although I felt she was emotionally 'somewhere else' for much of my childhood, I frequently witnessed her giving emotional and practical support to people in our family and neighbourhood. My mother saw the wellbeing of every child as being partly her responsibility (for example, she would help lone children cross the road more safely or stop children who were fighting). Although my mother was always tired from working (too) hard, she always had time and energy for her community, and her community was made up of everyone she came into contact with. I would walk past her in the street listening intently to one of the numerous people who came to her for counsel and advice. My mother's friends were and are the most loyal and loving I have met. I accompanied her (often begrudgingly!) to celebrations and funerals where I witnessed the ways communities can support each other in times of great joy and great sadness. Although I felt shy and out of place surrounded by adults who were part of my mother's life and not directly part of mine, I often felt deeply moved by collective demonstrations of love and connection.[11]

As a result of my parents' deep sense of community, I envisioned a kind of society in which diverse cultures existed and developed side by side in harmony rather than being melted together or ranked on a scale of evolving 'civilisation'. In my early teens I became interested in the parallels, differences and challenges inherent in attempting to address the diversity of issues related to forms of domination – from Australian Aboriginal history and culture to Irish history and culture – as well as an interest in the destruction of natural forms of life and ecosystems. I was aware that there are so many issues to address that it is easy for some to get lost or for a particular group to feel excluded from critical discourse. Yet I did not want to narrow my interest or focus purely on my experience of domination. Mutua (2006) argues that even when energies are focused on one issue of social difference, 'there is a difference between concentrating energies in one direction as a practical matter and assuming that this one effort is the whole' (p. 34). In addition, 'in our everyday lives we are undoubtedly presented with multiple micro-activities that strengthen multiple movements' (Mutua, 2006, p. 34), such as seeing offensive talk about Black men, Gay people, Muslims and so on as opportunities to challenge oppression.

I began to see a world in which much of what was intrinsically cruel, destructive and dehumanising was passed off as human nature. I searched for an alternative view to contrast the capitalist distortion of liberation as the generous and benign gift of 'development' to the 'developing' world; an alternative that would not obscure the cruelty of poverty, exploitation and greed. I wanted an alternative to the prevailing tendency to fragment oppression into different forms and therefore invite different allegiances, as well as an alternative to the tendency to make values associated with being subordinate to values associated with having. I wanted to move away from ahistorical, reductionist and apolitical analyses of injustice and oppression that saw domination as inevitable.[12]

Prior to studying psychology I worked as an auxiliary nurse on psychiatric wards in London. Some of the experiences I had there were horrendous (such as participating in helping ward staff pin down patients – sometimes with a history of rape – in order to forcibly inject them with medication), and highlights how easily and often with good intentions we enact violence for other people's 'own good'.

It is from this background that my passion for challenging oppression, abuse and marginalisation has become the foreground for my approach to being with clients (Afuape, 2004, 2006). I trained as a clinical psychologist and systemic psychotherapist in institutions that emphasised critical reflection on traditional forms of therapy, with respect to attention to power and social context. I did not see my role as a psychologist as helping individuals and families adapt to, adjust to and cope with the status quo, given that it is often within the status quo that causes of suffering and distress can be found. I became committed to challenging aspects of the mental health system that are oppressive, supporting user-empowerment and critiquing the medical model view of emotional distress. Unlike Lee (2005) I have not yet 'honed my ability to be impeccably articulate' (Lee, 2005, p. 109) which is necessary to survive a White middle-class male world and in a profession that continues to locate me as 'the other'. Writing is my means of articulating what I might find hard to say.

I have been influenced by Thích Nhất Hạnh's socially engaged Buddhism (Nhất Hạnh, 2003) and Dharmic socialism (Sivaraksa, 1992). My supervisors at the Medical Foundation, Nimisha Patel and Aruna Mahtani, supported me in using psychological theory to advocate for individual and collective liberation, such as getting asylum. I was fortunate enough to be clinically supervised by Glenda Fredman and Sharon Bond from a social constructionist systemic perspective. The ideas discussed in supervision were about living, so did not stay in the professional sphere, but influenced how I was in the world. Without this integration of my personal/professional connections to power, resistance and liberation, I might have separated out my commitments and obligations as a professional from my commitments and obligations as a citizen, subordinating the latter to the former, and thus separating out what I do from who I am. Although revolutionary social and community activity is always important, I believe that there is revolution under the surface of everyday living. As Babacan and Gopalkrishnan (2001) suggest: 'When oppression becomes the norm, resistance becomes duty' (p. 3).

Evidence-based practice and its critiques

Over the past two decades there has been increasing emphasis in all areas of applied psychology in the minority world (such as the UK, Canada, the US and Australia) on basing professional practice on evidence – what has come to be known as 'evidence-based practice' (Harper, Mulvey & Robinson, 2003; Marston & Watts, 2003; American Psychological Association (APA), 2005). Although this approach originated in medicine it has been adopted in many other health and social care fields such as social work, probation, education, human resource management, dentistry, nursing, physiotherapy and mental health (Trinder, 2000), and has been met with both enthusiasm and criticism. Despite the intuitive, common-sense logic that seems to be inherent in the idea, what is understood as evidence and what practitioners do in practice are fairly diverse (Harper et al., 2003).

According to Marston and Watts (2003), the term evidence-based practice 'is a catch phrase for 'scientific', 'scholarly' and 'rationality'' (pp. 144–5). The APA *Policy Statement on Evidence-Based Practice in Psychology* (2005) states the following: 'Evidence-based practice in psychology (EBPP) is the integration of the best available research with clinical expertise in the context of patient characteristics, culture, and preferences . . . Generally, evidence derived from clinically relevant research on psychological practices should be based on systematic reviews, reasonable effect sizes, statistical and clinical significance, and a body of supporting evidence' (p. 1).

Alongside this emphasis has been a comprehensive critique of the kind of evidence that promoters of evidence-based practice advocate, the notion of the applied psychologist as a scientist-practitioner, and whether the type of research that is currently done is the most useful for helping people in practice. In determining what evidence is, the views and experiences of service users and carers are relegated to the lowest category. In the field of health care, the randomised controlled trial (RCT) has come to be seen as a gold standard of evidence, and yet this form of research is not able to answer questions such as: what sorts of interventions lead to clients feeling liberated? How is power and resistance most effectively and ethically understood and utilised in clinical practice?

It has been suggested that we need to move towards practice-based evidence rather than evidence-based practice (Harper et al., 2003); the reflective practitioner who draws on research evidence but combines it with past experience and other knowledge, rather than the scientist-practitioner (Harper et al., 2003) and 'evidence-influenced'/'evidence-aware' as more realistic descriptions of what can be achieved and what is more often the case in practice (Nutley, Davies & Walter, 2002, 2003).

This international climate emphasising evidence-based practice with a focus on short-term, individual-focused interventions to treat social-psychological difficulties means that opportunities to work on wider systems (beyond families and other significant relationships) are becoming harder and harder to engage in and/or justify. Given the growing constraints of employing institutions as well as the ways in which traditional approaches of the 'psy' field[13] tend to operate on the assumption that social issues remain the same, I have in the past contemplated leaving the 'psy' profession and channelling my critiques of oppressive social structures and discourses into personal and political commitments at the edges of the discipline. In the end (at the risk of being viewed as not radical enough or too benign) I decided to look for ways of bringing ideas about power, resistance and liberation into the therapy room and integrate who I am with what I do.

Power, resistance and liberation

In November 1989, when I was 14 years old, Ignacio Martín-Baró – a Jesuit parish priest, psychologist, theologian and liberation theorist – was assassinated along with seven other people by US-trained Salvadorian government soldiers (Montero & Sonn, 2009). During his life Martín-Baró developed liberation psychology based on the suffering he witnessed in Latin America. Although liberation psychology is associated with Latin America, there were liberation theorists before Martín-Baró, such as the world-renowned African American sociologist, philosopher, historian, novelist, poet and editor Dr William Edward Burghardt (W.E.B) Du Bois, writing in the early decades of the twentieth century. Du Bois' thought-provoking and erudite body of work has often been left out of the critical canon despite the fact that he remains one of the most important proponents of critical and liberation theory. Among other insights Du Bois critiqued positivism (a philosophy of science that separates object from subject and argues that the only authentic knowledge is objective knowledge) and argued that human experience is not machine-like and research cannot be disinterested and neutral, for it is always informed by particular, albeit hidden, values.

Is liberation only possible outside of therapy?

Despite the culture of evidence-based practice, there is concurrently a growing interest in liberation and social justice approaches to therapy: so much so that I would not be able to do justice to them all here (see Waldegrave, 1990; McGoldrick et al., 1999; Bernstein, 2000; Mason & Sawyerr, 2003; McDowell et al., 2003; Vera & Speight, 2003; Waldegrave, Tamasese, Tuhaka & Campbell, 2003; Waldegrave, 2005, 2009; Almeida, Dolan-Del Vecchio & Parker, 2007, 2008; Kosutic & McDowell, 2008; McGoldrick & Hardy, 2008). As well as liberation psychology, other authors have written about interventions on wider systemic levels that are designed to address the social reality of oppressed clients, such as 'just therapy' (Waldegrave et al., 2003); network therapy (Copello, Orford, Hodgson & Tober, 2009) and multi-systems therapy (Boyd-Franklin & Hafer Bry, 2000). These approaches view vulnerability to emotional distress as compounded and mediated by social, political, cultural and economic factors that necessitate proactive interventions, rather than accepting the status quo and reinforcing inequalities (Patel, 2003). For example, McDowell (2005) argues that we need to go 'beyond being "weekend warriors" for social justice or viewing multiculturalism as an elective stance' (p. 2).

Liberation psychology, in particular, has led critical psychologists and therapists to argue that any form of counselling and therapy is inherently ineffective as it focuses on the individual at the exclusion of acting on social structures and systems. For example, Prilleltensky, Dokecki, Frieden and Ota Wang (2007) write that 'the convenience of working with individuals is not enough justification for a professional practice. In some respects, it is like looking for the penny where there is light, rather than looking for it where it got dropped' (Prilleltensky et al., 2007, p. 32). As a result liberation psychology tends to encourage radical forms of community psychology, in which the creation of a just society is the ultimate goal, rather than a focus on what happens within the confines of the therapy relationship.

Ideally social justice, liberation and social action approaches should guide intervention in all mental health practices and not just be associated with what community psychologists or radical/critical psychologists do. Otherwise it might be assumed that the vast majority of 'psy' clinicians, who are not community psychologists, absolve themselves of the responsibility of doing therapy in a socially responsible, socially engaged and transformative way.

Although I am aware that many types of therapy have discussed power – for example, talking about psychoanalytic psychotherapy Totton (2006) argues that '*by making the struggle over power a central focus of the therapeutic encounter*, we do as Freud did with transference: turn a structural problem into a creative aspect of therapy' (p. 83; emphasis in original) – I have mainly focused on systemic therapy because of certain opportunities and constraints. With respect to opportunities: psychologies of liberation have tended to borrow from the psychoanalytic tradition, in order to analyse the unconscious effects of oppression on the oppressed (e.g. Alschuler, 2006). There seems an opportunity therefore to change the focus by drawing more heavily on systemic theory and its links with liberation psychology. In doing so we might better understand the context that helps to give rise to acts of violence, prejudice and oppression, rather than attempting to understand the 'psychic structures' of 'perpetrators' or the 'internalised oppression' of 'victims'. With respect to constraints: there have been some bold claims regarding the issue of power being addressed and eradicated in systemic therapy (e.g. Anderson & Goolishian, 1990). Despite emphasising relationships and context, systemic therapy is still open to the trap of reducing socio-political issues to marginal concerns focused on the individual in interaction with their immediate environment.

I hope that the reflections I make will be of interest to all who embark on counselling and therapy regardless of their particular orientation. I hope to reflect on how we can enter into a space in counselling and therapy where our hearts can be touched by what we hear and we feel galvanised into action.

William C. Madsen (2007) refers to an *anthropological approach to intervention* that continually attempts to elicit and understand the particular perspective of the clients we see, and Ruth Behar (1996) has called for an 'anthropology that breaks your heart'; that is, a way of entering into each encounter with people 'not at a safe objective distance but up close' (Watkins & Shulman, 2008, p. 31). Watkins and Shulman go on to argue that 'we need a psychology that breaks our heart, because only that kind of psychology could awaken us to our entanglements in strategies of dissociation, to the despairs of trauma, to grief from mourning, and to potential joy in restoration and healing' (p. 31). This book is about the heart breaking; about the ways our encounter with life, in relationship with others, leaves open the potential to love, share, connect, harm and be harmed.

The breath and the heart

Buddhist ideas about interconnection, community and compassion heavily influence who I am and what I do. I have been particularly influenced by the heart and the breath, which are at the centre of Buddhist practice.

The breath

Breathing is an important part of meditation and Buddhist practice. The careful focus on the breath that connects me to the experience of my body and to the present moment helps me to create space around my experiences in order to act creatively, as well as reminding me that everything in life is interconnected and impermanent. Breathing is also a reminder that life is about give and take. The Benedictine monk Brother David Steindl-Rast puts it this way:

> Mere giving is as lifeless as mere taking. If you merely take a breath and stop there, you are dead. And when you merely breathe out and stop there, you are also dead. Life is not giving or taking, but give-and-take. Breathing is an obvious example, but the same give-and-take can be found wherever there is life.
>
> (Steindl-Rast, 1984, p. 199)

Sometimes when I am with clients I think about this quote and focus on my breathing as a reminder that I am in a relationship of give and take. Focusing on my body also connects me to the mystery of life, given that our bodies are a crystallisation of the fluid space between birth and death, in addition to the network of connection between all living things.

The heart

The heart, at least in most cultures in modern society, is the place where we most deeply respond to the world. The heart features in many cultural metaphors of how crucial a deep sense of connection is to our continued existence. Everyday sayings about the heart convey a rich range of metaphors describing its centrality in our understanding of ourselves, our experiences and each other. With our heart we decide what is important in our lives, what we have our hearts set on; we are more likely to do well at something if our hearts are in it; we have communicated deeply and with genuine affection if we enter into a heart-to-heart; to get to the centre, we go to the heart (Vessantara, 2006). Even without words, when we place our hand over our heart it is generally understood as a sign of deep feeling and sincerity.

Connecting the breath and heart

Breathing can be used to open our hearts by helping us to:

- pause and reflect
- get in touch with what we are feeling in the present moment
- face and stay with suffering rather than turning away.

When supervisees talk about feeling overwhelmed by the suffering they see and experience in sessions with clients and as a consequence feel stuck, I often draw on Buddhist practice to offer suggestions about ways of staying open to the experience in the room and open to the person suffering. This can be useful when supervisees:

- feel strong emotions in response to clients' suffering that they do not find helpful or know what to do with, such as anger, fear, numbness, disconnection or disbelief
- feel a blockage to compassion
- feel stuck in terms of what to do or where to go therapeutically
- do not know how to respond.

When strong emotions petrify supervisees I might suggest that they scan their bodies in the moment to locate and connect with where they feel stuck or tight (for me it is almost always my stomach; for others it might be their chest or jaw) and breathe into it. This can introduce space and warmth into the experience and enable them both to reflect on themselves and to be responsive to the client.

For people who feel tightness in their chest when they are stuck, I might suggest they imagine the area around their chest and heart becoming wider and more expansive as they breathe deeply and mindfully into it. For those who feel a blockage to compassion I might suggest that as they breathe deeply they imagine something like an umbilical cord connecting the client's heart with theirs.

I sometimes share my own experiences of using breathing when I am overwhelmed or disconnected. For example, if I am witnessing intense distress that I find myself shifting away from in some way, I sometimes imagine that my heart is expanding as wide as it needs to be in order to take in and accommodate whatever is present, and let it in completely (Chödrön, 2001). I breathe in the pain and breathe out compassion. If I am ashamed of or want to reject the difficult feelings arising in me in response to suffering, I might visualise my heart opening as I breathe in so that I take in fully all the unpleasant feelings arising in me and breathe out compassion towards myself. Rather than rejecting or denying my emotional experience in the room I try to connect with it in order to move from a self-preoccupation to responsivity to the other. Breathing in this way keeps me returning to the client's suffering, connecting with it as fully as possible.

Connecting the heart and breath also helps move me closer to pain so I can see it more richly – not just with respect to negative cognitions and erroneous internal dialogue but within the context of social disadvantage, isolation, abuse, oppression, violence, discrimination and so on. My heart opening pulls me to action in a way that shutting down or jumping into my head does not.

As Chödrön (2001) points out we never really know what someone else is feeling or what might help them. So I might simply breathe in and out with a general intention of being present and soothing rather than assuming I know what the remedy is.

The aim of this book is to explore how we do therapy as a fully heart-opening activity. Once our heart is open it can be broken, and anything that breaks inevitably changes. When I talk of broken hearts in this context I do not mean the anguish that comes with the end of an amorous relationship; or any type of romantic heartache. When I think of my heart breaking in therapy I think of the ways I deeply connect and deeply care. I think of the tensions of life, pulling us in different directions, threatening to tear us apart, but potentially expanding us. The metaphor of a broken heart reminds me of the importance of being moved both to feel and to act.

This book aims to explore power, resistance and liberation in ways that preserve or enhance the humanity of us all. I critically deconstruct the concept of trauma as an intra-psychic, individual and cognitive phenomenon in favour of a view of psycho-social trauma located in historical, social and political context. I hope to highlight a few of the ideas about power, resistance and liberation that I have drawn from and drawn together, which have been forged in multiple locations. My aim is to bring together liberation psychology, coordinated management of meaning (CMM) and narrative approaches that are not usually in communication with each other, to focus on what can happen within therapy towards a liberation agenda. In doing so, I hope to highlight possible ways of working that any practitioner can practice, rather than feeling defeated by the challenge of replicating in its entirety a community psychology agenda within the confines of the 'psy' systems in which we work. It is hoped that this book will act as a springboard that energises clinical practice with liberatory vigour.

It may come as a surprise to the reader that many of the ideas that have touched my heart I have critiqued in this book. My intention in doing this is to reflect on the potential misuse of *any* theory, particularly those that seduce us. Ironically I critically reflect on these ideas *because* they have moved and inspired me and because, like my father, they have done so by encouraging me to be critical.

This book is divided into four parts. *Part I* explores power and resistance in society and in therapy. I also reflect on the concept of trauma using a power, resistance and liberation lens, particularly with respect to people who experience complex psycho-social difficulties (often called people with mental health problems) and survivors of war, organised violence and torture, as these two groups have been written about extensively. By looking more closely at these specific client groups my aim is to introduce a way of working that can be applied more generally.

Part II takes a critical look at the theories I have been attracted to in my quest to ground liberation into the very essence and fabric of my clinical practice, as well as how I have attempted to draw them together.

Part III presents examples of how a focus on power, resistance and liberation might manifest itself in clinical practice, guided by the three tasks of a liberation psychology proposed by Martín-Baró (1996): (1) The recovery of historical memory, (2) de-ideologising everyday experience, (3) utilising the people's virtues.

Part IV draws together the ideas presented in the previous chapters and looks more deeply into the concept of resistance as creativity and therapy that breaks our heart. I reflect on the ideas I have presented and offer some final thoughts on these complex issues where final conclusions are almost impossible.

Part I

Therapy, power, resistance and trauma

Chapter 1

Therapy and social context

Systemic therapy[14]

Systemic theory and practice holds out enormous promise because of its focus on relationships and social context as well as a desire to be respectful of diversity and difference. Based on a belief in the importance of multiple perspectives, systemic therapists often work with reflecting teams (Andersen, 1997), which are two or more people other than the therapist in the therapy room who listen to the therapeutic conversation and, when asked, make reflections to each other about what they have heard (see Appendix for a detailed description of social constructionist systemic therapy). Liberation theorists explicitly highlight the need for a systemic approach to psychological difficulties. Martín-Baró (1996), for example, argued that 'there is no person without family, no learning without culture, no madness without social order; and therefore neither can there be an I without a We, a knowing without a symbolic system, a disorder that does not have reference to moral and social norms' (p. 41). Martín-Baró went on to say: 'no learning process, vocational guidance, or therapeutic counselling can hope to see the development or realisation of persons if it does not cast the individual in his or her social and national context' (p. 42).

Some bold claims about power being addressed have been made by proponents of systemic therapy. For example, Harlene Anderson and Harry Goolishian, in their collaborative language systems approach, comment: 'We . . . reject the position that power and control are essential concepts either to the understanding or the practice of the therapeutic process' (Anderson & Goolishian, 1990, p. 160). In addition, Anderson (2001) seems to suggest that therapists can choose whether or not to use their power.

Systemic therapy is interested in people not on an individual level, but in relationship to others and the social environment. Older forms of family therapy, such as strategic and structural interventions utilising a therapist's expertise and power to influence change, were criticised as imperialistic and patriarchal (McNamee & Gergen, 1992). Like any institution and social practice, family therapy was thought to support dominant values in ways that rendered invisible the workings of oppression based on gender, skin colour, sexuality, class, economic situation, culture, and so on. Critics argued that the corrective nature of structural and strategic interventions was disrespectful to clients' own meaning-making and expertise. It was argued that for therapy to be useful it has to make sense to all participants and not just the therapist.

Guided by social constructionist theory, systemic theorists proposed that narrative become a root metaphor to guide systemic intervention, making it a dialogical reflexive process where therapists and clients co-create what the relationship is (Goolishian & Andersen, 1992; Hoffman, 1992).

The table in the Appendix outlines the philosophical movement in family therapy from *positivism*, which viewed the world as having a fixed quality that could be observed objectively, to *constructivism*, which recognised that what we see is influenced by our individual perception, through to *social constructionism*, which went even further in explaining the inherently social interactional nature of reality.

Explaining social constructionism – the red rose

Undeniably reality is imbued with meaning that comes with emotional connection. Giving a personal example of this, the colour red has many powerful associations for me, representing compassion and revolution (I am a socialist), passion and fire (I am Aries) as well as love and romance (I am idealistic). My most meaningful connection is with my father's love of red roses that were always in my house growing up (a red rose forms part of the AMORC emblem; the symbol of the sacred feminine and of the heart). My father always buys red roses for my mother on her birthday and Valentine's Day and when his mother died he dropped a single red rose on her grave as she was buried. Red roses are important to me with respect to emotional memories and aspects of my identity; they are redolent of passion, love and respect.

Yet we could ask the rather strange question, what makes a red rose a red rose? A positivist approach might argue that red roses are an objective fact existing out there in the real world. However, Bracken (2002) points out: 'when I look at a flower and see it as red and beautiful I can do so only because my human physiology allows me to see (or reveal) a certain part of the electromagnetic spectrum and make contrasts with other colours' (p. 89). Constructivists would agree that this act of perception is determined by our individual ability to perceive the colour red, hence a colour-blind person would have a different reality of the rose. Social constructionists view this act of perception as never passive, but always a social, cultural and interactional act of creation. That is, we know a red rose as a beautiful red flower, and all the emotional associations that come with this knowing, 'only because [we] have the idea of a flower and the notion of beauty available to [us]. [We] experience the world with words, beliefs, emotions and patterns of thought that come from the social world' (Bracken, 2002, p. 89). The idea that things are what we agree to call them applies just as much to engrained social concepts such as 'man' and 'woman' as it does to everyday objects like a red rose.

This movement away from the idea of objective, quantifiable positivism to an understanding of experience as co-created and socially constructed changes the nature of how we understand the world. To say that reality is not discovered through objective means but agreed upon through social interaction is not to deny the emotional connections we have in the moment-to-moment experience of living. For instance, to talk about psycho-social difficulties and distress rather than mental illness is to challenge the view of a disease entity residing within individuals that has been objectively dis-covered, measured and researched by scientists. It is *not* to dismiss the meaningful experiences of individuals.

Given that systemic therapy is interested in individuals in context, it might be assumed that systemic therapists automatically consider and address power. There are many different traditions within systemic therapy all of which have slightly different approaches to the issue of power, resistance and liberation. Harlene Anderson was influenced by social con-structionist thinking and developed 'collaborative therapy' approaches, but reflected less on ways in which dominant discourses could be challenged in therapy. Steve de Shazer and Michael White are often compared as they both emphasised liberation from the problem with respect to 'exceptions' in the case of de Shazer and 'unique outcomes' in the case of White. However, unlike de Shazer, White acknowledged resistance as a response to power and talked about ways to deconstruct dominant discourses.

In the next chapter I hope to explore the nature of power and resistance further and argue that all therapies, regardless of their theoretical and epistemological starting point, should continually reflect on the complexity of power, resistance and liberation in counselling and therapy and the lives of clients. I argue that systemic approaches to counselling and therapy are just as much in danger of neglecting these issues as any other therapy.

With respect to *power*: I start by briefly describing some of the numerous ways we can think about power, before reflecting on power in society, with respect to poverty, prejudice and oppression. I then explore the concept of power in therapy, and start by critiquing traditional approaches in systemic therapy of either dismissing the importance of power or claiming to have overcome it; before reflecting on therapy as a form of social control and cultural imperialism. Lastly I reflect on power in therapy with respect to power bases, processes and outcomes (Proctor, 2002).

With respect to *resistance*: I start by critiquing the traditional psycho-therapeutic use of the term and outlining my definition of resistance as a political concept. I make brief reference to the distinctions between reactive/

destructive and reflective/creative resistance. I describe resistance as a fundamental theme in history, before exploring resistance as a creative process. I
then reflect on resistance in therapy, critiquing traditional family therapy
understandings of resistance, before describing a dialogical/collaborative
approach to resistance in therapy.

Chapter 2

Power

What is power?

There are various ways of thinking about power depending on our world-view, personal experience and philosophical standpoint. For example, Proctor (2002) describes four different types of power:

- power over: domination, coercion or authority
- power with: collective power
- power from within: personal resources, abilities and values
- power to: individual strength or influence.

Another way of describing the various guises power takes, with respect to its creative and destructive potential, is provided by Prilleltensky and Nelson (2002):

> Power refers to the capacity and opportunity to fulfil or obstruct personal, relational or collective needs. We distinguish among power to strive for wellness, power to oppress, and power to resist oppression and strive for liberation. In each instance, the exercise of power can apply to self, others, and collectives.

> (p. 7)

I argue in this book that by valuing resistance in therapy we might minimise the negative effects of power (such as domination) and maximise the positive ones (such as collective power; resistance against structures of domination and coordinating the power from within of both the client and the therapist).

Power in society

Poverty

Not to talk about poverty would be to ignore the most pervasive manifestation of power as a form of oppression that society knows. Poverty is our greatest crime. If I am wrong, and there *is* such a thing as evil, it is not an individual or group of individuals but a state we have collectively created. It is my belief that if evil exists, it exists as poverty: the material manifestation of the global asymmetry of power and privilege. The extent of global inequality is overwhelmingly tragic and should be totally intolerable, yet we in the minority world[15] (the West) seem to have become desensitised to it, enjoying our privileges in our daily lives largely without question, apart from the occasional pang of conscience. Celebrities who 'adopt' children from the majority world appear to grab the interest of the media and reduce solutions to global poverty to grossly simplistic and paternalistic actions. We could argue that the publicity surrounding these actions further marginalises global and political issues, such as grossly unjust and unequal distributions of wealth and capitalist exploitation, that underlie and perpetuate a situation whereby millions of people die needlessly every year and 800 million people worldwide are hungry (Green, 2008).

With respect to poverty in the UK, it is impossible to work in mental health with people who are experiencing complex psycho-social difficulties and emotional distress and not regularly come across issues related to the impact of social deprivation.

> Meena was a single mother living with her eight-year-old son José in a one-bedroom flat infested with rats and mice. Meena was referred for depression and anxiety in relation to her son's 'difficult behaviour'. José was withdrawn and 'defiant' towards his mother and described feeling that it was 'unfair' that he did not have his own room to sleep in and that at night mice ran over him and chewed his hair.

Women in the UK are more likely to be poor and live in poverty than men despite the fact that the true extent of their poverty is hidden (Bradshaw, Finch, Kemp, Mayhew & Williams, 2003). Life expectancy in the UK's wealthiest areas is seven to eight years longer than in the poorest areas (Green, 2008). Given this global and national picture, power can be viewed as having some effect and influence on the world as well as access to sought-after resources. It is clear from this definition that some groups of people have less power than others. In addition to this definition, we need to take account of how ideas and discourses serve to create and uphold oppressive social structures, such that those in power further narrow interests rather than those for the collective and greater good. According to Green (2008) it is not only a moral imperative but a viable possibility to eradicate poverty, given that the global economy has the resources to do so. One third of each year's global military spending would lift the poorest people on the planet above the extreme poverty line (UNDP, 2005). I would argue that what prevents the eradication of poverty is pervasive beliefs and ideas in society, such as racism and misogyny. Continents mainly made up of people with brown skin are more likely to be poor and exploited by powerful White nations. Within continents in both the minority and the majority worlds, the more Black you are identified as being, the poorer you are likely to be. For instance, Black Brazilians are twice as likely to die a violent death and three times as likely not to go to university as White Brazilians (Ciconello, 2007, quoted in Green, 2008). Due to discrimination against girls and women, the world's female population is lower than it should be compared to males, through selective abortions, nutritional and educational neglect as well as matricide, sororicide and filicide. A shocking 101.3 million women are estimated to be 'missing' in this way, mainly from India (7 per cent of its expected female population) and China (8 per cent of its expected female population) (UNDP, 2005).

Power and discourse

Discourses are the processes of interaction between people and the products of those interactions such as what we write, what we say and what we think. Discourses therefore help to construct meaning, shape behaviour and uphold structural inequalities (Burr, 2003). For example, racist representations of young Black men as violent legitimises the exclusion of Black males. Being Black and educated does not preclude one from experiencing racism; for instance, educated African men are five times more likely to be unemployed than their White English counterparts (Trade Union Congress, 2001). Hare-Mustin (1994) argues that 'meaning making and control over language are important resources held by those in power' (p. 21). That is, to define the world or a person in a way that allows you to do the things you want is to exercise power. Therefore power is enacted in what people think, say and do.

Representing women as sexual objects of male desire legitimises sexual exploitation and violence towards women and children. As a result of pervasive homophobia and heterosexism, Gay and bisexual men and women face discrimination, bullying, harassment, violence and hate crimes in their homes, schools, workplaces and within the wider community. *Breaking the Chain of Hate*, the National Advisory Group's 1999 survey of homophobic crime, found that 66 per cent of the 2,500 respondents had been a victim of a homophobic crime, of which only 18 per cent were reported to the police (Wake, Wilmot, Fairweather & Birkett, 1999). Gay people also face discrimination within the mental health system and in psychotherapeutic services (Wake et al., 1999).[16]

Kelly was a 33-year-old White English middle-class Gay woman. When she was at school she regularly heard other children referring to being 'so Gay', 'a poof' or 'dyke' as the most insulting thing that anyone could be accused of. Her peers would become defensive in the face of such accusations, further reinforcing the idea that being Gay was not normal or desirable. Kelly was shown every day of her school life that being Gay was not only unacceptable but shameful. At the same time she felt excited by her developing sense of herself as a sexual and emotional being. With every crush she had she experienced a fear of being disliked as well as the energy that comes from feeling whole. For Kelly to be fully alive in a homophobic society meant confronting contradictory expectations that she be happy while defining herself by other people's oppressive standards and staying connected to those who might want to reject and harm her.

Terence invited his brother Robert to therapy with him. Terence was a Black working-class Gay man of African origin, growing up in the East End of London, the youngest of five brothers and one sister. Terence was popular at school and in his neighbourhood until he became a teenager. Terence recalled that 'things seemed to change overnight', as he was suddenly seen as a threat, with adults looking at him with suspicion and crossing the road to avoid him. Terence was grateful he could talk to his parents about experiences of racism, but he could not talk to them about the prejudice he faced because he was sexually and emotionally drawn to men. Terence felt closest to his brother Robert, to whom he came out when he was 17 years old. However, Terence felt that Robert did not challenge homophobic comments when they came up despite knowing Terence was Gay. Robert felt that being heterosexual was one of the few privileges he had as a working-class African heterosexual man. As a result he tried very hard to avoid even the hint of suspicion of homosexuality and kept silent rather than challenging heterosexual privilege. In therapy Terence shared his feelings of betrayal that he could not expect to be fully validated, respected and celebrated within the relationships and social spaces that meant the most to him.

Hayfield (1995) pointed out that for Black Gay men and women, experiencing homophobia within their communities often cuts them off from support networks of family and friends, who are important to support a positive Black identity in the face of daily racism. Black Gay and bisexual women and men also face discrimination from the Gay community and organisations that exist to support them. The experiences and issues of people from Black and other minority ethnic groups can be ignored within political/campaigning groups and in social/support situations.[17]

With respect to the natural environment, most minority world belief systems define humans as unique and superior within nature. These assumptions shape the ideas that abound about the meaning of a good life for human beings, and the relationship we have with ourselves and nature. Peterson (2001, p. 28) argues that 'man is the only animal that . . .' is the start of centuries of assertions that create 'a singular and impassable barrier between humans, on the one hand, and the rest of creation, on the other'. The apparently unique qualities of human beings, unlike the distinct traits of other species, often justify human domination (Ani, 1994; Peterson, 2001). What appears to be in the short-term interest of a select group of human beings is often detrimental to the short-term and long-term health of the biosphere, *and* all human beings. Social discourses teach us that not only are we separate from other forms of life, but other forms of life exist for our convenience, in order to enhance our lives as resources to be exploited, rather than having intrinsic value and existing for their own sake. Thus we have been encouraged to view nature as something outside of ourselves. It seems as though only those environmental measures that will not significantly inconvenience the most privileged are to be favoured. According to the Special Eurobarometer (2008), although most Europeans have environmentally friendly attitudes and they are aware of their role as individuals in protecting their environment, their green attitudes do not necessarily translate into environmentally friendly behaviour and concrete actions.

I would argue that despite attempts to move away from these ways of viewing the world, to some extent we learn to accept harm to other forms of life, gross social inequality and exploitation of nature and poor people, despite reasonable alternatives. The above examples demonstrate how discourses can provide the context for direct acts of abuse and oppression to occur. Reflecting on power in this way is crucial if we want to understand the distress we come across in the 'psy' field and the ways in which therapy can be a tool of liberation rather than supporting the very causes of distress.

Prejudice, oppression and psychological distress

Clinicians in the 'psy' field have long been criticised for their tendency to pathologise the disadvantaged rather than the systems that oppress them (for example, Carr & Sloan, 2003). A plethora of research studies show links between being a member of a socially disadvantaged or oppressed social group and psycho-social difficulties (with respect to gender: Dulle, 1990; 'race': Patel & Fatimilehin, 1999; sexuality: Bridget & Lucille, 1996 and class: Gomm, 1996) as well as the impact of abuse of power, such as domestic violence, child sexual abuse and torture, on emotional well-being

(Başoğlu, Paker, Ozmen, Taşdemir, & Sahin, 1994; Read, 1997; Golding, 1999). Research shows that Black and minority ethnic (BME) people are overrepresented in mental health services and experience poorer outcomes than their White counterparts (Fernando, Ndegwa & Wilson, 1998). Similarly Proctor (2002) argues that the higher rates of women diagnosed with eating difficulties, depression and anxiety reflects our position in society with respect to power (Jonstone, 1989; Baker Miller, 1991; Williams & Watson, 1994). Smail (1998) points out that 'we suffer pain because we do damage to each other, and we shall continue to suffer pain as long as we continue to do the damage. The way to alleviate and mitigate distress is for us *to take care* of the world and the other people in it, not to *treat* them' (p. 1; emphasis in original). As Smail (1998) comments, clients of the mental health system are less people with whom anything is wrong than people who have suffered wrong. The effect of oppression by its very nature tends to be invisible to those who hold more power and privilege. Prejudice also impacts negatively on privileged members of society by making it harder to recognise and benefit from the diversity around them.

It is clear therefore that structural inequalities of the scale we see in the world could not exist or remain without certain ideas being perpetuated. At the same time power, such as corporal power,[18] can be experienced beyond the level of discourse (that is, physical power as experienced through muscular strength or bodily powerlessness as in the experience of physical violence). Power is obviously very complex. Across contexts people may engage in contradictory actions that promote personal or collective wellness in one place but perpetuate oppressive practices in another. Despite the obvious link between power and emotional distress, until recently (the past three decades) power was largely ignored by family/systemic therapists.

Power in systemic therapy

Power ignored

British anthropologist, social scientist, linguist and cyberneticist Gregory Bateson's work was very influential to the development of family therapy even though he was not a family therapist and he approached the nature of behaviour from a different perspective (Rivett & Street, 2003). Bateson[19] (1972) argued that the concept of power was an 'epistemological error' because one individual could not hold unilateral power over another, and argued for an 'interactional epistemology' (Reiber, 1989, p. 123).

It has been argued that Bateson's reflections on power influenced the ways in which power was ignored in family therapy at that time, despite the fact he wrote very little about power, and not very often. Power became defined within the family therapy field as a linear concept that failed to grasp the systemic and relational nature of the world. According to this perspective, those who experienced the effects of power had participated in 'bringing it forth'. Despite being an interpretation of what Bateson said about power, this widely accepted understanding became the notion in family therapy that power did not exist (Law & Madigan, 1994). Bateson's ideas did not arise out of a vacuum, but occurred in a social and political context in which power in relationships was not as comprehensively interrogated as it is now. Although in the 1970s the importance of deconstructing and challenging power as a form of abuse was promoted by critical voices, these were on the margins of mainstream society.

Bateson's resistance to following in his father William Bateson's footsteps as a leading biologist and geneticist, opting instead to study anthropology, influenced the lens through which he saw the world (Bateson et al., 1977). As an anthropologist Bateson was taught to question what we come to believe as concrete reality and fact. Myths became the essence of his worldview. This might make sense of his comment in *Mind and Nature* that 'It is not so much "power" that corrupts as the *myth* of "power"' (Bateson, 1979, p. 21). Bateson felt that '"power", like "energy", "tension," and the rest of the quasi-physical metaphors are [sic] to be distrusted and, among them, "power" is one of the most dangerous . . . as teachers we should not promote that myth"' (Bateson, 1979, p. 21). Bateson challenged our view of the world by arguing that when we dissect behaviour into parts and name these parts as though they are real we are deluded. He felt that 'the context – the relationship, order, form and pattern – are destroyed in the process' (Bateson et al., 1977, p. 90). He disliked using concepts such as force and power, choosing to reject them as incomplete and unhelpful. His experience of power would have been influenced by his social position as a White upper-middle-class man (Bateson et al., 1977). However, it might be simplistic to assume from his limited descriptions of something with multiple dimensions that Bateson had only one fixed idea about what power was. Bateson himself talked about multiple versions of the world (Bateson, 1979).

Bateson's comments about power were just a small part of the general picture between the 1950s and 1970s of systems theory implying that all problems were interpersonal in nature (Dallos & Draper, 2005). The 1980s saw challenges to the negation of power in family therapy by Black and ethnic minority family therapists, feminists and Gay theorists, as well as those working in the fields of child abuse and domestic violence (Goldner, 1993). These critics argued that systems and family therapy theories entailed an ahistorical and decontextual analysis of power. More recently, challenging the notion that unilateral power is not possible, Renoux and Wade (2008) argue that ordinary social acts, such as greetings, jokes and handshakes, are mutual because individuals coordinate their actions to accomplish them, but 'violent acts are unilateral in that they consist of actions by one person against the will and wellbeing of another' (p. 2).

It could be argued that different conversations were being had about power, all of which were valid, but words and ideas that are useful in one context may not be in another. So Bateson's comments about power focused us on the importance of context, but were not useful in helping us understand abuse of power. In recent years there has been a wider recognition of, for example, domestic violence as the perpetrators' power and control over women and children.[20] At the same time a broader and more complex understanding of power in therapy has also been developed and, in particular, therapy has been viewed as a form of social control and cultural imperialism.

Therapy as a form of social control

Many authors have argued convincingly that therapy has the potential to uphold hegemonic interests of dominant groups and can act as a form of social control, by influencing people to fit into pre-existing norms of acceptable behaviour (Nylund & Nylund, 2003). Therapists are often trained to see their worldview as rational and/or desirable and to lead clients in that direction. The therapist can therefore become a representative of the social norms, codes and rules of society (Spinelli, 1994; Smail, 2005). For example, psychologists might be asked to conduct an intervention (for example, cognitive behavioural therapy (CBT)) on a woman who is thought to have vaginismus (the medical term for a woman's inability to engage in any form of vaginal penetration, including sexual intercourse and gynaecological examinations) while not reflecting on social discourses about appropriate female (hetero)sexuality. Therefore, therapy has the potential to 'adjust individuals to that which is unjust' (Cross, 1994, p. 8).

As Masson (1994) points out:

> abuse of one form or another is built into the very fabric of psycho-therapy . . . psychiatric power corrupts just as political power does . . . Even more than politicians, therapists, by the very nature of their profession, are protected from usual forms of scrutiny. Psychotherapy is a self-policing profession.
>
> (p. 210)

Many of the interventions of psychologists and therapists are focused on changing the internal world of individuals to think and behave in more rational ways. This approach connects to a view of human beings as autonomous selves who have responsibility for making themselves feel better. This form of disconnected personal responsibility is often sold as developing 'personal agency'. Attempts to move clients beyond their problems, towards solutions that accept the reality of oppression and violence, may do little more than help people cope with their situation rather than challenge or change it. On the other hand, acting as agents of social control could be seen as an integral part of how we *should* work as therapists, for example when we report child abuse, write reports that advocate on behalf of clients and attempt to prevent harm like domestic violence. The issue therefore is not how we stop being social control agents but how we interrogate what interests we uphold, to whose benefit and to what cost.

Therapy as cultural imperialism

Where the outdated discourse of race inferiority/superiority fails, the more acceptable discourse of uncivilised/civilised nations succeeds in dividing the world into those who are advanced and those who are 'below' them. Cultural imperialism refers to the practice of promoting, separating or artificially injecting the culture of one society into another. Nearly always, the more economically, socially and militarily powerful nation imposes its cultural perspectives and values on the less powerful in an attempt to conquer it. Local culture is never totally destroyed but is often viewed as inferior, dangerous and not as progressive as the culture of the imperialist nation.

Cultural imperialism expresses itself when minority world cultures present themselves as having qualities that stand as a model for the rest of the world to emulate. The minority world's 'fanatical expansionism' requires the continuous search for new lands, people and objects to conquer (Ani, 1994). Gilbert (2006) argues that 'the speed of technological change and communication systems is simply one of the means' by which minority world culture 'now profoundly affects all areas of life worldwide' (pp. 10–11). For Gilbert, globalisation relies on 'a relentless drive towards cultural sameness which disregards and disrespects cultural and language diversity' (2006, p. 11). By expanding, minority cultural worldviews become universal, and everything relates to them, either in attempting to mirror them or being their reverse (Ani, 1994). This uncivilised/civilised dichotomy has substantiated a belief that 'other' cultures lack civilisation because they are at the early stages of development – a type of adult to child relationship between the minority world and 'other' people. Minority world culture can then be presented as synonymous with modern, and at a mature stage of universal cultural development, therefore representing that which will eventually be the form of all cultures (Ani, 1994).

Tseng and Hsu (1991) argued that four dominant ways of helping those in distress have always existed in all cultures: supernatural intervention, social interaction, principles of nature and bodily functioning. Historically, in many societies, healers/wise elders/witches/shamans addressed all four modes in their attempt to heal distress by, for example, listening to the distressed person (thereby performing a social dialogical function), appealing to gods and ritual for help (thereby addressing spirituality), giving the distressed person herbs, potions and other medicinal remedies (drawing on nature's knowledge) and recommending the person engage in certain activities (which served a behavioural/bodily function) (Lago, 2006). The development of professional specialism in the last century fuelled by the mind–body dualism of the minority world separated once-integrated systems into different disciplines – medicine, behavioural psychology, therapy/counselling, spiritual healing, homeopathy, herbalism and so on.

The emergence of helping based on dialogue alone is fairly new compared to these other systems of healing (Lago, 2006). According to Richeport-Haley (1998), belief in the influence of the social and spiritual environment on a person's health is the most common explanation of psychological problems throughout the world. Despite this, psychotherapeutic intervention has become the main form of help that can be offered to a person in emotional distress in the minority world, whether this distress results from social disadvantage, violence/abuse, illness, family conflict, physical pain/discomfort, relationship difficulties or bereavement. Despite the fact that every culture has conceptual frameworks for healing based on how it makes sense of emotional distress, the psy field and its underlying minority world assumptions continue to have global dominance. This legitimacy has been secured by a plethora of literature, training courses and media interest in the 'psy' professions. The global spread of the 'psy' field can be viewed as a form of cultural imperialism in much the same way as industrialisation based on exploitation of nature and poor people has come to dominate global politics. I will now explore power with respect to what happens within the therapeutic relationship.

Conceptualising power in therapy

To understand power as experienced within the therapeutic relationship, Proctor (2002) draws on Cromwell and Olson's (1975) domains of power, where *power bases* are the assets and resources of an individual or their *power to* and *power within*; *power processes* are the interactions between individuals and the potential for either *power with* (mutuality) or *power over* (domination); and *power outcomes* refer to the decision-making process and how outcomes are determined. Given that I have touched on the significance of power bases when discussing power as access to sought-after resources, I will now look more closely at power as an interaction with respect to therapy processes and outcomes.

Power processes

Proctor (2002) argues that if the therapist and client are unconnected, such as if the therapist closely guards against transparency or disclosure, they function separately without integration or cooperation, leaving the therapist and client entering into the relationship with potentially incompatible agendas that are not shared or negotiated. In another situation the therapist might totally dominate what happens in therapy such that the client does not feel that their voice is fully heard. Alternatively, the therapist and client can work collaboratively and mutually. A given therapeutic relationship might move between all three different ways of relating. The dynamics of power in the therapeutic relationship is processual and fluid. What is of interest is, who determines the shifts that take place and how do they do that? The expert position where therapists talk with certainty about what they know about clients, and how clients should think and conduct their lives, has been heavily critiqued. As Edward Said stated when talking about Western Islamophobia:

> Now it is often the case that you can be known by others in different ways than you know yourself, and that valuable insights might be generated accordingly. But that is quite different than pronouncing it as immutable law that outsiders ipso facto have a better sense of you as an insider than you do yourself.
>
> (Said, 1986, p. 219)

A therapy that emphasises distance and hierarchy between client and therapist could be termed a monological approach. Instead of new meanings being generated in conversation with clients, meanings already inherent in the therapist's store of expert knowledge are reproduced. Thus influence is unidirectional: while the client is influenced by the therapist, the therapist remains entrenched in an already established system of knowledge. As bell hooks says:

> no need to hear your voice when I can talk about you better than you can speak about yourself . . . I want to know your story. And then I will tell it back to you . . . in such a way that . . . I am still author, authority. I am still the colonizer, the speak subject, and you are now at the centre of my talk.
>
> (hooks, 1990, pp. 151–152)

Whereas a monological stance sees therapy as a relationship between an expert who has knowledge and a non-expert who needs help, a dialogical perspective involves dialogue between two different forms of expertise in constant interaction, as the therapist and client co-create new stories. Dialogue means much more than just exchange or negotiation of prior positions and identities. In dialogue all participants influence and are influenced, shape and are shaped by the interaction, and are mutually involved in making meaning (Seikkula, 2002).

What is curious is that certain therapies are assumed to have inherent 'monological' or 'dialogical' features. This assumption masks the ways in which any therapy might adopt either of these features regardless of the model being practised. Therapies assumed to be monological, such as CBT or psychoanalysis, can be practised with great attention to mutuality and learning from the client. Even the most collaborative systemic therapist may at times enter into an unhelpful expert position. It is possible, however, to take an authoritarian position, such as in the case of risk of harm, while enabling dialogue with the client about the impact of such a position and ways to move forward. There may also be times when the client wants the therapist to be an expert, such as when advice, direction and guidance are desired. Later in the book I describe how this might be done in a dialogical fashion.

Guilfoyle (2005) argues that associating monologue with power and dialogue with an absence of power is problematic because it implies that some therapy approaches can rid themselves of the problem of power. This idea conflates power with hierarchy, control and domination and therefore views power as wholly negative and something that can and should be removed from therapy. If we assume (like Proctor, 2002) that power can be positive as well as negative and is unavoidable, it becomes meaningless to distinguish monologue from dialogue on the basis of the presence or absence of power. French historian, social theorist and philosopher Michel Foucault (1980) argued that instead of being removed, power can only be concealed. Therefore monologue and dialogue represent two different kinds of power relations (Guilfoyle, 2003). In a monologue the therapist is dominant and influence is one-way from therapist to client. A dialogue is an interaction of voices in which the issue of who influences whom is never totally finalised either way. Power is not overcome in dialogue but operates in flexible and turn-taking ways (Falzon, 1998).

Power outcomes: The influence of wider systems

Discourses and practices in society help to define the client and therapist, client–therapist relationship and outcome of therapy. Generally speaking, the client expects to be helped by the therapist and the therapist expects the client to behave and define their problems in a way that will enable the therapist to 'treat' or 'cure' them. In fact all therapies contain these relatively fixed positions, which mean that the nature of the therapeutic relationship is powerfully modelled by and reproduces culturally dominant ideas about what therapy is.

From Foucault's (1982) definition, power does not necessarily mean domination. A powerful person acting upon the actions of another might be experienced by the person being acted upon as positive (for example being rescued by a fire-fighter from a burning building). Equally the person being acted upon might resist the actions of the powerful person (for example a survivor of abuse speaking out about their experiences despite attempts by the perpetrator to silence them). According to Guilfoyle (2003), the key to understanding the power/domination distinction is resistance. Domination in therapy occurs when the possibility of resistance does not have a legitimate place in therapy, leading to an authoritarian imposition of meaning from therapist to client. The acknowledgement of the possibility for resistance in therapy makes interactions dynamic and reversible. In other words, dialogue does not require the removal of power, but does require the acknowledgement and utilisation of resistance to the exercise of power (Guilfoyle, 2003).

Chapter 3

Resistance

What is resistance?

Dominant discourses always coexist with alternative discourses that challenge them. Similarly, whenever a person experiences abuse, oppression or violence they resist their experiences in some way. Hence, power and resistance can be viewed as two sides of the same coin. Wade (1997) argues that resistance is:

> any mental or behavioural act through which a person attempts to expose, withstand, repel, stop, prevent, abstain from, strive against, impede, refuse to comply with, or oppose any form of violence or oppression, or the conditions that make such acts possible. . . . any attempt to imagine or establish a life based on respect and equality, on behalf of one's self or others, including any effort to redress the harm caused by violence or other forms of oppression.
>
> (p. 25)

Resistance is not just a response to power but a form of power; hence, resistance, like power, is complex. It can be creative and expansive – opening up possibilities and embracing difference, or restrictive and destructive – closing down options and creating more oppression.

How we view acts of resistance depends on our position, the viewpoint we take and the issues we reflect on. For instance, there have been various views about suicide bombers in Palestine; strike action; women who kill their abusive husbands; the Irish Republican Army (IRA) and the African National Congress (ANC), depending on political position and personal experience. In order to attempt clarity where there is complexity, we could argue that destructive resistance is a misguided response to power that harms individuals and communities, particularly those in more disadvantaged and vulnerable circumstances (Jenkins, 2009). The revolutionary and creative power of resistance can be overshadowed if it manifests as abusive and reactive actions. Creative resistance opens up opportunities and possibilities rather than causing further limits and constraints on people's ability to live well with each other. Creative resistance also provides people with hope at times when hopelessness is pervasive. It reconnects people to life beyond suffering, reminds people of the experiences they cannot live without and the abilities/qualities that cannot be destroyed by oppression.

It is important to point out that resistance can of course have both destructive and creative elements at the same time. In addition, whether we can engage in reactive or reflective resistance is often heavily determined by the wider social context, such as the social circumstances, opportunities and restraints we experience (for example, living under military occupation).

Resistance as creativity

Whereas critique reveals the need for new ideas and action, creativity is required to envision and bring about better circumstances. Creativity can be viewed as a form of resistance and resistance as a way of living creatively. Creativity means transcending traditional boundaries, bringing into being new things that have not yet been and being moved by the everyday as though viewing it for the first time. Creativity in therapy is often described as social poiesis, which moves away from the inner reflections of the poet towards describing what gets created between people (McNamee, 2000). Poetry resists conventions of language and uses metaphors to bring together ideas usually kept separate, in order for new relationships to be constructed. Similarly, therapy can be a co-construction of meaning in improvisational and creative rather than expert-driven repetitive ways, such that something new is always brought into existence, based on the power of the dynamic between, rather than the power of any one participant. Like therapy, resistance might also be viewed as a type of poiesis – creative liberation from tradition.

Spirituality, sexuality and creativity are often repressed and targets for oppression by dominant groups in society. Resistance to oppression can therefore lead to greater access to means of self-expression and collective expression. Resistance gives energy to hope and the capacity to move beyond what we experience to extend ourselves towards possibilities.

Resistance in history

American resistance historiographers Terence Ranger and Herbert Aptheker have highlighted how resistance to oppression has been obscured from history books and popular knowledge throughout history. African people enslaved in the US in the 1800s were often portrayed as stupid, submissive and passive. With a few exceptions (for example the film *Amistad*, 1997), less attention has been given to 'slave sabotage, strikes, and slowdowns' (Aptheker, 1986, p. 16). Aptheker wrote: 'the present generations of [Black] men and women now shaking the very foundations of racism . . . [were] the inheritors and continuers of a great tradition of militancy' (Aptheker, 1969, pp. 3–5). The Ningi Hills of Northern Nigeria were refuge areas where fugitive slaves hid, as was the Olumo rock in Abeokuta (meaning 'town under the rock') where my parents grew up. Common forms of slave resistance were arson, poison, abortion, suicide and infanticide (Toni Morrison's *Beloved* is an example).

Cora Ann Presley (1986) argued that studies of African independence movements seldom gave evidence of the active participation, achievements and sacrifices of women. For example, women organised rural resistance to colonialism in the Central Province of Kenya and were active in every aspect of the Mau Mau resistance movement. As famous as Harriet Tubman and Sojourner Truth are as leaders of slave revolts, many more women resisted in many different ways (Fox-Genovese, 1986).

Aptheker argued that White people's resistance to slavery had also been squeezed out of history books until recently. The schoolteacher Joseph Wood was hanged in New Orleans in 1812 for complicity in a slave rebellion. Delia Webster and others were jailed in Kentucky in 1804 for participating in efforts to free slaves and rebel against slave oppressors (Aptheker, 1988). Aptheker (1988) argued that 'The whole matter of black–white unity in struggles against racism brings dimensions to the history of resistance that are fundamental' (p. 19). With respect to the British context, Fryer (1988) states that:

> nowhere within the British Empire were Black people passive victims . . . Far from being docile, they resisted slavery and colonialism in every way open to them. Their resistance took many different forms, both individual and collective. It ranged from a watchful and waiting pretence of acceptance . . . right up to large-scale mass uprisings and national liberation movements.
>
> (p. 85)

Resistance in systemic therapy

Why is any of this important? Well, it is clear in reviewing history that resistance has formed the backbone of political struggles, liberation movements and social and cultural transformation. It is curious then that resistance has traditionally been viewed negatively within the 'psy' field as the opposite of engagement, rather than a necessary and important part of the process of collaboration and liberation. Here I will move beyond constructing resistance in therapeutic terms, and make links with a political conceptualisation of resistance.

In therapy literature client resistance has tended to be perceived in pathologising and individualistic ways; as resulting from denial, inner conflict, ambivalence, self-destructive tendencies, aggressive impulses, ignorance, apathy, refusal to change, narcissism, sadism, and so on. Given the tone of much of the traditional therapy literature, whether psychoanalytic or family therapy text, we would be forgiven for believing that people who come for therapy quite often do not want their difficulties to change and therefore resist any movement towards it.

Family therapy theories of resistance

A variety of ways of understanding resistance are presented in family therapy literature. A homeostatic metaphor used in traditional family therapy proposed that families are systems that view change as a threat and respond with attempts to maintain stability even if this sustains the problem. This concept of homeostasis originated from a physiological term to explain the body's ability to regulate itself and maintain internal constancy in the face of external changes (Cannon, 1932). Given that clients are viewed as often reluctant to change, it is assumed that therapists who seek to bring about change in the client's system will encounter resistance. Nichols (1984) pointed out that 'tactics to outwit resistance are the very essence of strategic [family] therapy' (p. 466), which developed sophisticated strategies to get around people's opposition. These approaches to resistance ran the risk of blaming families for not doing enough to challenge the problem, and gaining something from it, which potentially added 'therapeutic insult to economic injury' (Madsen, 2007, p. 93). This perspective might lead us to view clients as adversaries who, given any opportunity, will attempt to manipulate, exploit or trip up the therapist in order to prevent them reaching their aim of effecting change. This might orient the therapist to the family in a way that may encourage responses from clients that are then viewed as resistance (Madsen, 2007).

Steve de Shazer was a family therapist, psychotherapist and author who developed solution-focused brief therapy and founded the Brief Family Therapy Centre with his wife, fellow family therapist Insoo Kim Berg. In reaction to the prevailing view of resistance as an individually located phenomenon originating in the client's psyche, de Shazer (1984) argued in *The death of resistance* that the concept of resistance was a negative one because it made us think of therapy in terms of force or power, turning the therapist and client into opponents, with the therapist needing to win in order for therapy to succeed. De Shazer argued that it was more useful to talk in terms of 'cooperating', such that a client's resistance was utilised as part of a therapist and client co-creating process.

On one hand the idea of resistance as part of a cooperative act fits with my central argument that resistance is a useful part of a collaborative therapy. On the other hand, if the term 'resistance' is killed off, the workings of power in therapy are masked and the ways in which clients might actually experience therapy as unhelpful or even harmful get factored out. Negative experiences of therapy have been described (Sands, 2003) and there have been reports of therapists abusing their power by engaging in sexual relationships with clients (Rutter, 1989; Juhu, 1994). In fact Totton (2006) argues that:

> Outright therapeutic abuse is serious and widespread. According to the UK charity POPAN [Prevention of Professional Abuse Network] (2004) 50 per cent of calls to their phone helpline are alleging abuse within the talking treatments; this amounts to around 300 people each year and – since many clients have never heard of POPAN – must represent only a small proportion of what actually occurs.
>
> (p. 84)

Madsen's (1999) suggestion that 'invitational interventions may provoke less resistance' (p. 94) is in danger of positioning resistance as something undesirable and avoidable. As a Black working-class woman I cannot help but believe that neither power nor resistance is dead. If we cannot address power by finding ways of eradicating it, neither can we do so for resistance. Rather than replacing resistance with another term that conceals the working of power, I prefer to reclaim the idea of resistance as integral to thinking about power in society and in therapy. I would argue that being open to the reality and necessity of resistance in therapy can lead to creative options for collaborative and empowering practice, particularly given that it is highly unlikely that we can be helpful and fit with clients at all times. Instead we might be curious about what client resistance tells us about:

- the client's values, principles, hopes and fears
- the therapeutic relationship
- the therapeutic approach of the therapist in relation to the social position and worldview of the client
- social/cultural/historical constraints impacting on the client's world and the therapeutic relationship.

Dialogical approach to resistance

A dialogical approach sees resistance as stating a difference and taking an alternative standpoint to the dominant position. When clients are described as 'treatment resistant', for example, rather than buying into the client-blaming discourse we can see this term as telling us two things: (a) the treatment is not helpful to the client and (b) the client is in some ways able to resist it. Rather than a reason to pathologise the client this is an opportunity to talk with them about what would be more helpful and what resources they are drawing on to resist that which is not helpful.

Understanding the therapeutic significance of resistance is important, because while the workings of power are often invisible, resistance is generally more evident. Foucault argued that the success of power 'is proportional to its ability to hide its own mechanisms' (1976, p. 86). I have written elsewhere about the ways in which resistance to racism is often pathologised as 'draconian, extreme or without foundation' in the face of the at times invisible power of racism (Adetimole, Afuape & Vara, 2005, p. 11). Similarly, a client's resistance might be more visible yet weaker against the power of the therapist, the therapeutic relationship and the societal expectation that therapists know best. At the same time client resistance can profoundly determine the course and outcome of therapy. It can be dismissed and pathologised or acknowledged and utilised, depending on the stance of the therapist. How we understand resistance shapes how we respond to clients, how clients then respond to our responses, and the progress of the therapeutic relationship (Madsen, 2007). As Madsen (1999) points out: 'Our understanding of resistance may invite connection, appreciation, and respect or evaluation, judgment, and criticism' (p. 87).

Power is already present within the therapy relationship as a product of the institutional and contextual forces that position persons categorised as therapists differently to those categorised as clients (Hare-Mustin, 1994). A therapy that acknowledges and centralises the possibility for client resistance might make therapeutic interactions more dynamic and reversible. Thus power and resistance can work together to infuse dialogue with an interplay of forces (Falzon, 1998).

Resistance arising from therapy can be thought about from different positions:

- *the resistance of the client* to power in different forms – against the therapist and therapy; against violence, abuse, oppression in relationships outside of therapy
- *the resistance of the therapist*, for example against being positioned as expert, diagnoser, arbiter of truth; against linear explanations of the nature of problems and solutions to them
- *the resistance of the therapist and client* together against unhelpful and/or oppressive discourses.

Chapter 4

Understanding trauma with respect to power, resistance and liberation

The original title for this book was *Power, resistance and liberation in therapy with survivors of abuse, oppression and discrimination: To have our hearts broken*. As well as this being too many words for a title, I decided to engage with the very popular concept of trauma rather than bypassing it. In this chapter I will look into the concept of trauma through power, resistance and liberation lenses, focusing particularly on people who experience 'psychosis' (also referred to as people with severe and enduring mental health problems) as well as people who are survivors of war, organised violence and torture. Given that trauma has become shorthand for the effect of all types of painful experiences, it seems important to engage critically with this term, to go deeper into the assumptions that guide our practice around it, before going beyond it. I start by reflecting on trauma with respect to power (abuse), resistance (renewal) and 'psychosis'. I then attempt to go beyond the concept of trauma to reflect on social, cultural and political dimensions of human experience. Despite focusing on these client groups I believe this critical approach to our theories and practices is applicable to any issues emerging in our work.

What is trauma?

'Trauma' was originally a word used in medicine to describe a physical wound. Over the past 100 years it has become 'fully psychologised' (Rose, 2003, p. 35) and refers to damage to our internal worlds. I use the term 'trauma' in this book to refer to the emotional distress we experience as a result of emotionally painful circumstances often linked to forms of oppression, prejudice and/or abuse. According to Papadopoulos (2002), originally trauma referred to the injury left as a result of the skin being pierced (trauma means wound or injury, and comes from the Greek verb *titrosko* – to pierce). Papadopoulos (2000, 2001) also suggests that *titrosko* comes from the verb *teiro* which means 'to rub', and in ancient Greek meant both to rub in and to rub away (Papadopoulos, 2002). This implies two possible outcomes of trauma:

from 'rubbing in' an injury or a wound; and from 'rubbing off' or 'rubbing away', as in cleaning a surface where there were marks previously. [People] . . . might be either injured (psychologically) as a result of being exposed to traumatic events ('rubbed in'), or alternatively, they may experience (in addition to the distress) a sense of renewal when the traumatic experiences erase previous values, routines and life styles and introduce new meaning to their lives.

(Papadopoulos, 2002, p. 28)

Inherent in any experience of abuse of power is always some form of response, and this resistance to power has the potential to be transformative. My aim is to reflect on issues related to the lived experience of people in relationship to others and the wider world, with respect to the contexts of trauma as injury and trauma as renewal.[21] Of course experiences of injury and renewal are often not separate and distinct (the same individual, for example, might talk about their experiences with respect to fragmentation and integration; disconnection and harm; as well as unity and love), but for the purpose of clarity I will reflect on them in turn.

The experience of 'psychosis' *and* the subsequent responses of others to such experiences can undoubtedly be traumatic. They might also lead to a search for meaning that is potentially transformative. This search for meaning can be viewed as forms of resistance against crazy-making experiences of abuse, oppression and prejudice as well as against living in a mad-phobic society, compelled to separate people out according to how well they make a clear distinction between socially acceptable and socially unacceptable reality.

Trauma as injury: abuse and 'psychosis'

Although I use the term 'psychosis' I do so reluctantly and with many reservations about a term that perpetuates assumptions that people who have 'unusual' beliefs and experiences are fundamentally flawed, different and indecipherable. The term 'psychosis' is predominantly used by those in the 'psy' field but is not always the term used by clients of the mental health system who have personal experience of it. In using this term I do not wish to feed into colloquial usage of terms such as 'psychotic' and 'psycho' that are synonymous with 'madness'. As will become apparent, I do not view humanity as split between sane and mad people (a distinction I find unhelpful, simplistic and dehumanising). Meaning, values, experiences, relationships and emotions are more useful ideas in helping us to understand each other. By using the term 'psychosis' I hope to play with its common usage and highlight ways of thinking about it differently.

There is a plethora of research (e.g. Romme & Escher, 1989; Eaton, Romanoski, Anthony & Nestadt, 1991; Tien, 1991; Poulton et al., 2000) suggesting that there are people who hear voices, have heterodox beliefs and experiences who have not used psychiatric services, and that these might actually be widely prevalent human experiences. Whether or not people experience significant problems as a result of 'unusual' beliefs/experiences seems to be influenced by the meaning attributed to the experience, whether the messages within it are thought to be helpful or hostile, the degree of interference or acceptance experienced, past experiences of trauma, and the reactions of others (Romme, Honig, Noorthoorn, & Escher, 1992; Beavan, 2006; Romme & Escher 2000; Romme, Escher, Dillon, Corstens & Morris, 2009). I also wonder how much social privilege plays a part; that is, access to resources to support the client's ability to turn their difficulties into opportunities and become a valued member of society.

It has been suggested that people who receive psychiatric interventions for 'psychosis' are more likely to have a history of trauma than those who do not seek professional help (Ellason & Ross, 1997; Read, 1997; Read, van Os, Morrison, & Ross, 2005). Many have reported high rates of childhood sexual abuse and other negative life events and/or aversive environmental conditions such as poverty, racism, sexism and homophobia (Kingdon & Turkington, 1999; Romme & Escher, 1989; Romme et al., 1992) in the lives of this population (Goff, Brotman, Kindler & Waites, 1991; Ross & Joshi, 1992; Masters, 1995; Mueser et al., 1998; Read, Perry, Moskowitz & Connolly, 2001; Mueser, Rosenberg, Goodman & Trumbetta, 2002). Associations have been reported between past trauma and the actual content and themes of psychotic experiences (Read, Agar, Argyle & Aderhold, 2003; Romme & Escher, 2006). It has also been suggested that a history of child abuse meant that clients were more likely to hear malevolent rather than helpful voices (Offen, Waller & Thomas, 2003).

In addition, research suggests that experiences of acute 'psychosis' and/or psychiatric hospitalisation can be traumatic in themselves (Shaner & Eth, 1989; McGorry, Chanen, McCarthy, van Riel, McKenzie & Singh, 1991; Lundy, 1992; Williams-Keeler, Milliken & Jones, 1994; Shaw, McFarlane, & Bookless, 1997; Meyer, Taiminen, Vuori, Aeijaelae & Helenius, 1999). Psychotic experiences can disrupt the person's sense of themselves, the world, and others (Bayley, 1996; Davidson & Strauss, 1992; Shaner & Eth, 1989). Additionally, the response of others to the person experiencing 'psychosis' might lead to social isolation and discrimination. Psychiatric hospitalisation and its associated invalidating, humiliating and oppressive experiences, which may include witnessing/experiencing verbal, sexual, and physical abuse (Shaw, McFarlane & Bookless, 1997), in conjunction with sensationalist media coverage, can also be traumatic (Beveridge, 1998).

To highlight the ways in which resistance may lead to renewal, I will briefly explore spirituality.

Trauma as renewal: spirituality and 'psychosis'

Not all experiences associated with 'psychosis' are experienced as negative, and even if experienced as such they have the power to reconnect people to what is important to them. Rather than a complete shattering of a sense of self, 'psychosis' can lead to the emergence of a deeper sense of being connected to something meaningful.

A sense of social failure is not an inevitable result of psychotic experiences but more likely to result when psychiatric labels are applied that imply biological, social and moral defection. Hospitalising someone who feels overwhelmed, lost and confused and forcing them to take medication is one response to 'psychosis' based on the illness model predominant in Western medicine. Of course there are many other possible responses based on other understandings (spiritual support, physical rest, nutritional healing, social action and challenging oppression, vocational and therapeutic activities, exercise/movement therapy, homeopathy, among others). What seems important is that the response of others reinforces the total humanity and complexity of the distressed person.

There is also a growing recognition that talking to people about meaning and values might mean reflecting on spirituality. This is particularly significant considering the common preoccupation with people experiencing 'psychosis' with religious and spiritual ideas.[22] Stanislav and Christina Grof, associated with transpersonal psychology,[23] founded the Spiritual Emergency Network in 1980 (Prevatt & Park, 1989) (now the Spiritual Crisis Network) and coined the term 'spiritual emergency' referring to what happens when spiritual emergence or awakening becomes a crisis or emergency (Grof & Grof, 1989, 1990).[24] They define spiritual emergencies as:

> Crises when the process of growth and change becomes chaotic and overwhelming. Individuals experiencing such episodes may feel that their sense of identity is breaking down, that their old values no longer hold true, and that the very ground beneath their personal realities is radically shifting. In many cases, new realms of mystical and spiritual experience enter their lives suddenly and dramatically, resulting in fear and confusion. They may feel tremendous anxiety, have difficulty coping with their daily lives, jobs, and relationships, and may even fear for their own sanity.
>
> (back cover)

Greeley (1974) defined spiritual experience as a spiritual force that seems to lift you out of yourself. It is a transient, extraordinary experience marked by feelings of unity, harmonious relationship to the divine and everything in existence, euphoria, sense of noesis (access to the hidden spiritual dimension), alterations in time and space perception, and the sense of lacking control over the event (Allman, De La Roche, Elkins & Weathers, 1992). Assagioli (1989) argues, for example, that people may become inflated and grandiose as a result of intense spiritual experiences: 'Instances of such confusion are not uncommon among people who become dazzled by contact with truths too great or energies too powerful for their mental capacities to grasp and their personality to assimilate' (p. 36). An emphasis on spirituality can help practitioners understand the explanations given by some clients for the intrusion and boundary-less experiences of 'psychosis'. It also highlights the fine line between spiritual emergence and emergency, influenced by experiences outside the individual such as the isolation that can ensue when our way of understanding reality is not shared by others.

What seems important is recognition by those in the 'psy' field that there are different types of 'logic' – that is, different ways of connecting to and understanding reality – other than that which is 'rational' and concrete. Given what seems to be an increasing preoccupation with science and rationality, talking about spirituality can be as difficult for clients, and therapists, as talking about other intimate yet taboo issues, such as sexuality. The idea that spiritual emergencies are part of a process of spiritual emergence suggests that despite the distress, they can have beneficial transformative effects on individuals who experience them. It also highlights that whether or not clients experiencing psycho-social difficulties talk about or understand their difficulties through a spiritual idiom, a search for meaning is an important part of being able to 'move on'.

In December 1991 David Lukoff, an American clinical psychologist, and his colleagues Francis G. Lu and Robert P. Turner made a proposal for a new diagnostic category entitled Psychoreligious or Psychospiritual Problem[25] (Turner, Lukoff, Barnhouse, & Lu, 1995). The category was approved by the DSM-IV Task Force in 1993, after changing the title to Religious or Spiritual Problem. It is included in the fourth edition of the *Diagnostic and Statistical Manual of Mental Disorders* (DSM-IV) under the heading 'Other Conditions That May Be a Focus of Clinical Attention', Code V62.89 (APA, 1994; Lu, Lukoff & Turner, 1997).[26] According to Chinen (1996) the inclusion marks 'increasing professional acceptance of transpersonal issues' (p. 12). However, I would argue that, recognising the importance of spirituality in people's lives, whether they are experiencing emotional distress or not, is not about distinguishing between 'real madness' and spiritual beliefs/spiritual problems. It is about deconstructing how we come to understand our experiences and how we might be open to the many ways of understanding reality, supporting people who want support and addressing multiple levels of context, of which spirituality for many people is an important part. It does not make sense to me to make distinctions between 'rational' and 'irrational' knowing. Rather than developing new categories aimed at trying to decrease 'misdiagnosis' and increase the 'accuracy' of psychiatric labelling, I would challenge the epistemological foundations of psychiatric categories all together.[27] What links all human experience is a search for meaning, and yet people viewed as 'ill' or 'irrational' often are not listened to, have choice and decisions taken from them and are not viewed as having anything to offer our view of humanity or reality. Listening to clients who have experienced 'psychosis' we come to better understand that these experiences, although often distressing, are meaningful, decipherable and linked inextricably to a person's lived experience.

I have by no means exhausted the myriad ways of understanding 'psychosis'. In fact, rather than attempting to show any simple cause–effect link (for example, between trauma and 'psychosis') my intention is to bypass this debate altogether and focus on what ethical positions an emphasis on power, resistance and liberation might encourage us to take. Given the different explanatory 'models' of 'psychosis', it seems important to accept this diversity[28] and find ways of engaging with 'psychosis' in ways that validate the person's intimate experience of it. This may not require having a model at all, but rather require a particular emotional posture and moral stance.

Liberation as recovery

It could be argued that the term 'recovery' reinforces an illness model of psycho-social difficulties. However, I embrace the term, given that historically 'psychosis' was associated with chronicity, incurability and deterioration and viewed as occupying the person's whole identity. I use the term to highlight the growing demand for alternative perspectives to this view that centralise first-hand personal accounts of clients who have experienced psychosis and moved on in positive ways from it. Although there are service users who are happy with a medical model view of their distress, many are not and very few, if any, would welcome the pessimistic life-plot that often accompanies it.

In the past four decades the service user movement has shown great resistance to aspects of the 'psy' field that are abusive (particularly psychiatric and pharmaceutical dominance). There has been a shift towards reclaiming 'mad' experience and the right to take authorship over it, as well as the establishment of unconventional belief groups, such as Mad Pride, the Hearing Voices Network, The Paranoia Network, the Evolving Minds group, the Spiritual Crisis Network, Mind Freedom International and the Icarus Project.

Bacigalupe (1998) argued that it is often those who have been privileged by mainstream discourse that are in a position to critique it and create alternatives. However, the idea of recovery from psycho-social difficulties has been introduced by those who have experienced them rather than mental health professionals. Recovery is about people living a full and satisfying life in the presence or absence of what doctors might describe as 'symptoms' (Repper & Perkins, 2003). What seems to be important in the recovery process is supportive others and meaningful life experiences. This challenges the location of distress within the minds of individuals. Instead, recovery is viewed as happening in people's lives rather than their psychologies, and is thus a social, cultural and spiritual process (Deegan, 1993; Barker, Campbell & Davidson, 1999; Coleman, 1999; May, 2000, 2004; Russo, 2001). Given that recovery is rarely linear, what is often called 'relapse' might better be conceptualised as part of a wider process of growth. Where clients do not experience their lives moving in preferred directions, the chronicity of psycho-social difficulties could result from (a) experiencing, telling and being told static stories, with a pessimistic life-plot where a person's complex identity is replaced by a stigmatising label, and (b) constraints (interpersonal, familial, cultural) on an individual's ability to live his or her preferred life that are so strong that he or she struggles to experience coherence and coordination in the world of others.

Lanzmann (1995), talking about blindness as a form of 'not understanding' obscene cruelty, said he 'clung to this refusal of understanding as the only possible operative attitude' and argues that 'blindness has to be understood here as the purest mode of looking . . . the only way not to turn away from a reality which is literally blinding' (p. 204). Similarly, psycho-social difficulties and emotional distress might be viewed as a reasonable response to living in a context that is literally maddening. Hannah Nelson (quoted in Gwaltney, 1980) notes, 'I have grown to womanhood in a world where the saner you are, the madder you are made to appear' (p. 7). Mary O'Hagan (1996) juxtaposed excerpts from her journal with excerpts from notes made in her hospital file while she was admitted to a psychiatric ward, comparing different descriptions of the same event. The words in italics are what Mary wrote about her experience. The words in bold are what was written about Mary in her hospital notes:

> *I am lying face down behind a chair in the waiting room of the hospital.*
> *I am a long piercing scream*
> *All screaming on the inside of me*
> *And out of the pores of my skin.*
> *My screaming and myself are one.*
> *This is pure pain.*
>
> *The doctor comes along and snaps at me to get up. He tells a nurse to put me to bed. I have never ever been in so much shame.*
>
> *Guilt swoops down on me*
> *And pecks my sense of being good to bits*

as I lie here snared between my sheets
like a whimpering animal.

I am full of red hot blame at myself for everything
I cannot bear being so thoroughly bad.

I am carrying hell around inside of me.

On arriving on the ward – spent the entire day curled up on the waiting room floor behind a chair. Could not talk. Impression of over dramatisation but with underlying gross psychological turmoil. She is difficult to engage and to that effect I have admitted her a period of two weeks in order to consolidate her working relationship with us.

(O'Hagan, 1996, p. 46)

These juxtapositions highlight how the more unusual the behaviour of another person, the harder it is to think of non-dispositional factors contributing to it. They also demonstrate how our inability to form an empathetic appreciation of a person's experience can become our proof of their madness.

Therapy can be a process of co-creation and mutual discovery that centralises the client's voice with respect to the ways in which their experiences and feelings are real even if their story is difficult for anyone else to relate to or participate in. As a result, we end conversations changed in some way by them, such that both therapist and client are not in the same place as when they started. These conversations enable what might start out as our anecdotes to develop into fuller, richer stories about the client's lived experience. By better understanding experiences of abuse, social isolation and prejudice we might better understand how to make the social world one that is worth connecting to.

The relationship between distress and social circumstances has helped to promote the idea that people who are psychiatrically labelled are not distinctly different from the rest of the population and that recovery from emotional distress is possible, particularly if experiences of trauma are acknowledged, oppressive circumstances challenged and values validated. This draws our attention not to mad individuals but to oppressive social contexts as well as the resourceful (albeit distressing) ways people resist by searching for and finding meaning.

Beyond trauma: Survivors of war, organised violence and torture

There has been a striking increase in published work on trauma in the past two decades and many specialist clinics have opened up in the minority world aimed at treating it (Blake, Albano & Keane, 1992; Bracken, 2002). Refugee people and survivors of war, organised violence and torture seem to be the fastest growing client group being written about with respect to clinical models of trauma. Increasingly psychologists and therapists have an interest in working with this client group. I will now elaborate on how a power, resistance and liberation lens can shift our focus and challenge our assumptions about working with trauma – an analysis that can be applied to other client groups and their experiences.

Despite the repeated assertion that post-traumatic stress disorder (PTSD) 'was created at a particular time, in a particular place, according to a particular moral and political agenda' (Bracken, 2002, p. 47), it continues to be widely understood by lay people, health professionals and 'psy' clinicians alike as the main response to trauma. PTSD is a psychiatric diagnosis – found in the psychiatric manuals *Diagnostic and Statistical Manual of Psychiatric Disorders* version 4 (text revision) (DSM-IV-TR) and *International Classification of Diseases* (ICD-10, 2nd ed.) – given to an individual who develops a particular set of symptoms as a result of a traumatic event, which persists for more than a month (APA, 2000; World Health Organisation, 2004). PTSD symptoms are thought to include the following:

- re-experiencing trauma through flashbacks, intrusive memories and nightmares
- efforts to avoid any reminders of the traumatic event
- emotional numbing and restricted range of affect, such as dissociation and low mood
- hyperarousal such as difficulties remembering or concentrating, severe anxiety, and exaggerated startle response.

A person who has experienced a traumatic event is thought to be suffering from PTSD if they complain of, for example, insomnia, memory difficulties, frightening nightmares, frequent flashbacks of traumatic events, increased irritability and proneness to anger and fear. Because these characteristics of PTSD are now widely known in the general population and commonly accepted as a human response to trauma, it is believed that the existence of PTSD gives evidence of past trauma. The search for simple and reproducible models of intervention for PTSD has become an international, cross-cultural enterprise. I call this the burgeoning 'trauma industry', using the term 'industry' deliberately to reflect its pervasiveness and influence. I will now deconstruct the concept of PTSD before describing alternative ways of making sense of the experiences of survivors of torture that go beyond the focus of this industry.

Deconstructing PTSD

Adaptive, not pathological

The diagnosis of PTSD contradicts the notion that it is normal to react severely to extreme events, and suggests the existence of a cut-off point whereby distress changes from being a response to being a pathological response. Alternatively, 'symptoms' can be viewed as adaptive responses to oppressive and abusive experiences. For example, exaggerated startle response can be a learned adaptation to living in the context of war. Withdrawal from others and lack of trust may be lifesaving when one is living in situations of political violence.

PTSD is history-, event- and culture-specific

History-specific

PTSD first entered the diagnostic system after the Vietnam War and served to position veterans as victims of trauma although some of them were also perpetrators of atrocities in Vietnam. The antiwar movement lobbied for war veterans to receive specialised medical care based on the concept of PTSD, succeeding earlier definitions of shell shock and war neurosis. This legitimised immunity from blame and afforded financial awards such as compensation (Summerfield, 1999a, 1999b).

Event-specific

PTSD applies to survivors of single traumatic events that are sudden and unexpected (Terr, 1991), whereas many people experience traumatic events that are multiple, predictable and cumulative (Herman, 1994; Summerfield, 1999b). While PTSD could be seen as a good fit in the case of somebody surviving a car accident whose life was normal before and could potentially return to normal after the accident, the situation for asylum seeking and refugee people in the UK for example could hardly be described as post-traumatic with respect to an oppressive asylum system, discrimination and enforced helplessness.

Culture-specific

PTSD is seen as a universal reaction to traumatic experiences, observable in both children and adults. It is further assumed to be 'expressive of conflicts and disturbances happening within individual minds' (Bracken & Petty, 1998, p. 39). However, psychiatric diagnoses are minority world labels that describe certain types of behaviour from a Western perspective, based on an individualistic view of self. Underlying the concept of PTSD is the view of trauma as an individual-centred event confined to intra-psychic experience. For cultures that emphasise interdependency rather than autonomy, maintaining a connection to family, community, dead relatives and ancestors may be more significant than individual thoughts and feelings.

Expressions of distress and the ways in which people cope differ both between and within cultures. For instance, Guatemalan Indians in the midst of the conflict in Guatemala felt that their 'collective body' had been wounded, 'one which included the ants, trees, earth, domestic animals and human beings gathered across generations' (Summerfield, 1998, p. 17). It is a 'category fallacy' to assume that because behaviours are identified in different social settings they mean the same thing in those different settings (Kleinman, 1987). For one person recurrent nightmares may be insignificant, revealed only under direct questioning; to another they may represent the need to visit a mental health professional; to a third person they may represent a message from his/her ancestors or other spirits. The prevalence of PTSD in the majority world is often measured using methods developed in the minority world, with norms that have not been established on people from different cultural backgrounds.

Limited description of trauma

There can be a wide range of responses to traumatic events not exhausted by the four groups of 'symptoms' described in the DSM. Moreover the 'refugee trauma' discourse tends to emphasise only part of the wide spectrum of refugee experience. In contrast, Papadopoulos (2002) divides the refugee experience into four phases: *the anticipation* of impending danger and trying to avoid it; *devastating events* characterised by actual violence; *survival* in exile and the *adjustment* and grief of the refugee person living in exile.

Exposure to war, organised violence and torture as well as its aftermath is not generally a private experience, but disrupts social and cultural institutions often leading to survivors feeling isolated. Beyond the devastating material and economic losses refugee people experience, Eisenbruch (1990, 1991) emphasises the significance of 'cultural bereavement' – the loss of things that give meaning to life, such as social structures, cultural values, community rituals and relationships. Papadopoulos (2002) suggested the term 'nostalgic disorientation' to refer to the loss of all the various dimensions of home 'from a physical and geographical community, to a psychological locus of relatedness and communion; from a seat of origins, to the ultimate goal, the place of rest, beyond conflict' (Papadopoulos, 1987, p. 7).

The essence of home assumes a space where one's presence and entitlement are taken for granted; an assumption that is disrupted by experiences of racism, hostility and oppression in the receiving country. For example, the Kumusha in Shona cultures is more than home or a place to live, but refers to a site of identity and belonging, as well as a geographical and spiritual point of reference to ancestral spirits (Bourdillon, 1991). Hence strong emotional bonds to regions in Zimbabwe form the context for the highly charged debates about land (Parsons, 2006).

The concept of PTSD does not adequately conceptualise insidious or additive forms of trauma, whereby not being ensconced within a dominant and valued group means repeated exposure to covert and overt oppression, the penalties of which can range from annoying to life-threatening (Brown & Ballou, 1992). In addition, Papadopoulos and Hilderbrand (1998) note that positioning refugee people within victim discourses overshadows their resourcefulness and resilience. Yet 'refugee people present the maximum example of the human capacity to survive despite the greatest of losses and assaults on human identity and dignity' (Mueke, 1992, p. 520).

'Post' suggests that traumatic events are limited to a certain moment in the past. The cumulative and continuous nature of the multiple traumas refugee people experience means that neither the beginning nor the end of a traumatic process can be clearly determined.

The focus on 'trauma' diverts attention away from the important social, cultural and political aspects of refugee people's experience, as well as the social, cultural and political foundations of how emotional distress gets understood. Medicalised constructions of the experience of organised violence present a mechanistic view of human experience that suggests that the effects of war and organised violence are to be found *inside* a person (Summerfield, 2004).

Whereas 'stress' causes inconvenience and distress, oppression, persecution and violence challenge the ways we live and come to know ourselves, others and the world.

Describing people who have experienced persecution, violence and war as having a 'disorder' pathologises human responses and adaptations to abnormal, oppressive and abusive experiences. The PTSD diagnosis cannot take account of the magnitude, depth and complexity of refugee peoples' experience in its entirety. Such multiple difficulties cannot be meaningfully separated, nor can we predict which experiences are the hardest to cope with.

Aims of torture

Reflecting on the aims of torture (Patel, 2008) rather than the effects of torture focuses us on perpetration, as opposed to the inner world of the person who has been tortured. Patel (2008) argues that the aims of repressive regimes are often to create psychological and physical debility and dependency; annihilate without death; maximise helplessness, power-lessness and unpredictability; heighten a sense of vulnerability; keep in a constant state of fear; disorient, create confusion and uncertainty as well as to dehumanise and degrade (ethnic, political, sexual, religious) identity. Torture tends to be an ongoing repeated act that terrorises whole communities.[29] Thus torture is rarely just an assault on the individual but more usually on the links and connections between people.

In addition, people seeking asylum in the UK continue to be violated by an oppressive asylum system. In the process of seeking asylum their life stories are often distorted in a deeply shaming and dehumanising way. Therapy can help refugee clients reclaim the stories that have been thrown back at them, having been scrutinised, pulled apart and invalidated. A power, resistance and liberation lens can radically challenge our taken-for-granted views about emotional distress and move us away from a preoccupation with intra-psychic damage towards a fuller understanding of the interpersonal, social, cultural and political processes that might lead to liberation.

Part II

Liberation and therapy: Theory

Chapter 5

Liberation psychology: An overview

Before we think about liberation, it seems necessary to reflect on how we understand oppression, empowerment and justice. Given the complex ways oppression works, we have to hear fully the effects of inequality and prejudice in order to fully understand and appreciate people's responses and resistance to it.

What is oppression?

The terms 'oppression' and 'injustice' are closely linked and often used interchangeably. The word 'oppress' comes from the Latin *opprimere*, which means to press on or press against (Pearsall, 1998). For Watts, Griffith and Abdul-Adil (1999) oppression is the unjust use of power by one socially salient group over another in a way that creates and sustains inequality. With respect to injustice, Gil (1998) provides the following definition: 'coercively establishing and maintaining inequalities, discrimination, and dehumanising, development-inhibiting conditions of living . . . imposed by dominant social groups, classes, and people upon dominated and exploited groups, classes and peoples' (p. 10). Van Wormer (2004) argues that injustice refers to a general lack of rights or justice, whereas oppression refers to the mistreatment of people.

What is empowerment?

Parker (1999) challenges the concept of empowerment, and Lowe (1999) critiques the attempt to bring 'empowerment' into the therapeutic relationship through collaboration and transparency, which have become new tools for the 'armoury of the already powerful' (Lowe, 1999, p. 83). Parker (1999) argues: 'the word "empowerment" betrays something of the position of the expert who thinks that they have been able to move an enlightened step beyond 'helping' people but cannot give up the idea that it is possible to bend down to lift someone lesser than themselves up a step, to give them a little empowerment' (pp. 9–10). In addition, Lowe (1999) writes: 'How collaborative can collaborative be, and how transparent can transparency be, if they are institutionalised within a particular mode of practice? It is one thing to offer clients a voice within a professional therapeutic discourse, but it might be quite another thing to allow them a discourse of their own' (p. 82).

Similarly, Read and Wallcraft (1992) argue that no-one can give power to another person but they can stop taking power away. Therefore, moving beyond the collaborative approach, client resistance can be linked to empowerment in therapy, if clients' resistance to having their power being taken away is legitimised and their own power is able to breathe.

What is justice?

The word 'justice' is derived from the Latin *jus*, which means right, especially legal right (Ayto, 1990). However, how we define justice and rights depends on the cultures we grow up in. For some justice refers to individual achievement, for others it arises from collective liberation and redress and for others justice is linked inextricably to liberation of all life forms, including the environment. For example, the 'principles of environmental justice' adopted at the First National People of Colour Environmental Leadership Summit,[30] Washington, DC, October 1991, described justice and liberation as the re-establishment of 'spiritual interdependence to the sacredness of our Mother Earth' (First National People of Color Environmental Leadership Summit, 2005, p. 429).

Van Wormer (2004) quotes Menninger's (1966) book *The Crime of Punishment* in arguing that justice does not always entail fairness to all parties and can even mean punishment and mistreatment, such as in the case of imprisonment. What is clear is that justice and liberation are not uncomplicated ideas. The term 'liberation' conjures up images of freedom, happiness and joy, and yet the pursuit of liberation can lead to experiences of more injustice.

Throughout this book I reflect on the importance of community, connectedness in relationships and a respect for shared humanity. However, investing in communities, groups or relationships that do not respect the preferences of individuals, ensure equality and correct injustice is likely to be detrimental to individuals. Liberation therefore is an essential component of community, as much as community is essential to liberation.

What is liberation?

Liberation is that which connects the total and full humanity of all people. It can be viewed as a process of resisting oppressive forces and striving towards psychological and political wellbeing, rather than an endpoint

(Prilleltensky, 2003). Although a psychology of liberation is not new to the majority world (Latin America, Africa and Asia), it has only recently begun to influence the theory and practice of psychologists and psychotherapists in the minority world (Europe, Australia and North America). Liberation psychologists go beyond the psychology knowledge-base and break down the boundaries between political, sociological, historical, psychological, economic and cultural disciplines. Liberation psychology starts with the assertion that the 'psy' professions have neglected the collective and political. This critique could also be directed at systemic therapy, despite its focus on context and systems.

Proponents of liberation psychology seek to integrate psychology's core aim, the psychological wellbeing of people, with the stark reality of oppressive systems that undermine this aim (Du Bois, 1906/1994; Freire, 1973; Martín-Baró, 1996; Hollander, 1997; Comas-Diaz, Brinton Lykes, & Alarcon, 1998). Liberation psychologists believe that the root causes of oppression lie in social structures and discourses that create the everyday experiences of violence, poverty and prejudice. One of the major aims of liberation psychology is to develop an understanding of the role of the psychologist in social transformation (Martín-Baró, 1996; Comas-Diaz et al., 1998). Hence it emphasises social action to alleviate personal and collective distress (Du Bois, 1906/1994; Martín-Baró, 1988; Albee, 1992; Freire, 2006), and integrates individual models of therapy with broader models of oppression (Kessler & Goldston, 1986; Martín-Baró, 1988; Hollander, 1997; Comas-Diaz et al., 1998).

Liberation psychology is most commonly associated with Latin American liberation theology, founded by the Peruvian priest Gustavo Gutiérrez, which confronted the wealthy and racist elite and committed itself to the poor and oppressed. However, there has been a non-consideration of African voices in the international discourse on liberation psychology. Despite the multiple, diverse cultural, religious and social influences occurring there, African liberation psychology has been largely ignored outside of the continent. As other authors have pointed out, there are striking similarities between the field of Black liberation theology, originating in the African social movements of the 1950s and 1960s, and the liberation psychology of Latin America (Azibo, 1990, 1994).

Personal connections to liberation theory

My eldest sister Tayo introduced me to W.E.B Du Bois and Frantz Fanon when I was a teenager, which ignited my desire to meld my interest in the politics of oppression with my passion for supporting psychological wellbeing. I then came across Martín-Baró as an undergraduate psychology student when I read *Readings for a Liberation Psychology*. This interest was concretised on my final placement as a clinical psychology trainee at the

Medical Foundation, for the care of victims of torture. When I was studying systemic psychotherapy at the Kensington Consultation Centre (KCC) there was a room named after Brazilian education activist and scholar Paulo Freire, and I remembered that Martín-Baró based his theories on Freire's work and decided to read *Pedagogy of the Oppressed*. At the same time I read bell hooks' *Teaching Community* and *Teaching to Transgress*, which made reference to her admiration for Freire.

Reading these great critical theorists connected me to the heart-centre of my passion for justice and equality. It was a belief in love and compassion that drove me and I could taste that same desire for collective love in their work. The theories of Du Bois, Martín-Baró and Freire, as well as Memmi and Fanon (whom I will talk about later in this chapter), and their emphasis on the dynamics of oppression were deeply validating of my experiences growing up in a society that routinely denied racism.[31] I particularly welcomed their descriptions of oppression as forms of violence, given that I was surrounded by suggestions that racism was at worst inconvenient, rather than directly and indirectly abusive. My desire to contribute to changing oppressive discourses was reinforced by the social transformatist nature of their text. As Martín-Baró (1996) argued, 'the concerns of the social scientist should not be so much to explain the world as to change it' (p. 19).

W.E.B Du Bois and Franz Fanon

The origin of Black liberation psychology is often traced back to the writings of Martinican psychiatrist Franz Fanon (1963, 1967). However, Black liberation psychology can also be traced back further to W.E.B. Du Bois (1868–1963). A forerunner of critical and liberation theory, a significant amount of his work was produced before the development of liberation psychology.

W.E.B Du Bois' background

Du Bois was an African American man born on 23 February 1868. The Du Bois family were among the very few Black people growing up in Great Barrington, Massachusetts. Du Bois' experience of racism helped him develop a keen concern for the liberation of Black people. At 15 he became the local correspondent for the *New York Globe*, a platform for his lectures and editorials.

Between 1885 and 1888 Du Bois made his first trip to the southern states of America to attend Fisk College having received a scholarship. Du Bois' experiences as a Black person in the South further ignited his passion for challenging racism, as a writer, editor and passionate orator (Du Bois, 2007).

Du Bois received a PhD from Harvard University in 1895. His doctoral dissertation, *The suppression of the African slave-trade to the United States of America*, was published in 1896. For more than a decade he devoted himself to sociological investigations of the Black experience in America, producing 16 research monographs published between 1897 and 1914 at Atlanta University where he was professor. In 1899, at the age of 26, Du Bois published *The Philadelphia Negro: A Social Study* (Du Bois, 1996), the first case study of a Black community in the United States. This study was also the first time such a scientific approach to studying social phenomena was undertaken, and as a consequence Du Bois is acknowledged as the father of social science. He set the standard for emancipatory forms of research long before the term was used by critical research theorists.

Du Bois also studied at the University of Berlin in Germany. In 1903 he published his famous book *The Souls of Black Folks*. Du Bois started writing for *Crisis* magazine, where he continued to highlight and deconstruct racism. He never relented in attacks on imperialism, especially in Africa. His book *The World and Africa* was written as a challenge to historians who consistently omitted Africa from world history.

Du Bois also critiqued American foreign policy a century before the searing critiques of anarchists such as Noam Chomsky. As a member of the left-wing American Labour Party, Du Bois told a world peace meeting in Paris: 'Drunk with power, we [the US] are leading the world to hell in a new colonialism with the same old human slavery, which once ruined us, to a third world war, which will ruin the world' (Du Bois, 2007, p. 17). He later moved to Ghana and in the final months of his life became a Ghanaian citizen and an official member of the Communist Party (Du Bois, 2007).

W.E.B Du Bois' theories

Du Bois' history of the slave trade, written in the 1890s, is still viewed as one of the smartest and most comprehensive studies of the topic. His scholarship on a variety of topics continues to inform critical pedagogists with respect to his belief that schooling should ground itself on a transformative vision of the society we want to construct rather than simply reinforcing the social arrangements of the status quo.

Du Bois argued that Black people had been situated as 'the other' by slavery. In this position they had been stripped of their cultural consciousness in ways that served to perpetuate their sense of inferiority. Consequently, education for Black people should restore self-consciousness, self-realisation and self-respect and should allow Black people to see themselves through their own eyes instead of through the eyes of their oppressors.

Du Bois asserted that ghettoisation is not the creation of poor Black Americans but of wider social, political and economic forces. He pointed out the existence of structural and institutional racism 70 years before these concepts were understood in mainstream sociology. Du Bois also anticipated the work of post-structural theorists such as Michel Foucault on subjugated knowledges.[32] Du Bois argued that we are ever-confined by our social, cultural and historical position in the world but potentially emancipated by our appreciation of our predicament. That is, empowered by our knowledge we can begin to understand and disengage ourselves from the powerful narratives that are oppressive in our lives (Du Bois, 2007).

In a celebration of subjugated knowledge, Du Bois wrote about traditional West African education, which, he contended, began very early as children accompanied their parents in their daily tasks. Du Bois argued that the purpose of ancient education, particularly in pre-colonial indigenous African societies, was to contribute to the development of authentic human beings who could master the ethical, spiritual, emotional as well as cognitive and mental skills for living and, as such, African education was completely integrated with everyday life. No education existed in this context that was not concurrently usable for living a good life. Du Bois argued that American education had much to learn from the culture, history and spirituality of people from the African continent (Du Bois, 2007).

Franz Fanon

Franz Fanon (1925–1961) was a psychiatrist born into a middle-class Black family on the Caribbean island of Martinique. He practised as a psychiatrist in Algeria. Given his own exposure to violence – fighting in the French army against Germany, witnessing military and police brutality as well as exposure to colonialism and racism – violence became central to his theories about the impact of oppression and ways of ensuring liberation (Bulhan, 1985). He argued that institutional violence divided the world into 'us' and 'them', 'good' and 'bad', 'Black' and 'White' and formed the basis of racist ideology. As a psychiatrist Fanon was interested as much in the impact of this violence on the psyches of individuals as in its impact on everyday relationships between people and cultural practices. He argued that anger was an inevitable response of the colonised but tended to be directed towards each other, given that they lived in a cultural context that prohibited reacting to the violence of racism more directly (Moane, 1999).

Black liberation theology was conceived as bringing about the transformation of Africans out of 'wretchedness' into a rebirth of dignified and free Black humanity (Fanon, 1963; Azibo, 1994). Lincoln (1974) put forward a definition of Black liberation theology as 'the affirmation of Black humanity that emancipates Black people from White racism . . . [and] confronts the issues which are part of the reality of Black oppression' (p. 191).

Martín-Baró, Paulo Freire and Albert Memmi

Latin American liberation psychology is associated with Jesuit priest Ignacio Martín-Baró – often credited with developing the approach based on the work of Paulo Freire – and Maritza Montero, a Venezuelan social and political psychologist who is now regarded as the leading theorist in the field after the murder of Martín-Baró. Latin American liberation psychology developed from a particular cultural, social and political context (Burton & Kagan, 2005). Latin American societies are not identical, but have in common endemic poverty and social exclusion affecting the majority of the population as well as a much larger discrepancy between the rich and poor than in the UK or North America. Academics are often less ensconced and integrated into the state's systems than in the UK or North America, and therefore health professionals often have more freedom and autonomy to develop approaches to social problems that are directed more by the needs of local people than by government policy.

Martín-Baró (1996) did not see liberation psychology as a specific knowledge or approach to clinical work; instead he viewed liberation as the only ethical way to practice psychology and therefore the task of all psychologists (Montero, 2009). Despite this, liberation psychology in the UK and North America tends to be associated with critical social/community psychology, as opposed to linked to the task of all clinicians in the 'psy' field. Martín-Baró's interest was in what psychological theory and therapy would look like from the point of view of those who experience oppression rather than those in dominant social groups. He argued that only from the oppressed can we understand fundamental truths about society.

Of course these two groups (the oppressed and the oppressors) cannot always be easily delineated in modern society, as we are all part of many social groups at once and thus can be both dominated and dominator. However, Martín-Baró makes an interesting point about the viewpoint we tend to legitimise in the 'psy' field. Few textbooks, theories or training courses in mental health base their ideas on the experiences of those from minority or oppressed groups other than learning how to 'work with difference'. Members of subjugated groups rarely get accepted as having anything useful to say about the general concerns of psychology and therapy without there being a surrendering of their origins and identity (Martín-Baró, 1996). Martín-Baró (1996) called for psychology to examine itself critically so that it could be a force for transformation rather than conformity. He proposed three essential elements for the building of a liberation psychology: a new horizon, a new epistemology and a new praxis.

By a new horizon, Martín-Baró meant that psychology must 'stop focusing attention on itself, stop worrying about its scientific and social status, and instead propose an effective service to the needs of the majority of the population' (Martín-Baró, 1996, p. 26)

For Martín-Baró psychology should have a new perspective (epistemology) centred on being able to have a vision of what is possible that 'requires a new way of seeking knowledge . . . for . . . truth . . . is not in . . . present oppression but rather in the tomorrow of . . . liberty' (Martín-Baró, 1996, p. 27). This did not mean throwing out our knowledges, but revising our knowledges by critiquing what we have come to know.

Paulo Freire's (1973) notion of praxis combined reflection with social action. Psychology's attempt at scientific purity has meant taking the perspective of those in power and acting from a position of dominance. Directly linked to a new epistemology, a 'new praxis' (action) referred to placing ourselves alongside the dominated rather than alongside the dominator, which requires taking a stand and taking sides (Martín-Baró, 1996).

Stages of political consciousness

Freire developed the idea of critical consciousness (or *conscientización*), which became central to liberation psychology. Critical consciousness referred to an awareness of the socio-political context of daily life. It involved illuminating the often taken-for-granted realities about the way the world operates. Writer and essayist Albert Memmi grew up as a Jewish person in Tunisia colonised by the French, and described in his classic *The Colonizer and the Colonized* the context in which the psychology of the oppressed and oppressor develop and interact dialectically.[33] Freire described a process of moving from 'oppressed consciousness' towards 'critical consciousness'; whereas Memmi described a process towards 'decolonisation'.

For both Memmi and Freire the psychology of liberation was intimately linked to the psychology of colonisation, with an emphasis on the effects of political, economic and psychological domination on both the coloniser and the colonised. In Freire's model liberation was the process of humanisation; that is, becoming more authentic. For Memmi liberation was the process of decolonisation; breaking free from colonial oppression. Black liberation models are also based on developing critical consciousness, moving from oppression to liberation. Fanon (1967) argued that racism is a form of colonialism in which oppressors inscribe a mentality of subordination in the oppressed. He felt that the oppressed need to find their own voice and language to name and describe their conditions for liberation. Both Freire and Memmi described similar stages towards critical consciousness, each stage characterising the ways in which a person (a) names the problem, (b) reflects on the causes of the problem and (c) acts to resolve the problem. Martín-Baró (1996) delineated three tasks for psychology based on these stage theories of critical consciousness. First I will outline the stage theories of Freire and Memmi before delineating Martín-Baró's three tasks for psychology.

To achieve critical consciousness, Freire described three stages of a progressive development towards the desired endpoint. Stage 1 was called 'magical' because people feel powerless against an awful reality experienced as an irresistible force that changes or maintains things; hence people find themselves conforming. A person with *magical consciousness* will describe poverty and oppression as facts of life. Freire (2006) argued that 'magical consciousness is characterised by fatalism, which leads men to fold their arms, resigned to the impossibility of resisting the power of facts' (p. 39). Similarly Memmi described how the colonised person at the first stage initially accepts himself/herself as inferior and accepts colonial rule.

Stage 2 of Freire's model is *naïve consciousness*, which is reforming rather than conforming. At this stage people readily name problems but only in terms of problem people, whether this is individual oppressors or the oppressed themselves. People at this stage have a fragmented understanding of the causes of problems and therefore do not understand that individual oppressive acts are the result of oppressive systems (Smith, 1976). At this stage, reflecting on problems leads to reflecting on oneself in accordance with the ideology and value system of the oppressor that has been internalised as one's own. Action in this stage involves an attempt to become more like the oppressor or attempting to reform individual oppressors rather than tackle the system of oppression. Similarly, Memmi sees Stage 2 as the colonised person rejecting themselves to become like the coloniser in order to assimilate.

An important part of this stage is the notion of internalised oppression and double consciousness.[34] Freire (1973) borrowed from Du Bois' notion of double consciousness when he talked about the 'duality' found in 'the oppressed who "house" the oppressor in the form of a shadow that they "project" in two parts' (p. 40). Freire (1973) argued that 'suffering from a duality that is implanted "inside" of their being, they discover that, not being free, they cannot become authentic beings . . . They are themselves and at the same time they are the other, projected upon them as oppressed consciousness' (p. 26). As long as this inner oppressor remains undetected and predominates, the individual is unable to become their authentic being; that is, their own consciousness.

At Stage 3 individuals see instances of oppression as the normal functioning of an unjust and oppressive system. Individuals name oppression as the problem, as well as the failures of their collective group to challenge it. Similarly, for Memmi in Stage 3 the colonised person rejects the coloniser and colonial rule to reaffirm himself/herself and problems are viewed with respect to community rather than individuals. People in this stage understand how they collude to make the unjust system work; they reject the oppressors' ideology and seek liberation. Cooperation and collective solidarity replace conflict with fellow group members. Isolated actions against individual oppressors are replaced with self-actualisation and collective acts of social transformation. Memmi (1974) described this stage as decolonial-isation and revolution in which the colonised attain liberation through a recovery of the self.

Critical consciousness and the tasks of psychology

Martín-Baró (1996) described *conscientización* as a term coined by Paulo Freire related to Latin American people becoming 'literate in dialetic with their world' (p. 40). He goes on to say: 'for Freire literacy does not consist simply in learning to write on paper or to read the written word; literacy is above all learning to read the surrounding reality and to write one's own history . . . [and] say the word of one's own existence, which is personal but, more significantly, collective' (p. 40). Freire (2006) argued that as critical consciousness develops we no longer see current realities as the unchangeable nature of things. Instead, we see options for change. Critical consciousness or *conscientización* is therefore about 'learning to think critically about accepted ways of thinking and feeling, discerning the hidden interests in underlying assumptions' (Hopper, 1999, p. 21).

Martín-Baró (1996) linked the three-stage model of critical consciousness to the three tasks of psychology, which were as follows.

- By politicising memory and placing it in historical context, individuals are helped to transform by changing their social reality.
- Through gradually decoding their world, individuals are supported to grasp the mechanisms of oppression and dehumanisation so that they no longer view these as natural.
- To help people's new knowledge of their surrounding reality carry them to a new understanding of themselves with respect to strengths, resources and values. This enables them to discover the roots of what they are and what they can become.

These tasks go beyond simply changing how people think. As Martín-Baró (1996) puts it:

conscientización does not consist of a simple change of opinion about reality, a change of individual subjectivity that leaves that objective situation intact; conscientización supposes that persons change in the process of changing their relations with the surrounding environment and, above all, with other people.

(pp. 40–41)

The transformative process of liberation requires a process of transforming human relationships and not merely transforming cognitions. As well as describing this perspective that has influenced my ways of working with power, resistance and liberation in therapy, it is also important for me to reflect critically on its opportunities and constraints.

Chapter 6

Liberation psychology: Critical reflection

Despite the undeniable merits of a liberation psychology approach, any theory has the potential to be used in ways that are unhelpful to clients. In order to do justice to Martín-Baró's emphasis on the need for the 'psy' field to critique itself continually, the following is an exploration of the limitations of liberation psychology theory.

Development model

Parallels can be drawn between models of psychological development and the emphasis in liberation theory on the political development of a person, progressing along a given continuum towards a common and universal goal. These ideas about change make sense within a minority world context with a proliferation of models of development, based on moving through particular stages of growth. In these theories sequential stages of change are laid out like stepping stones on a path towards culturally preferred ways of being (Watkins & Shulman, 2008). This approach to liberation has influenced the emergence of other stage-based models that became popular in the 1970s through to the 1990s, such as Gay and lesbian identity development (Cass, 1979, 1984; Troiden, 1989), White racial identity models (Helms, 1984, 1995), a feminist identity development model (Downing & Roush, 1985), cross-cultural awareness model (Christensen, 1989), a Chicano–Latino ethnic identity model (Ruiz, 1990), a biracial identity development model (Poston, 1990), the Black racial identity development model (Cross, 1991), minority ethnic and sexual orientation identity development (Gutierrez & Dworkin, 1992; Morales, 1992), the nigrescence model of Black identity (Cross, 1995) and multiracial identity development (Root, 2002). More recently critics have argued that identity is a complex process with multiple aspects that can be flexibly chosen, depending on social context; as well as that there are many, often intersecting factors contributing to identity (Root, 2002; McDowell et al., 2005).

The stages of critical consciousness described in liberation psychology potentially reinforce the notion of 'progress' as growth and maturation towards what is considered ideal (Watkins & Shulman, 2008). From this perspective, raising political consciousness is a linear movement towards wholeness and liberation. However, Freire (1973) used the Portuguese term *conscientizaçäo*, which translates into Spanish as *conscientización*, which has 'no straightforward English translation' (Burton & Kagan, 2005). Although 'consciousness raising' is often cited as the term's meaning, Burton and Kagan (2005) refer to it as a possible translation. This translation lends itself to viewing Freire's concept as a process of increasing awareness. In fact Freire stopped using the term in 1974 because of its improper use and the implications of it (Burton & Kagan, 2005). Similarly Montero (2009) argues that there should be no techniques, methods or approaches associated with *conscientización*, as *conscientización* is 'not a unitary process' (p. 74).

As an anarchist/socialist, it is difficult to think about the idea of 'progress' in the context of globalisation without conjuring up notions of hierarchy, superiority and power – notions that need not be synonymous with liberation. We are so indoctrinated into the ideal of progress, and the corresponding notion of improvement, that we rarely critically reflect on the metaphor of moving forward as an understanding of liberation. Although delineating liberation into identifiable stages might be very helpful, it might also encourage us to take a position in therapy that is less than collaborative. We might come to believe that movement in the direction of liberation happens as a result of a top-down, hierarchical education of those who are less critically conscious by those who are more. This might manifest itself as therapists advocating an education approach to therapeutic intervention in which they act like mainstream teachers, choosing books for their clients to read and topics for discussion in therapy. If we want to join people where they are and help them be where they want to be, how helpful is it to see others as more or less socially insightful and politically aware than we are?

On a personal level, I have often observed that, rather than focusing blame outwards towards the social conditions and ideas that uphold oppression, it is all too easy solely to blame individuals for enacting social discourse; hence women blame other women, Black people blame other Black people, and so on for not embodying liberated consciousness.

Taking an expert position

When Freire talked in terms of educator and student, mythify and demythify, what might be understood is that in order to be liberated, people need to be re-educated. As a result, there seems to be a curious double position. On the one hand Martin-Baro (1996) argued that to develop a new praxis, psychologists should work *with* people developing their own strategies for transformation. On the other hand the emphasis on expert knowledge being passed down to those who have not yet been educated into critical consciousness runs the risk of replicating the oppression of imperialism. Ironically, the politics of liberating others and bringing them what we think they need for their own sake is very often the politics of domination. Powerful nations have spent decades referring to liberating countries from themselves (played out most often in the Wests' Islamophobic relationship to Muslim countries).

Any theory that purports to demonstrate how dominant groups misrepresent social reality must by definition claim some superior knowledge of that reality. If the expert knows reality then it makes sense that they have a duty to educate those blind to it. If we hold the view that people have to move from 'oppressed consciousness' to 'critical consciousness' to be liberated, our task in therapy is more likely to resemble education than collaboration, therefore taking on the very imperialist and paternalistic positions liberation theorists criticise. If a therapist or psychologist takes this expert position, any criticism or resistance on the part of the client might be viewed as ignorance. It is possible from this position to gently coerce clients to fit an agenda not of their making.

Given the inherent diversity of human experience and meaning making, reaching any kind of 'consciousness' would inevitably lead to different ideological outcomes, as it is not possible for there to be a single set of conclusions that everyone would reach (for example, some women might see liberation as being free to expose their body but not being defined by it, while other women might view liberation as covering up their body in order to be defined in other ways). To expect uniform outcomes might turn the process of critical consciousness into indoctrination.

Focus on internal world

The concept of liberation is by no means the sole province of liberation psychology. Freud himself focused his efforts on the poor, believing psychoanalysis would lead to their liberation. During the 1920s and 1930s psychoanalysts created free clinics and dedicated their time to those who could not afford analysis. As Danto (2005) argues, 'Freud always believed that psychoanalysis would release the reasoning abilities in oppressed individuals and that personal insight (combined with critical thinking) naturally led to psychological independence' (p. 302). Sándor Ferenczi, a lifelong friend of Freud's, argued that psychoanalysis should address the real conditions of society, in contrast to other psychoanalysts who argued that clinical objectivity was central to its science and therefore demanded distance from politics and social policy (Danto, 2005).

Many psychoanalysts at that time were also Marxists (for example Erich Fromm, Barbara Lantos, Käthe Friendländer, Wilhelm and Annie Reich) or identified themselves as socialist (for example Bruno Bettelheim, Helene Deutsch, Ernst Simmel). Liberation in their sense was about freeing people from oppressive internal states (for example from neurosis), which would positively impact on their experience of their world and their relationships. As well as liberation being a concept shared by liberation psychology and psychoanalytic theory, so too is an emphasis on the internal world of individuals.

Despite emphasis on social transformation, there is a concurrent focus in liberation theory on the internal world. Paulo Freire's *Pedagogy of the Oppressed* (Freire, 1973) and Frantz Fanon's *Black Skin White Masks* (Fanon, 1967) used this focus to examine how oppressed consciousness is created and maintained. This required the world be split into 'the oppressed' and 'the oppressor', as expressed in Freire's quote below:

> The oppressed suffer from the duality which has established itself in their innermost being . . . The conflict lies in the choice between being wholly themselves or being divided; between ejecting the oppressor within or not ejecting them; between human solidarity or alienation; between following prescriptions or having choices; between being spectators or actors . . . between speaking out or being silent, castrated in their power to create and re-create, in their power to transform the world.

> (Freire, 1973, pp. 32–33)

I am curious about the position Freire was writing from with respect to this dichotomy of 'the oppressed' and 'the oppressors'. Was he writing from the position of a critically conscious oppressed person? In what ways might Freire have had privilege? Much of Freire's descriptions of those who have yet to reach critical consciousness assumes that the oppressed have submitted to the will and power of the oppressor and that their sense of self and identity is only in relation to that which oppresses them (Wade, 1997). Freire repeatedly refers to the oppressed as 'inauthentic beings' and 'spectators' because an 'inner oppressor' remains undetected. Freire writes that 'self-depreciation is another characteristic of the oppressed, which derives from their internalisation of the opinion the oppressors hold of them' (1973, p. 49). From this perspective psychological patterns act as a barrier to liberatory social action and are part of what maintains oppression. Similarly, Martín-Baró believed that liberation 'involves breaking the chains of personal oppression' (1996, p. 27) and Fanon (1967) described how 'in the man of colour there is a constant effort to run away from his own individuality, to annihilate his own presence' (p. 60).

Terms such as 'internalised racism' or 'internalised homophobia' imply that individuals are stuck in their oppression because it has become a fixed state but also because it comes not just from the outside, but from within. Freire wrote that 'the oppressed, who have adapted to the structure of domination in which they are immersed, and have become resigned to it, are inhibited from waging the struggle for freedom' (1973, p. 32). With respect to racism, Thompson and Neville (1999) argue that 'putting an end to pathology that surrounds racism entails a struggle . . . the struggle requires the individual to examine the aspects of identity that relates to one's socialisation[35] as a racial being and to daringly confront how one has succumbed to the malignancy of racism' (p. 200).

In contrast, I would argue that homophobia, racism and other discourses of domination are social rather than individual traits. I believe that forms of oppression are processes and enactments and not located within individuals as intra-psychic characteristics. It might be important, therefore, to make sense of the link between social abuse and individual distress in ways that focus us *away* from the internal world and not towards it.

Limited and restrictive view of resistance

Given that society tends to value the big and the grand, the types of action that get viewed as constituting resistance are often 'contaminated by spurious notions of heroism' (Brown, 1994, p. 26) and focused on moments of collective protest. Such a view of resistance neglects:

- the ways people always resist oppression
- the ways we all struggle with contradictory positions and ways of responding to oppression that can coexist
- the back and forward movement towards liberation that is forever shifting and changing
- the place of our relationships and social circumstances in supporting or constraining movements in our preferred direction
- the possibility of being both oppressor and oppressed.[36]

If we focus purely on periods when overt protest and organised struggle directly challenge domination, we reinforce a view of resistance that is narrow. We assume that domination enjoys an unchallenged life until moments of societal upheaval. We also assume that the cultural practices and identities of the dominated remain firmly grounded in a terrain mapped by the dominant. Stage models of liberation are in danger of implying that movement towards liberation is linear, rather than what seems to be the case – that people often move in and out of positions, or occupy more than one position at once.[37] There is a danger that liberation theology leads us to focus on overt forms of resistance as more sophisticated than covert forms, which ignores the creativity of everyday acts of resistance. Gail Valaskakis argues that for first national people 'resistance is cultural persistence . . . continually negotiated in the discourse and practice of everyday life' (1993, p. 293).

As well as examples of overt resistance such as the Ndebele and Shona risings against Rhodesian imperialists and colonialists in 1896 (Ranger, 1986, p. 32), Paul E. Lovejoy charts untold stories of everyday acts of resistance among people classed as slaves in Sokoto Caliphate. This was the largest state in nineteenth-century West Africa, where slaves undermined the wealth and authority of their 'masters' through escape. This absolute loss of 'property' meant that even if captured their worth was reduced as a result of having been fugitives. This is in contrast to more 'dramatic examples of slave revolts and sabotages' (Lovejoy, 1986, p. 72). Although escaping slavery was ultimately about freedom from cruelty and bondage, the idea of human beings as 'property' was so fundamental to slavery that a by-product of escaping meant using 'their chattel state as weapons against their masters' (Lovejoy, 1986, p. 71). Resistance in whatever form reduced the worth of slaves to their 'master', so slaves worked more slowly than their 'masters' wanted, feigned illness, 'misunderstood' directions, stole crops and other valuables, burnt fields, broke equipment, and so on. As Lovejoy (1986) argued, 'by manipulating their value as commodities, slaves invariably asserted their identity as human beings, even if they suffered as a consequence' (p. 73). This resistance was viewed as a psychiatric illness by White slave owners and psychiatrists, who labelled the incongruent desire for 'non-humans' to be viewed and treated as humans as drapetomania.[38] Similarly, dysaesthesia aethiopis was a psychiatric diagnosis given to slaves who 'break, waste and destroy everything they handle . . . raise disturbances with their overseers' and generally refuse to work (Cartwright, 1851, p. 321). Craton (1986) argued that 'resistance has always been far more common than usually described . . . anything other than resistance is scarcely history at all' (p. 96). Resistance is often not organised, collective and overt, but localised as a response to everyday conditions of living where domination and oppression can have their greatest influence.

A limited view of resistance limits our view of social action. It is important to develop broader definitions of social action because narrow definitions can themselves serve to alienate and marginalise people who do not see overt forms of political protest as anything to do with their everyday lives. Martín-Baró (1996) dismissed the definition of 'political' as 'to do with the functioning of the state and its various branches' as too narrow (p. 53). He concluded that 'behaviour is political when it plays a role in the social confrontation of class and group interests' (p. 55). This opens up a variety of possibilities for taking action in the interpersonal, family, local community, government, and other spheres of society. It would therefore be incomplete to view a lack of overt public activism as a sign of passive resignation, satisfaction or insufficient dissatisfaction with the status quo. Social activism is obviously important and yet it is only one of many manifestations of resistance.

Approaches to 'justice' in therapy

A well-founded frustration with the ways in which social justice values, while often spoken, rarely translate to clinical practice has led some clinicians to take what they term a social justice approach to clinical intervention. Rhea Almeida's cultural context model (Almeida et al., 2007, 2008) offers a model for social justice practice that 'revises the endeavour of family therapy to include the pursuit of justice at every level, using tools and techniques' (Almeida et al., 2007, p. 6) that invite critical awareness and consciousness of diversity and power; highlight how hierarchies of power, privilege and oppression perpetuate suffering; and link social activism and accountability to therapy. Almeida et al. (2008) describe a commitment to 'bringing justice, fairness and equality to the centre of clinical work' (p. xiv) and site Freire's educational pedagogies, liberation theology and critical psychology, among others, as influences in their approach.

In their case studies Almeida et al. (2008) describe clients being shown video clips of films the therapists have chosen that address pertinent issues; urging clients to take responsibility for their abusive behaviour; therapists telling clients what restorative action they should take and clients being confronted by people in culture circles.[39] The text refers to clients being 'exposed to social education' (Almeida et al., 2008, p. 11), suggesting a one-way hierarchical relationship between people who know and those who do not. Such an approach is in danger of underestimating the client's own realisations and potentially invites adversarial protest or passive accommodation from clients (Jenkins, 2009).

The following excerpt from Almeida, Dolan-Del Vecchio and Parker's case study seems to reveal signs of client resistance. Tim and Mary were a White upper-middle-class heterosexual couple married 25 years, who entered therapy because their daughter was hospitalised with anorexia nervosa and 'because of Tim's long history of extra-marital affairs' (Almeida et al., 2008, p. 8). The authors go on to describe how convincing evidence emerged of Tim's latest affair and, as a result, Tim's culture circle 'helped him to explore the ways that he, like many men, placed his own desires over those of his partner and children' (Almeida et al., 2008, p. 8). The case example continues:

> This admission was difficult for Tim, but it was made easier by the voices of other men who reminded him that this pattern resulted more from their shared socialisation into manhood than from Tim being a 'bad' or 'sick' individual. At one point *Tim threatened to leave treatment and seek a 'more responsible' therapist*. His men's circle . . . challenged him to consider the possibility that the real issue was his reluctance to confront issues openly and honestly. He decided to stay. Therapists and sponsors began urging Tim to take responsibility for

disregarding Mary on many levels . . . The therapists encouraged Tim to . . . claim full responsibility for his actions by informing Mary and their children of his affair. *He balked initially*, but then agreed.

(emphasis added) (p. 8)

The case goes on to describe how Tim 'with support from the other men' wrote a letter to 'the other woman' terminating their affair (Almeida et al., 2008, p. 8). Then surrounded by members of both his and Mary's culture circle, Tim revealed his affair to his family. On first reading I was impressed by an approach motivated by a deep sense of social justice. From a liberation psychology perspective social issues such as gender power and fairness are directly addressed as central to therapy and not a peripheral concern. When I read the extract again from the perspective of power and resistance I reflected on what was missing from the description, such as:

- how collaboration was created between the therapists and clients
- how the therapists and culture circles continued to critically reflect on their approach with respect to power, privilege and oppression and how they facilitated and allowed for multiple voices to be heard
- how the therapists were accountable for the power of their position and its effect on others.

The culture circles were presented as though they represented one critical voice saying the same thing, for the same purpose, towards the same goal – to re-educate Tim. Tim's forms of what could be viewed as resistance (what I have put in italics) seem only to be a backdrop to the real work at hand. In my own practice, I have reflected on how a confrontational approach with a facing-up agenda might invite from clients reactive rather than creative responses; for example, passive attempts to avoid criticism and gain approval from the therapist or withdrawing into denial or defensiveness (Jenkins, 2009).

Given that in writing up clinical interventions it is often very difficult to capture the complexity of the therapeutic process, my criticism is not of the clinicians or their intervention *per se*, but of the issues that get privileged in describing social justice-oriented clinical work and the issues that get left out. The danger is that we start to view the confrontation of oppression as the primary goal in therapy and the potential for therapists to abuse their power as secondary to this primary goal. When we are guided and driven by our passion and ethics there is an energy and motivation that is very satisfying. It is very easy in this context to be more wrapped up in our values than connected to the world of the client – a world that may be very different from our own. Examples of how I fell victim of this in my own practice are found in Part III.

Jenkins (2009) makes a useful distinction between shaming individuals and helping to create the context in which individuals themselves face shame. He argues 'When a man faces shame, he comes to his own real-isations through recognising a contradiction between his ethics and his actions. By contrast, shaming others is [an abuse of power] and not sur-prisingly, tends to further exacerbate avoidance of responsibility' (p. 20). Confrontational practices might lead us to become insensitive and dis-respectful of the client's experience while expecting them to become sensitive and respectful to the experience of others (Jenkins, 2009).

What is useful about liberation psychology?

Despite these potential pitfalls, liberation psychology is undoubtedly useful in developing therapeutic approaches that honour the complexities of power, resistance and liberation. Liberation psychology ideally focuses on people developing their own strategies for action, which suit their capabili-ties and interests, and which give them a sense of control and agency. As Watkins and Shulman (2008) point out, the aim of liberation psychology should not be to move towards a fixed utopian goal that is universal or known in advance; but to continually develop and sustain relationships that are experienced by as many people as possible as liberatory. This is there-fore an 'on-going revolution . . . a continuing practice of dialogue and restoration with the goal of building more humane communities' (Watkins & Shulman, 2008, p. 25). What we reach for, according to Martín-Baró (1996), is 'an opening against all closure, flexibility against everything fixed, elasticity against rigidity, a readiness to act against all stagnation' (p. 183). Similarly, Comas-Diaz et al. (1998) suggest that the liberation psychologist accompanies those living in conditions of oppression, where they define 'accompany' as 'standing alongside people, working with them, seeking to develop collaborative relations that recognise power inequities' (p. 779). This is not a matter of thinking for other people or imposing our ideas about how to solve their problems; 'it has to do with thinking and theor-ising with them and from them' (Martín-Baró, 1996, p. 28). The important question, therefore, is who is author of the process? An interest in power has to take into account not just the outcome or goal of intervention but the processes we engage others in. My understanding of Paulo Freire's seemingly contradictory premise that no one person liberates another and yet no-one is self-liberated (Freire, 1973) is that this is not contradictory at all. If we view this statement through a circular rather than a linear lens, and relate it to a collaborative dialogical process, liberation is what happens *between* people; not against, for or on behalf of others.

Rather than viewing people as being at various stages towards liberation, with respect to what is not yet the case, we could enquire about *what already is*. This curiosity in and of itself may encourage people to make further moves in their desired direction. The difference in emphasis is that we do not aim to help people realise what they are not doing. As Esteva says, 'for two thirds of the people on earth . . . "development" . . . is a reminder of *what they are not*. It is a reminder of an undesirable, undignified condition. To escape from it, they have to be enslaved to others' experiences and dreams' (1992, p. 6). Instead we might help people connect to the ways in which they already orient towards liberation if we focus on liberation psychology's three tasks of therapy:

1. politicising memory and placing it in historical context
2. highlighting, reflecting on and challenging oppression
3. noticing, validating and amplifying people's strengths, resources and values.

I will reflect on these three tasks in more detail in Part III of this book and describe examples of clinical work that demonstrate how the three tasks might guide our intervention. Before I do this, the following chapter reviews narrative, communication and social context approaches to liberation arising from therapeutic conversations.

Chapter 7

Narrative approaches to liberation

From a systemic, narrative and communication approach, liberation might be viewed as the ability to move on in a preferred direction towards a preferred goal, identity or way of living based on the client's values. Therapists from this perspective contribute to collaborative conversations that elicit, acknowledge and elaborate on client abilities, resources and values that have previously been obscured. These conversations might open up new possibilities for being and action that impact on the world of the client. Values are not neutral or inherently positive. Participating in oppression, for example might become a more attractive option because the oppressor is promised something they value, such as power or prestige. Not all values lead to positive actions. A violent and abusive partner may value control and mastery at the expense of respect and kindness. Therefore, it is important to supplement an enquiry into values with a systemic focus on how we coordinate with others; such that we reflect on the consequences of our preferences on our relationships and what gets created between people.

I will now briefly describe liberation with respect to narrative practice, particularly with respect to a focus on multiple stories and ways of story-telling. Following this I will describe how the communication theory known as coordinated management of meaning (CMM) can be viewed through the lens of liberation theory.

Liberating stories

The narrative view of self is intrinsically a social view, so it is no surprise that collectivist societies have strong storytelling traditions. Narratives have the power to provide individuals and communities with a sense of connection to others past and present, human and nonhuman. Peterson (2001) describes the Chipko (tree hugging) movement that resists logging in India and relies on tales of past heroes and martyrs as well as traditional Hindu sacred stories. These narratives provide Chipko activists with 'an identity between themselves and the trees they embrace' (Callicott, 1994, p. 223).

Narrative practice draws heavily from Michel Foucault's work on power and knowledge (White & Epston, 1990). Foucault argued that society has 'normalising truths' that have the power to construct how people see the world, and therefore their lives. These normalising truths create dominant knowledges for those who have power, and keep other truths that do not fit these dominant accounts subjugated. Because no one story captures the complexity of life, there are always alternative, more enabling and liberating stories open to us, which also have the potential to shape and guide our lives in preferred directions.

Narrative practice is about joining with clients to co-construct new stories that lead them to act creatively into the future, in ways that sustain preferred identities, activities and relationships. Narrative therapists look for the patterns that connect the stories we live and the stories we tell.[40] Given that we cannot be sure of what a useful story or direction might be for a client, a narrative therapist might ask questions about preferences. What are the person's preferred ways of being? What stories might they want to suspend/eradicate/put aside? What stories might they want to enhance/make more prevalent/allow space to breathe? How do they want to live? How do they want to relate to others? What kind of person do they want to be?

Deconstruction is central to a narrative therapy approach and aims to unpack the assumptions within discourses, examine the function and effect of discourses on clients' lives and facilitate access to more empowering narratives (White, 1995). Similarly, Martín-Baró (1996) argued that 'the healing power of any psychotherapeutic method depends on the dosage of its break with the dominant culture . . . [and] the veil of lies we move about in' (p. 120). Not surprisingly, narrative therapy is often called a therapy of resistance (Guilfoyle, 2005).

The power of stories

We hear stories, remember stories and re-tell stories. Our understanding of ourselves, others and our relationships is significantly influenced by the stories we tell as well as the stories that we do not tell. In attempting to make sense of ourselves and our lives we arrange our myriad experiences into a coherent account of what we are experiencing. Peterson (2001) points out that narratives have the power both to guide life as it is and to challenge life into being what it could be. As a result, stories can be transformative or oppressive; and yet stories are never fixed or finished, but can be challenged by new events.

When I think about the power of stories I think about my relationship with my mother. I am very close to my mother and value my relationship with her immensely. Although we are very loving and affectionate with each other now, when I was growing up my mother often seemed emotionally absent. This made little sense to me given that she was obviously a loving and generous person, evidenced by her relationship with my father and her commitment to supporting other people. I often felt as a child that I was difficult to love because I felt that my mother did not always hold me in mind. This feeling that I was difficult to love carried into adulthood. I saw numerous counsellors and therapists who seemed to want me to 'get in touch with anger' about my mother's emotional absence, but I did not feel angry. I longed to understand her. I longed to be lovable.

When I left home and went to university I witnessed how much my mother missed me. I started asking her questions about her life and heard stories that surprised and moved me. During one conversation my mother told me about the pain of losing both her parents in her twenties and not being able to see them before they died because they were in Nigeria and she was in the UK. My mother told me about the indescribable trauma of a number of miscarriages and the death of her baby son Jidé, before my twin sister and I were born. I noticed how neither one of my parents could talk about Jidé without visibly crumbling with grief. I realised through these conversations that my mother was not emotionally absent. The depth of the fear she felt about losing people she deeply loved matched both the depth of her love and the distance she created in order to protect herself from that love.

More recently I decided I wanted to see a therapist and asked friends to recommend someone whose approach differed from the counsellors and therapists I had previously seen. My conversations with this new therapist helped me realise that my mother experienced me as so lovable that she could not help but love me, despite the enormous fear of loving and losing. I discovered that I was not difficult to love. The power of this new story meant I experienced a type of emotional liberation I had never felt before. When my mother expresses love towards me now I am reminded of this new understanding. Soon after this revelation in therapy two things happened – 'letting go' and 'connecting with':

1. I let go of depression (as a fixed part of my identity) and gave up cigarettes
2. I sought permission from my mother to write about these experiences in this book. Not only did she happily give me permission, but she began to talk about her miscarriages and losing her son Jidé, only this time she looked relaxed and content, as though she was happy that sharing meant being close to me. This painful story had become a story with the power to connect our hearts rather than being a reminder of her pain.[41]

The nature of stories

The story metaphor is one of many possible ways of enabling us to make sense of our experiences. Rather than viewing some metaphors as 'good' and others as 'bad' or as less or more correct, we could ask the question, which metaphors are useful in creating contexts for liberation? Moving away from metaphors of human beings as machines that work well or break down, narrative as a metaphor has transformative power, because stories are constructed and can be deconstructed and reconstructed. This metaphor is not predicated on there being an objective reality. It is fluid rather than static, requires authors and audiences (a community), tellers and listeners, and is therefore inherently social.

The word 'story' has different associations and understandings for different people, not all of which are positive or enabling. Stories are often associated with childhood, with theatre, drama and entertainment. Stories are also associated with less useful concepts for a collaborative therapy, such as fabrication, fantasy and triviality. In a narrative sense stories are simply the events of our lives, linked in a sequence across time in a coherent way and in accordance to a plot (Morgan, 2000).

In order to author a story, certain events are selected out and privileged over other events. Once privileged, they are linked with other events across time, to form a story about a particular issue such as 'being difficult to love'. When a person goes to see someone in the 'psy' field, often the stories they have for their lives have become dominated by problems that oppress them – what narrative therapists call problem-saturated stories. Problem-saturated stories can also become identities that have a powerful negative influence on the way people see themselves (for example, 'I'm unlovable'). There are always other events that are outside of this dominant story that remain hidden or less significant. Because our lives are multistoried – that is, there are many stories occurring at the same time and different stories can be told about the same events – no single story can be free of contradiction and no single story can encapsulate or handle all the complexities of life (Morgan, 2000).

From a narrative perspective people are never the problems they face, and there is always a context in which the stories of our lives are formed. This context of gender, class, 'race', culture and sexuality contributes to the meanings that we give to events and to the plot of the stories by which we live (Morgan, 2000). For example racism and sexism, and my responses to them, have impacted on my life in ways that have both strengthened and challenged the story that I am not lovable. How we tell our stories is also important. For example, we might tell and live our stories as though: the end is predetermined; the end is yet to be written and we write the end; they are accurate descriptions of an unchanging reality; or reality is fluid and subject to revision. We might tell stories as if they are devoid of cultural and political context. We might tell stories that leave out our agency and responses to our experience. We might have difficulty telling our own story while being profoundly open to the stories other people tell. The client in therapy is assisted to develop a different story and a different way of telling stories that might better fit how they want to see themselves and live their lives (Pearce & Pearce, 1998).

Beyond the story metaphor

Narrative metaphors are not without their potential difficulties, depending on our approach. Rather than a worldview, narrative therapy might be practised as a set of techniques, or as permission to dismiss a person's experience as 'just the story they tell themselves'. Bertrando (2007) says that realities are but the conversations we have about them. However, given that there is always a 'more' to meaning, the story metaphor can only ever be a partial meaning. There is also a vast material reality that impinges on how we feel and behave with each other. Although there may be liberation in words, it is just as true to say that there is liberation beyond words. A woman survivor of sexual torture, for example, may change her story of herself from victim to empowered survivor, but she may still have to live in poverty, with ongoing physical pain and racist experiences. In addition to re-authoring stories, people often need actual systemic changes in order to experience liberation from the constraints of structural inequalities, such as fair wages, educational opportunities, access to life-saving treatment, clean water, sanitation, safe living conditions, and opportunities to express their views and talents.

Oppressive and abusive realities can carry a destructive force separate from the meanings and stories attached to them. For instance, poverty is a reality beyond stories. Amartya Kumar Sen, the eminent Indian economist and philosopher who won the Nobel Prize for Economics for his passionate and compassionate work on the underlying mechanisms of poverty, inequality and oppression, frames poverty in terms of both capabilities and entitlements. Without the latter, the former cannot thrive.[42] Hence there is a dialectical relationship between personal capacities and social factors (Sen, 1999a, 1999b). Poverty can impact on people silently, in their wordless experiences, as structural oppression becomes the quiet fabric of people's life. There is no doubt that poverty creates inexplicable limitations. Highlighting this reality is not to say that poverty can totally eradicate the ways in which stories are often used to live beyond limitations.

The social GRAACCCEESS

The social GRAACCCEESS is my extension of Roper-Hall's (1998) social GRACES acronym reminding us to reflect on gender, religion, age, ability, class/caste, culture, colour (skin), ethnicity, education, sexuality, spirituality,[43] which are the many social influences that mediate experiences of power, resistance and liberation. Without a focus on the social

GRAACCCEESS, understanding the workings of power and the meaning of resistance might become simplistic.

Take for example a dual-heritage family where the father is a working-class African Caribbean city worker and the mother a White middle-class British artist. The mental health service is told that the mother feels neglected and depressed because her husband is working long hours. The therapy team might focus so heavily on gender – for example hypothesising that father is using his power as a man to distance himself from his partner by not centralising her emotional needs – that the impact of skin colour and class on what happens in the family gets neglected. Does the father feel he has to 'overwork' in order to survive as a Black male in an exclusively White middle-class profession? A focus on skin colour to the exclusion of gender, class or other issues might also oversimplify how power gets played out between people.

In our attempt to address issues of power we may inadvertently silence subjugated voices, reducing a more complex picture to only one of its significant dimensions. In the same way that we might excuse the most unspeakable acts of cruelty – such as war – provided they occur far enough away as to pose no personal threat, it is all too easy for us to pay less attention to forms of oppression and discrimination that do not directly impact on us. A focus on the social GRAACCCEESS supports our ability to move beyond what we know and experience directly, and reflect on different worlds.

> Jamie is a 14-year-old boy who lives with his single mother Judy. Both Jamie and Judy claim that the other is domineering and oppressive. Jamie is taller than his mother and has clear physical advantage. However, Judy is an adult with a status and privileges that Jamie does not enjoy. Given that power hierarchies may be contradictory, ambiguous and inconsistent, what would it mean if we focused on the parameters of gender and physical strength, but ignored the adult–child dimension? What would it mean if we focused on the power disparity between adults and children and ignored gender and physical strength as issues that influence how Jamie and Judy relate to each other? What if I then told you that Judy is a White woman of Scottish descent and Jamie is dual-heritage, of Scottish and West African origin? What would be the repercussions of ignoring the significance of skin colour on the experiences Jamie and Judy have of the world and each other?

We might need to develop our relationship to aspects of the GRAACCCEESS we are not so comfortable or familiar with or feel less able to reflect on. For example, a male therapist may understand the importance of reflecting on his gender and what it might mean to a woman who has experienced sexual or physical violence to be seen by a man, while having to develop his ability to reflect on the impact of being White in therapy with Black clients who have experienced the repeated abuse of racism. Similarly, a Black therapist may find it easier to explore and address issues related to 'race' than to sexuality.

I will now describe a communication theory developed by Cronen and Pearce (1985) and further developed by Cronen (1995) and Pearce (2007) separately, which explores levels of context more fully.

Chapter 8

Communication/Social context approaches to liberation

Coordinated management of meaning (CMM)

Coordinated management of meaning (CMM) has been described in detail elsewhere (Pearce & Cronen, 1980; Cronen & Pearce, 1985; Pearce, 1989, 2007), therefore my intention is to explain my understanding of how CMM fits with the aims of a therapy oriented by concepts of power, resistance and liberation. CMM is a social constructionist theory of communication developed by Cronen and Pearce (1985) which explores how meanings and actions emerge in context. It is a useful framework for exploring the experience of power and resistance, as it considers how wider social forces shape individual perceptions and how the individual as agent shapes the world. Individuals neither stand outside their social world nor are passive receivers of it.

In the process of living and telling the stories of our lives, we are always involved in communication and in doing so co-construct social realities with each other. In *Communication and the Human Condition* Pearce (1989) argued that forms of communication in which we participate either liberate or enslave us. The process of communication is about making /managing meaning *and* coordinating our actions with others. Pearce (2007) argued that both sides of this complex process should be considered equally important and given full consideration. With respect to power, CMM follows on from Foucault's notion of power discussed in Chapter 2. Foucault argued that an individual's actions cannot be considered totally autonomous, therefore exercises of power are merely power's 'ultimate destinations' (Foucault, 1980, p. 96) as they originate in social discourses. Given that power is enacted in the interaction between, rather than a possession within, context and meaning become central to our understanding of it.

Before we can fully understand what Cronen and Pearce mean by the centrality of communication, it is first important to explore different ways of understanding what indeed communication is. Pearce does just this in his 2007 book *Making Social Worlds*. He argues that the dominant way of viewing communication in the minority world since the Enlightenment is the transmission model that regards good communication as when we understand exactly as intended what is meant, despite 'the imperfection of language' (Pearce, 2007, p. 32). That is, 'good communication occurs when the meanings in "your" mind are exactly the same as the intentions in "mine"' (p. 31). Communication from this perspective is bad when this clarity and agreement is not achieved. This leads to the assumption that the message was not clear (and the speaker/writer/performer should explain further); or the message was distorted in the transmission; or the problem is with the person who interpreted the message incorrectly (Pearce, 2007). Therefore anyone who continues to disagree with us, or to feel hurt once we have made our intentions in communicating clear, must have something wrong with them and it is their fault they have misunderstood. Given the ethereal quality of words, there is no word that inevitably 'excites in the hearer the exact same idea which it stands for in the mind of the speaker' (Pearce, 2007, p. 32). Pearce argues that 'if we rely on this concept of communication we will strive to explain ourselves more and more clearly, but this may make our conflict worse rather than better, and then we are stuck' (Pearce, 2007, p. 32).

Kevin and Sidney came to couple therapy after Kevin had an affair and his boyfriend Sidney could not understand why. In therapy Kevin explained that he was feeling lonely and abandoned by Sidney, who was away from home a lot. In each session Sidney brought up the affair as an example of why he was feeling unhappy in the relationship, and each time Kevin tried to explain by re-telling the same story. Until one session Kevin got angry and said to Sidney: 'Why do I have to keep explaining the same thing to you? Do you not yet get what I am telling you?' Kevin felt stuck and hurt because he felt that his partner could not forgive and forget his mistake, despite his having apologised many times. Sidney felt hurt and confused because Kevin could not under-stand that he was not after a clearer and clearer explanation of what happened, but a way of feeling Kevin still loved him. It was not until Kevin arrived home one day and hugged Sidney saying: 'I've really really hurt you, and you really don't deserve it', that they were able to move on.

Initially Kevin and Sidney could not coordinate their different meanings. While Sidney was trying to communicate that he wanted Kevin to validate his hurt and show him that he still loved him, Kevin wanted Sidney to accept his justifications. When Sidney could not accept Kevin's explanation, Kevin felt that Sidney did not care about his feelings and would never forgive him. Acting out of these different contexts, Kevin and Sidney missed the other person's meaning.

There are many ways this scenario could have panned out, and I am not suggesting there is a right or wrong way. However, in understanding how the couple were able to move on, it is possible that when Kevin apologised to Sidney, Kevin had moved from his meaning towards connecting with Sidney's hurt. It is equally possible that Kevin's intention in apologising was to try a different way to get Sidney to forgive him. Despite the possibility that their positions had not changed very much and they were still approaching the issue in the same way as previously, they found a new way of being that involved co-ordinating their actions. As a result of this coordinated action they changed their stories about the other. The mutual act of hugging meant that Sidney felt Kevin loved him and Kevin felt Sidney forgave him.

This example illustrates how relationships are by-products of particular forms of communication. People can coordinate their actions and create new meanings, even when they do not agree about their meanings. This is equally true of the therapeutic relationship.

A social constructionist model of communication is based on the notion that there are an infinite number of social worlds and we are making them in each minute we interact with others. CMM practitioners believe that meaning, like everything else in the social world, is bound by the context it happens in (Pearce, 2007). CMM describes the complexity of communication and its relevance to understanding our experiences in a number of ways. In particular, I will describe (1) coherence, coordination and mystery; (2) levels of context and (3) the daisy model.

Coherence, coordination and mystery

Cronen and Pearce (1980) described the human need to make sense of the world with respect to *coherence* (the ways in which we interpret the world and our experiences), *coordination* (the ways we interact with the world and each other) and *mystery* (there is more to life than what we think we know and how we make sense of the immediate moment).

O'Hagan (1996) describes the importance of *coherence* when she describes her experience of emotional distress: 'Before, my thoughts were sliding off into nonsense. This terrified me so I tried to make some sense of things by taking bits out of nonsense and putting them into a story' (p. 49).

Coordination is not simply fitting in or complying but acting with, in dynamic and infinitely changing ways. This model does not assume that one way of coordinating is always better than others but simply asks the question: what are we creating together and does it meet our individual, relational and collective needs?

Mystery reminds us that there is more to life than what we come to view as the facts of existence and more to existence than the tangible and rational. The ways in which we experience our world as meaningful are a source of wonder. Almost all cultures have a view about the mystery that lies beyond the ordinary aspects of life and often grapple with this wonder through a spiritual idiom (Bracken, 2002).

Pearce (2007) argues that either we tend to focus on coordinating our actions at the expense of managing meaning or we attempt to make meaning without coordinating our actions. The following is an example of an attempt by me as the therapist to make meaning without coordinating my actions with the client, and therefore coming up against what could be viewed as client resistance.

> Victoria was an East African woman who came to see me after she witnessed the man who raped her sentenced to prison. Victoria made numerous irrefutable assertions that she was 'dirty' as a result of being raped and would have nothing but this filth to pass down to her children. Victoria would become upset and insist that she did not just feel as though she was 'dirty', she actually was. I found that any desire on my part to reflect on this idea, look into this word, deconstruct it, or link it to powerful discourses was strongly resisted by Victoria. She was adamant that this feeling would not and should not change. It was important for me to reflect on my own personal, professional, political biases towards wanting to challenge her view of herself as 'dirty' as well as to find ways of repositioning myself such that I would be more useful to Victoria and fit with her better.

My strong desire to deconstruct Victoria's negative view of herself did not fit with what she found helpful. Although I was well intentioned I was not respecting the idea of creating an 'us' and was thus experienced by her as oppressive. It was important to remind myself that there was a logic that I did not yet fully understand. So rather than trying to challenge it I needed to try and connect to it. Resistance in this instance was an invitation for me to be more curious than certain.

In later chapters I revisit this case example and explain how coordinating with Victoria led to more collaborative and respectful practice. An important part of this coordination was being able to reflect on the levels of context that made sense of her position and mine, why they were experienced as incompatible and how I could shift in my position in order to fully join Victoria and her journey towards liberation.

The levels of context

There are many different sorts of stories we live by, such as stories about the past, present and future; stories belonging to individuals and/or communities; family and relationship stories; and stories informed by culture,

POWER **Contextual Force:** The effect different levels of context have on communication. The greater the weight of the contextual force, the more a person can feel obliged to respond in a certain way.	**Political** – Meanings that are influenced by global/political context* **Spiritual** – Meanings related to systems of belief** **Culture** – Meanings that are shared within a community **Family** – Meanings that are shared within a family **Interpersonal relationship** – Meanings derived from relationships **Identity/life script** – Personal/professional/autobiographical experiences **Episode** – The event which adds meaning to what is communicated **Speech act** – The act and/or utterance and meanings that are communicated **Bodily sensations** – The bodily feelings/experiences that affect interpretation **Content** – of a statement	**Implicative force:** The effect the communicated response has on higher levels of context. **RESISTANCE**

Framework for thinking about contextual and implicative forces on levels of context, as power and resistance – adapted from Cronen and Pearce (1985). *Addition made by Nimisha Patel, November 2005, personal communication. **Addition made by Karen Partridge, May 2007, personal communication.

Figure 8.1 CMM multiple levels of context.

gender, skin colour, class, sexuality and so on. CMM levels of context (Figure 8.1) help us explore what contexts are influencing our actions in interaction with others; they illustrate the ways in which some stories have a stronger force in shaping our actions than others and how changes in one domain of life or level of context have a flow-on effect on others.

CMM levels of context have tended to be presented as having two primary uses, aimed at supporting the development of better patterns of communication by (a) discerning critical moments and (b) choosing how to act into them in ways that are most likely to lead to coordination rather than conflict (Pearce, 2007). CMM levels of context in this form are interested in specific situations, not situations in general. In this book I propose another use of CMM levels of context using ideas from liberation psychology and with a power and resistance lens.

CMM proposes that contextual forces at a higher level can directly influence the activities described within more specific levels. For example, it could be said that the contextual force of culture has a powerful and direct influence over the context of family relationships. In addition, an implicative influence from a more specific level of experience can influence more general (higher) levels. For example, behaviour at the episode level can have a far-reaching impact over time on future personal identity, interpersonal relationships, family dynamics and even ideas that are perpetuated and exist in communities and wider society. With respect to the lenses of power, resistance and liberation, the implicative force might be viewed as a type of resistance or counter-power against the power of the contextual force. With this framework we ignore neither structures of power nor personal agency and a person's identity is shaped not merely by what happens to them but also by how they respond to what happens to them.

Traditionally the language used in psychological literature has tended to focus on the effects of power. For example, we might say that bed-wetting is an effect of sexual abuse. Whereas an effect does not influence or change its cause, in the circular framework of CMM there are always implicative forces that impact on the contextual force. For example, bed-wetting might have made abuse less likely to occur, and is therefore not just an *effect* of abuse but a form of resistance to it. Similarly, Collins (2000) critiques the prevailing approach to studying oppression which does not take account of 'Black women's everyday acts of resistance' (p. 184). She argues:

> Sojourner Truth, Anna Julia Cooper, Ida Wells-Barnett, and Fannie Lou Hamer are but a few names from a growing list of distinguished African American women activists. Although their sustained resistance to Black women's victimisation within interlocking systems of race, gender, and class oppression is well known, these women did not act alone. Their actions were nurtured by the support of countless ordinary African American women who, through strategies of everyday resistance, created a powerful foundation for this more visible Black feminist activist tradition.
>
> (p. 183).

Scott (1985) critiques the Marxist claim that false consciousness makes the working classes unable to penetrate the hegemony of the ruling classes, and argues that this underestimates what people do 'between revolts' to defend themselves from dehumanising attacks (p. 29). It would be a grave mistake to overly romanticise 'weapons of the weak' (Scott, 1985) given that economic and social forces prevent the majority of people from being able to effect lasting social structural changes. However, it seems important to acknowledge everyday acts of resistance as these acts point to people's values, hopes and resources. Everyday forms of resistance may not change structures but they are not trivial.

CMM and the social GRAACCCEESS remind us that people continuously reconstruct themselves in their relationships. I might find it difficult at times to speak up in a group where I am one of few Black people present. What mediates the presence or absence of my voice is many interacting factors in the context I am acting into, such as the quality of listening and the responses of others, and acting from, such as my personal values and family stories. As well as being influenced by the social context of racism and sexism I might also be resisting it with respect to my values, opinions and beliefs. Reflecting on the impact of gender and 'race' on my confidence would be appropriate in some moments. However, in another moment I might speak with great confidence and passion and draw on a family and identity story about the importance of ethics or by a desire not to be silenced.

Hence, CMM levels of context help us view the constraints on people's lives at the same time as viewing their abilities as responses to these constraints. This framework fits with Stanton-Salazar's (2001) social capital framework in which 'people make their way in the world by constantly negotiating both the constraints placed on them and the opportunities afforded them, by way of the social webs of which they are part' (p. 18).

So far I have described how we might think of levels of context as having a fixed hierarchy that enables us to reflect on the ways in which wider and wider systems form the context for the experiences we have in our everyday lives. Figure 8.2 shows how CMM can be used to take a static look at social forces affecting the experience of a fictional client who would like to change some of her responses to her girlfriend in public that cause them both distress.

These levels of context help to make sense of this woman's responses as well as give her avenues for action, with respect to challenging the contexts that impinge on her right to love and be loved. Clinicians in the psy field can also use levels of context to reflect on the various levels of intervention that they can engage in to effect change.

- **Political** – Changing the political context through consultation, influencing policy, advocacy, collective power, social action
- **Spiritual** – Helping clients develop spiritual connections and resources that are supportive of who they want to be
- **Culture** – Community psychology, teaching/training, creating reflective spaces to challenge attitudes
- **Family** – Family intervention, systemic focus
- **Interpersonal relationship** – Systemic therapy, facilitating mutual respect, communication, understanding within relationships

POWER
Contextual Force

Political – It was only 36 years ago that homosexuality was taken out of the DSM, which classifies mental disorders. *I go to Pride, as it is important for me to be visible and celebrate my life*

Spiritual – My faith is very important to me but I have been told all my life that Gay people are sinners. *I am a member of Quest, a Catholic Gay group that is supportive of me*

Culture – The cultures I live in do not fully accept me as a Gay woman, do not see me as equal to a heterosexual woman, and may even want to do me harm. *I am part of a community of friends who encourage me to connect to Gay culture*

Family – Most of my family do not know I am Gay and would not approve. *I told my uncle and my sister I am Gay because they are the most supportive. I have a 'family of choice'*[44]

Interpersonal relationship – This is a new relationship and I do not know yet how to fully express myself. *This relationship feels really good so far*

Identity/life script – My identity is rich and varied, including, but not exclusively, being Gay

Episode – Girlfriend attempts to kiss me in public and I pull away

Speech act – I ask her not to kiss me. *I smile at her apologetically*

Bodily sensations – Raised heartbeat, shortness of breath. *I take deep breaths*

Content – I say 'No don't do that'. *In private I express my love freely*

Implicative force
RESISTANCE

Figure 8.2 CMM levels of context: Example of a fictional client. Implicative force is in italics.

- **Identity/life script** – Individual therapy, developing empowering narratives
- **Episode and speech act** – Attending to our positions in the therapeutic relationship, reflecting on process, eliciting client feedback, reflecting on ourselves
- **Bodily sensations** – Being connected to our physical self and bodily sensations and using these connections to connect to clients[45]
- **Content** – Being mindful of the language we use.

In the following chapters I suggest ways of using CMM to:

- highlight power (contextual forces) and resistance (implicative forces)
- work with wider systems and with different professional perspectives
- Ask clients questions that highlight the ways in which they are influenced by, comply with or resist higher levels of context.

Daisy model

The daisy model (first described in Pearce, 1994) departs from the monologous and expert voice of many dominant discourses. In this model words or concepts are the target for curious enquiry. The daisy model assumes 'that each event or object in the social world is a nexus of many conversations' (Pearce, 2007, p. 179) and can be used to highlight the complexity of an issue and the various influences, discourses or stories linked to it. The issue, event or object is in a circle in the centre of the daisy and each petal represents different ways of thinking about the central issue (Figure 8.3). For example, if a client says they are depressed, the word 'depressed' might be written in the middle of a daisy figure with each petal representing other words that help make sense of the centre word.

Given that we collapse a multitude of experiences under the term 'depression' (anger, guilt, oppression, powerlessness, deprivation of experience, confusion, resistance, shame, disconnection, marginalisation), we might need to look inside the word to understand fully what it means to the person using it in that moment. We might then ask: As you hear yourself say that word, is there anything else there in your words? Any other comments, feelings, ideas, images, experiences? If you imagine that word in your mind and you imagine yourself crawling inside of it, what (or who) else is in there? Given that we carry with us the residues of many other voices, representing the accumulation of our relationships (actual, imagined, and virtual), we might also use the daisy model to explore the various relationships and perspectives that influence how we come to understand the world.

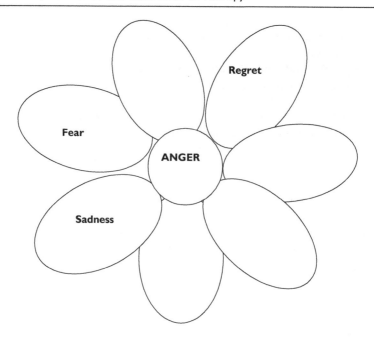

Figure 8.3 CMM daisy model of 'anger'

As well as looking inside a word, the daisy model might be used:

- to explore the influences on a person's identity
- with each petal representing one of the social GRAACCCEESS as a way to reflect on a particular issue
- with each petal representing a different person and their voice/influence on an issue
- with each petal representing a level of context
- with each petal representing different times along a time line influencing the development of an issue.

This enquiry helps us to enrich thinking about an issue and the social influences on it. An individual's actions and beliefs are rarely just their own but bear the mark of myriad others. Reflecting on the many stories available to us may open up perspectives and opportunities for action that were not available from the positions we were taking. Once the daisy is drawn, examples of what the client might want to do are:

- share their initial thoughts and feelings on viewing their daisy diagram
- darken petals of relationships that are more important, or more influential

- reflect on how some petals are similar or different
- talk about each petal separately or compare them all
- reflect on the self they are called to be in each relationship depicted in the petal (a fuller example of using a daisy diagram is given later in the book).

When working with clients we might unwittingly reinforce oppressive ideas about the inferiority of beliefs that originate in other cultures and the expertise of the minority world model of living. For example, a client might ask 'this is what we do in our culture, what do you think? Is it right?' My preference in this situation is to show curiosity about the diversity of perspectives available in their own lives and within their own culture, and to ask other system members present about their thoughts. I believe that all opportunities should be taken to validate pre-existing knowledge, experience and understanding, and the assumption should be that *all* cultures contain diversity and therefore hold solutions to difficulties arising in them.

Pearce argues that 'the test of CMM lies not in the truthfulness of its claim but in how useful it is in helping us understand the social worlds we live in' (Pearce, 2007, p. 226). CMM is not just about describing the world but about 'how well it guides action into the world' (Pearce, 2007, p. 226). The value of CMM for me is that it offers a way of bridging the psychological and the sociological through engaging in different levels of analysis: the micro level of day-to-day living, the meso level of communities and organisations, and the macro level of social structures and ideology (Bronfenbrenner, 1979; Kelly, 1987; Trickett, 1996).

Chapter 9

Drawing the theory together

To do justice to all the ways I wanted to reflect on power, resistance and liberation in therapy I needed a coherent framework that enabled me to move easily from the macro to the micro level and vice versa, and that would enable me to combine approaches and reflect on what they afforded each other. Any concept within a theory is open to misuse, such as the systemic notion of circular causality. In the case of unilateral power such as in a violent relationship, the search for circular causality might direct people away from taking responsibility for their violent actions and could be viewed by the victimised person as tantamount to condoning the inexcusable. Similarly, ideas from liberation psychology are open to misuse if not accompanied by a collaborative approach that reflects on the ways we can do harm in an attempt to challenge domination.

The contribution of liberation psychology

Terms such as 'empowerment' are so vague and have become so widely used that they can be co-opted and neutralised by the 'psy' profession, who focus mainly on the individual level. With liberation theology comes language that is overtly political. We are reminded that individuals are always part of relationships and thus empowerment is always more than individual achievement.

Liberation psychology serves as a bridge between a desire to support individuals and the need to transform relationships and environments, and uses psychological/psychotherapeutic theories to advocate for social change. One outcome of drawing on liberation psychology is to move power, resistance and liberation from the margins to the centre of the field of counselling and therapy. Liberation psychology approaches psychotherapeutic talk with clients from a desire to shift clients from defining their problems as individual pathology to talking about their problems in terms of structural conditions. However, this approach does not adequately explain what to do in therapy if the client does not find recasting their problems in this way helpful. How do we co-create stories that are liberating without holding on too strongly to our ideas about what form liberation should be?

The contribution of narrative approaches and CMM

Coordinated management of meaning (CMM) and narrative approaches to therapy keep the focus of the therapist on working collaboratively with clients rather than expertly on them. Both CMM and narrative therapy emphasise the power of language and context, and the importance of reflecting on the terms we take for granted, and whether our meaning works with or against others. As Watkins and Shulman (2008) point out, 'liberation' has often been used as a misnomer for military invasion and occupation:

> when the desire of the victor is proclaimed to be the desire of the oppressed . . . [which suggests] that a group can be 'liberated' by another group working on its behalf . . . to become not what they desire for themselves but what the 'helper' desires . . . The liberators . . . have already arrived at some pre-established height in a hierarchy of their own construction.
>
> (p. 46)

Instead Watkins and Shulman (2008) refer to 'a type of liberation that people can do with one another, but that no one can do for another' (p. 47). In relation to this:

- systemic and narrative approaches focus on the client as expert, rather than the therapist as educator
- the narrative approach shifts the metaphor of liberation from 'moving forward' (in a linear stage based way) to 'moving on' in a preferred direction based on client values
- the notion of contextual and implicative forces in CMM challenges the idea of absolute domination by one group and absolute subordination by another. CMM highlights the ways in which everyday acts can impact on wider levels of context.

What CMM adds to narrative approaches

Multiple stories

CMM is a useful complement to the narrative therapy focus on stories, because each word or story we share with others 'embeds a larger story' (Pearce, 2007, p. 164). CMM suggests that communication occurs at several levels simultaneously, and that our stories function as contexts for other stories (Pearce, 2007). Therefore, 'we never only mean one thing at a time in our actions' (Pearce, 2007, p. 141). CMM highlights that we can both resist and be complicit with dominant cultural norms, sometimes at the same time.

As well as offering power and privileges, dominant cultural norms can also oppress those who enact them. For example, an effect of over-conforming to dominant masculine practice, especially when it involves abusive treatment of others, usually results in becoming isolated and disconnected from self and others.

The difference between ability and opportunity

Narrative therapy can be used to focus on people's abilities despite their material reality, which is undoubtedly important. However, a concurrent focus is needed on people's real-life opportunities, which are often deter-mined by social factors based on the dynamics of power and difference, highlighted in CMM. For instance, poverty, discrimination and war are massive factors in determining people's opportunities to move towards their preferences for living. Rather than just putting onus on the client to change their relationship to their difficulties, we can invite others in the client's system to respond differently and challenge structures of domination.

A focus on relationship

Despite the benefits of the narrative approach there is the possibility of using narrative ideas on individuals as though they are not part of wider systems and relationships. For instance, a person moving in the direction of their preferred self might come across opposition, discontent or discour-agement from others who do not share the preference with the client. The daisy model might be used in this instance to look at the interaction between the client's preferred self and their relationships with significant others.

Ms Marie came to decide that she no longer wanted to take medication for her 'mental illness.' Ms Marie understood her experiences in ways that made her feel able to move on in her life, but was worried about what other people in her life would think about her decision. This led to a conversation using the daisy model about the different positions various people in her life took in relation to where Ms Marie was and where she wanted to be. Each petal represented a significant relationship – her mother, her husband, her daughter, and her psychiatrist, Dr Barlow:

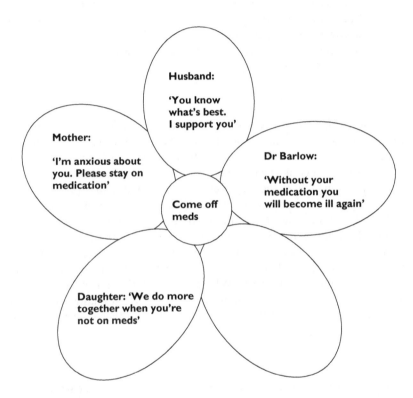

Figure 9.1 Ms Marie CMM daisy model

- 'What would Dr Barlow say about this shift and where you want to be?'
- 'What type of conversations can you have with him about that?'
- 'What would your mother say about this shift and where you would like to be?' 'What type of conversations can you have with her about that?'
- 'What resources can you recruit to help you in this task?'
- 'What resources might they need to help them understand how this shift came to be and why it is important to you?'
- 'How would you like them to contribute/participate in the direction you are going in your life?'

CMM and liberation psychology approaches remind me to stay emotionally connected to the stories I hear, by reflecting on the contexts the stories make sense in. The narrative therapy approach reminds me to be collaborative and connected to the worldview, values and preferences of the client. At a time where the 'psy' field is increasingly under pressure to turn complex processes into identifiable and concrete procedures that can be evidenced, we may need reminding that what we are doing is not an apolitical technique for ridding a client of problems, but a political act that can potentially re-enact or counteract prejudice and oppression. Stories are the hearts and souls of people, linking them to everything in their social world. We might ask ourselves: Where do the stories our clients tell us take us? What commitments do they make us have? What changes do they call us to make in the world? What type of activists do they challenge us to be, if we *really* listen?

Integration challenges and opportunities – strong irony

It is clear from the above descriptions that all three approaches have much in common and much to contribute to liberation. Despite the commonalities, integrating different approaches can be a challenge. I have found the concept of 'strong irony' (Leppington, 1991) helpful in enabling me to draw the usefulness of these approaches together by:

- reflecting on how to combine theories that have slightly different emphases but common concerns, in a way that maintains the potential value of each
- reflecting on how we might be both passionate about what we believe in AND aware of the constraining nature of final conclusions as to what is correct.

What is strong irony?

Irony refers to an expression of one's meaning by language of the opposite. Therapy is often a place where irony can have expression by exploring the contradictions in our personal, interpersonal and collective experiences. Strong irony refers to how we can do or be two seemingly opposite things at the same time and mean them both. In therapeutic practice this means the therapist moving in and out of varying positions, not picking one version of reality, but communicating equal respect for more than one. This is in contrast to an either/or position that forces therapists to choose between. Strong irony is the site where many possible ways of being and understanding intersect and can be explored. The more we explore, the more we notice what we do not know and the more mysterious and complex the phenomenon becomes. We are more concerned with what gets opened up or closed down and the ethical consequences of our positions than with accuracy.

An example of strong irony is the view that power concerns both a social context of violence, abuse and oppression in society and an illusion maintained by discourse. This both/and rather than either/or position suggests that power is something we at once are embedded in and attempt to move beyond. The therapist's professional obligation is often to be knowledgeable and have some expertise, and yet we can be a non-knower and non-expert (Guilfoyle, 2003). As therapists interested in power, resistance and liberation we both preserve and critically question the institution of therapy.

Given the complexity of life, we often live in the dynamic of both/and and in-between, rather than either/or. We might feel both happy and sad; want to open up our hearts and fiercely guard against doing so; value an intervention and feel uncomfortable about it, and so on. Oppression and privilege often comingle. The facts of life can be experienced as real, but they can also be experienced as other than what they are. These different competing perspectives seem to coexist and may even fit together, and yet there may be a tension between them as they try and make us see the world in different ways at the same time. Game and Metcalfe (2001) argue that it is in the in-between-ness of life that we can be knowledgeable and creative.

Jacques Derrida (15 July 1930 – 8 October 2004) was a French philosopher born in Algeria whose theories further elaborate on the concept of the in-between-ness of life. Although Derrida became uncomfortable with the popularity of the term 'deconstruction', how it became understood and the corresponding tendency to reduce his vast philosophical work to it, he is most known for developing this critical technique (Larner, 1995, 1999).

According to Larner (1999), unlike postmodern philosophers, Derrida did not want to overthrow the narratives of modernity or structuralism so much as to open them up to critical dialogue. Deconstruction is about moving away from either/or understandings, to get beyond the language and philosophy in which duality is set and work out of both (Larner, 1999). In Derrida's terms all theories, disciplines and schools of thought become closed systems of exclusion, dominance and the suppression of difference. Even the movement towards deconstruction involves taking a position against another and taking a path that excludes other possibilities. Hence Derrida was concerned with the potential oppression of his own position and argued that deconstruction itself required deconstructing for the sake of ethics (Derrida, 1994). In advocating an ethical foundation for deconstruction, he pointed out that justice is an ethical relation to the other which is 'undeconstructible' (Derrida, 1994).

Derrida talked of putting an 'x' through words to show that the words were both that and not that. This type of intermediate meaning, rather than having a lack of meaning, referred to an abundance of meaning; that is, meaning many things at once. Power, resistance and liberation can also be said to have multiplicity of meaning which continuously invites new avenues for understanding and action. Strong irony is an approach to tensions that cannot be completely resolved if we want to hold many parts of a tension because each part reveals something important.

As a therapist I am concerned with how I can believe that violent, abusive and oppressive behaviour is often deliberate and abusive individuals must take responsibility for their actions, while also believing in the inherent potential for compassion in everyone. I am interested personally and professionally in how I can condemn violent and abusive acts while understanding that oppressive discourses were not invented by those who enact them. Without wanting or intending to do so we are all learning oppressive and discriminatory ideas about people we are told are 'different' from us, and yet there are always spaces to move into created by alternative descriptions. Given that we are at once bound and free, I am interested in how we transform our experiences of being harmed into a commitment to do no harm.

Although strong irony breaks down the either/or, it is not thrown out. Sometimes the either/or needs to exist without the both/and. As Burnham (1992) points out, 'If one adopts a reflexive posture towards both-and then we would not always choose the position of both-and, since this would be taking an either/or position between either both-and or either-or' (p.17). There are clearly times when we have an ethical imperative to participate in an either/or position in order to take a stand against abuse or address risk. At the same time we do not stop interrogating the effects on others and the ethics of the positions we take. Burnham (1992) argued that 'always taking the position of not giving advice and indeed saying to clients "I do not give advice" is a form of advice, and so the position contradicts itself. Placing this apparent incoherence within the context of both/and creates a context for systemic practitioners to become curious' (p. 16). Clients from other parts of the world often have a culturally supported expectation that the therapist is an active and advisory expert. If the therapist is only non-directive this may be experienced as disinterest, lack of experience or a sign that the intervention is not helpful.

One response to being asked by a client to give advice is to give a range of options, invite the client to choose among them, and then ask questions about the choice they have made, such as: 'What made you choose that option rather than one of the others?' 'Who else would agree with your choice?' 'Who might disagree?' This response both respects the client's wishes as part of a collaborative relationship and honours the idea of multiple perspectives. I might reflect with the client about when it is useful to give advice and when not, and how I can orient myself to the effects of either position.

When therapy is experienced as a mutual exchange of words and a co-creation of meaning, it may not make sense to some clients that the relationship is professional and not personal. This is particularly pertinent with clients who have lost a significant proportion of their intimate relationships through war and forced exile. In this situation I have found it useful to ask:

- 'What relationship in your country/culture of origin does this relationship most resemble?'
- 'In what ways is this relationship similar and different?'

The concept of strong irony enables us to work with the irreducible plurality of experience that no one approach or idea could hope to totalise. By creating static caricatures of our approach to counselling and therapy we may miss an opportunity to acknowledge the contradictions that often render our positions fluid and not fixed.

Taking a stand AND being open to other perspectives

I have found the concept of strong irony helpful in working with the dilemma of how to balance the certainty of taking a stand against injustice with the fluidity of being open to other views. Taking a political position and aligning myself with the voices of the oppressed replicates the type of definitive knowing of dominant groups. How one takes a position of power in order to deconstruct power is a paradox. By being transparent we might share these dilemmas, assumptions and contradictions with clients and demystify the process of therapy, laying bare our not-knowing.

When I have been able to do this I have learnt more, not just about other positions but also about my own position (which might be immutable or subject to revision). For example, I used to feel that responding to people who experience complex psycho-social difficulties with psychiatric medication was misguided and at times abusive. Now I am able to enter into respectful conversations with clients who take a variety of positions on medication (want to take their medication and find it helpful; have mixed feelings about taking medication; or want to come off medication), without imposing my opinions. I am able to do this while also being critical of pharmaceutical power and the medicalisation of distress.

Strong irony, oppression and liberation

Although Du Bois originally believed that social science could provide the knowledge to solve racism, he gradually came to the conclusion that in a climate of virulent racism social change could only be accomplished through agitation and protest. This view clashed with another influential Black leader of the time, Booker T. Washington, who, preaching a philosophy of accommodation, urged Black people to accept discrimination for the time being and elevate themselves through hard work and economic gain. Similarly Martin Luther King and Malcolm X held some differing views about how to bring about Black liberation. The 1971 debate between Noam Chomsky and Michel Foucault (chaired by Fons Elders) is another case in point, which I will now review in more detail. Both Chomsky and Foucault had an 'equal commitment in philosophy as in politics' (Chomsky & Foucault, 2006, p. 1), despite fundamental differences in their ideas about human nature. Whereas Chomsky's background in linguistics led him to review the nature of language with respect to innate structures, Foucault was interested in how language was used, the power of language and the language of power.

With respect to oppression and liberation, Foucault argued that his task was to elucidate the often hidden workings of power, from 'neutral' institutions such as education, family, and religion; *not* to propose what an alternative better world would or should look like. Chomsky on the other hand argued that in order to critique institutions of power we need 'to create the vision of a future just society' based on 'some firm and humane concept of the human essence or human nature' (Chomsky & Foucault, 2006, p. 41). For Foucault human nature had no essence as nothing was fixed and innate. For Chomsky we should reflect on what social structures would bring about the type of human nature that gives full scope to freedom, dignity and creativity. Foucault argued that in defining this human nature we risked doing so in terms borrowed from our oppressive society. Chomsky argued that we should engage in social activism even when we are uncertain about its effects. He argued that despite the dangers in undertaking an act of social action it is equally dangerous not to.

I find this debate intriguing because it mirrors a familiar internal debate between my desire to strive for freedom and justice for all and the understanding that the more strongly I hold on to a particular position, the more I block from my view. Strong irony seems to create a third position that neither resolves nor dissolves the apparent duality, but incorporates it.

Part III

Liberation and therapy: Practice

Chapter 10

Ways of working with power, resistance and liberation

Recognising client responses as meaningful

In Chapter 6 I reflected on how liberation psychology might be thought about in ways that reinforce a development model based on a constraining notion of progress, takes an expert position and focuses on the internal world of people split into oppressors and the oppressed. I have argued that such a perspective might render invisible everyday acts of resistance. To avoid the trappings of this expert approach to liberation, we might:

- avoid talking about liberation with respect to numbered sequences and stages, which insinuates a particular order and direction
- be just as curious about and appreciative of what is – how the client currently responds to their experiences – as what should be
- reflect on the client's own preferences and values and how these might shape future experiences, with respect to preferred ways of being and social action.

Trauma has the potential to create a rift in a person's treasured values and sense of who they are and where they are going. If therapeutic conversation can bring forth how a person's actions were congruent with their values despite abuse and oppression, clients can experience themselves as resourceful, coherent and having integrity. Rather than reinforcing the idea that there were actions that were not taken that would have indicated critical consciousness, curiosity about a client's actual actions might assist the client to draw more appreciative conclusions about their choices.

People often ascribe negative meanings to their responses to abuse, prejudice and oppression when they compare their actions unfavourably to an unrealistic standard. Therapeutic conversations might explore and deconstruct these 'not taken' idealised actions. Beaudoin (2005) argues that popular culture propagates overly heroic images of resisters who 'accomplish the impossible' (p. 42). As Beaudoin (2005) points out, 'There is always a reason why these clients did not engage in the later generated options. Always' (p. 42). If clients compare their performances to an idealised scenario they are likely to continue to dismiss their actual expressions of resistance and what they tell them about (a) their values and (b) the social context of constraints and opportunities. Reflecting on the social context might enable clients to move away from a personalised sense of failure. In addition, therapy might explore what the idealised actions reveal about what continues to be important to them even when wider factors make it difficult for them to express their values the way they prefer.

A model that views people as being on a liberation continuum towards right-being and social activism (away from wrong-being and social inactivity), might further pathologise clients and feed into a sense of failure and incompetence. What might appear to be non-actions may in fact be actions in disguise. Given that we always respond and resist experiences of oppression, prejudice and abuse, we could take the existence of apparent non-activity as a cue to enquire about actions taken in their place. The therapist might connect the client to forms of resistance that might not be valued, acknowledged or noticed by them and those around them. The conversation might also highlight the 'non-actions' (such as thoughts and feelings) that are actually actions in the service of resistance (Beaudoin, 2005; Wade, 2007). Thus the client comes to see that what they did and did not do in response to abuse and/or oppression was in fact meaningful rather than meaningless.

Sarah was a 27-year-old White working class single parent with three children under eight years old. Sarah explained that she was unemployed because she wanted to spend time bringing up her family. She was well supported by her mother, who had also been a single parent, and her friends. In describing what she called her 'low mood', Sarah explained that she felt that people outside of her close-knit network saw her as a 'chav'[46] and 'waste of space'. In particular when she went to the job centre and was told she had to look for work, she felt that they looked down on her because she left school with few qualifications and had not been in work since her children were born.

We explored the term 'chav' and where she first heard it. We talked about the British media's apparent contempt for the White working class and the many examples of patronising and ridiculing images and portrayals. Sarah said that her mother was always telling her that she should be tougher and 'stand up for herself more'. This made her feel 'low' because she worried that she was passive in the face of prejudice, choosing to be 'cheerful' and smile even when she felt angry and dismissed.

In one session I explored what being 'cheerful' and smiling meant to her. Sarah said 'it means that I care more about giving my children a good life that is happy than what people think about me. They don't know that even though I struggle we have a good life.'

I asked about Sarah's anger and what happens to it when she is smiling and being cheerful. Sarah said that 'people think I am simple because I am cheerful, but there is more going on behind my smile than they realise . . . being angry lets me know that I am worth something . . . smiling reminds me of that too . . . I'm not a "chav".' Sarah began to talk about her 'knowing smile' as a representation of the valuable qualities she owned rather than passive resignation.

Reflecting on power, difference and privilege

For Memmi (1974), privilege was 'undoubtedly economic' (p. 8), such that the 'deprivations' of the underprivileged are the direct consequence of the advantages secured by the privileged. As a result of multiple group membership, most people function in some settings where they benefit from being in a dominant group. Watts, Williams and Jagers (2003) argue that any hope for the formation of alliances across the divide of oppression requires that the beneficiaries of privilege critically analyse their status and its impact on their experiences, values and beliefs.

When I was going to Gambia in 2008, some people I spoke to said that it was a nice place but 'it's a shame because they are so poor they hassle you for money'. I remember wondering if the issue was that *they* are so poor or that *we* are so rich. This made me think about the ways in which we tend to focus on 'the other' when we think about power and rarely reflect on our privilege. Power and privilege are complex experiences. Although we are all privileged to some extent, that is not to say that we are equally privileged. Privilege is not an inherently bad thing. A lot of privileges are things that all people should have and do not. However, those with membership of privileged groups often feel entitled to their privileges and likewise entitled to impose their interests and cultural practices on those who are less privileged.

Even though I know I am privileged, I do not always feel like I am. I have at times felt powerless and frustrated and yet I am an earner, I have my own property, I have friends and a loving family, I am not beset by war and violence and in the therapy session I am the person called 'therapist'. Just because we do not always feel privileged does not mean that we are not. We understand this when we work with men who abuse their partners and do not feel privileged. We may understand this less when we reflect on our own privilege.

Michael Kimmel's chapter 'Towards a pedagogy of the oppressor' beautifully articulates the dynamics of power and privilege when he writes:

To run or walk into a strong headwind is to understand the power of nature. You set your jaw in a squared grimace, your eyes are slits against the wind, and you breathe with a fierce determination. And still you make so little progress. To walk or run with that same wind at your back is to float, to sail effortlessly; expending virtually no energy. You do not feel the wind; it feels you. You do not feel how it pushes you along; you feel only the effortlessness of your movements . . . It is only when you turn around and face that wind do you realize its strength. Being White, or male, or heterosexual in this culture is like running with the wind at your back. It feels like just plain running, and we rarely, if ever, get a chance to see how we are sustained, supported, even propelled by that wind.

(Kimmel, 2006, p. 63)

The power of wind is a great metaphor for privilege because, as Kimmel states, privilege is both ubiquitous and invisible. Kimmel argues that if you are a White person you are 'everywhere you look. You are the standard against which everything and everybody else is measured' (2006, p. 64). He goes on to explain that 'Any college course that does not have the word woman or gay or minority in the title is, de facto, a course about men, heterosexuals, and white people. But we call those courses literature, history, or political science' (p. 64).

White privilege

W.E.B. Du Bois was ahead of his time in the study of White privilege, arguing that White people drew on the unearned 'wages of whiteness'. Such benefits comforted them with the knowledge that no matter how far they fell down the socioeconomic ladder, how alienating and exploitative their work might be, they were still White; they were still not slaves. Du Bois' work encouraged White people to understand their privilege and listen to the wisdom of those people subjugated by the ideal of Whiteness. Even when privilege is acknowledged by White people, it may be difficult to process the individual responsibility that comes from reflecting on everyday acts of oppression. To be asked the question 'What do you do to sustain racist discourse and participate in the re-enactment of racism?' might be too challenging. This prompts the question, how useful is it for White people to reflect in part on Whiteness while disassociating themselves from being White?[47] Indeed, how useful is it for any of us to talk about power and privilege without reflecting on our own?

My privilege

As I write this part of my book my stomach is doing summersaults because I have just received a bill for more than £1,000 for work done to a communal garden area where I live that I did not ask for, and I am worrying about how I will pay for it. As I get myself into a state about it I remind myself of the thousands of people in this country who regularly worry about not having money; of the thousands living in abject poverty in the UK and across the globe. I wonder about the many anxieties my parents experienced about supporting not only their family of five children but also their families of origin back home.

Despite my family's financial struggles, my parents always reminded us of our privilege and our duty to do something with it that helped others.[48] For me, remembering our privilege is not about feeling grateful for what we have and sorry for those who do not have, but about challenging inequality and addressing the implications for others in the real world. As a Black working-class woman I am undoubtedly oppressed *and* I am undoubtedly propelled by the invisible wind of privilege. I can walk down the street holding my partner's hand and not risk being beaten up or killed because of the gender of my lover. As a woman who earns money I have power over my destiny in a way many women across the globe do not. Wind as a metaphor is also apt because winds change; the direction changes; the flow and force are not static and not always in the same direction. The force of wind is not fixed, and the person with wind flowing behind them one minute can experience it from in front the next. Running against the wind is harder and takes more effort, but also makes you stronger.[49]

Coordinated management of meaning (CMM) does justice to this complexity and reminds us not to see the ethereal and mutable (privilege) as concrete and fixed. In addition, CMM reminds us to reflect on what happens between us, and what we can do to challenge the circumstances that uphold privileges for some at the expense of others. Whenever I experience myself moving away from the sensitivity, connectedness and understanding I want to guide me as a therapist, I imagine myself being propelled by the wind of privilege further and further away from clients. Reflecting on our privilege could connect us more deeply to our sense of responsibility as people in a global world; our responsibility to change the circumstances that contribute to distress and not be content with just helping people find ever more ingenious ways of surviving.

> I had been seeing Mary, a 29-year-old homeless single woman from Cameroon, for almost three years. When Mary first came to the UK four years previously, it was late October and the days were getting shorter, something Mary had not experienced before. When she first came to see me she had been asked to leave her aunt's family home where she was staying, after a dispute, and was living in a hostel in an area of London that had little street lighting and was frequented by sex workers and people addicted to drugs.
>
> At first Mary was so afraid of the outside world she would not leave her hostel, so I visited her there, until she was able to come and see me. Mary did

not make many friends outside of therapy and insisted I was her only true friend. Mary said she would never stop seeing me and my attempts to talk about community outside of therapy did not go anywhere. Mary did not want to talk about or 'work on' her fears. She just wanted our therapeutic relationship to continue. As time passed my sense of frustration and fears about the ethics of not sufficiently challenging what I saw as her dependency began to dig deeper in me and I found myself not listening to her assertion that she was afraid and that this fear remained no matter what we talked about. It became harder and harder to talk about the fact that one day our relationship would come to an end.

One night as I lay asleep alone at home I was woken by a loud bang coming from my kitchen. Because I was half asleep I did not put this noise down to my cat exploring my work tops. Instead I feared that an intruder was in my flat with access to knives! For only a few seconds I felt intense fear. As the fear subsided I thought about the fear Mary experienced in her hostel. I realised that my privilege as someone who can sleep easily at night meant that it was hard for me to understand why Mary was so connected to what for her was the one place she felt safe.

The next session I stepped into Mary's experience of fear and talked about it with her in a new way. This new way did not have undertones of anxiety about reinforcing dependency. This new listening believed her story of fear in a deeper way. Mary started talking about her hopes for the future, to work with young people who have no family, and to be their family. As well as exploring Mary's future vision I spent some time writing housing letters trying to help get Mary moved to an area that was less isolated and frightening. It was not that I had finally understood the complexity of what it meant to be Mary, or that Mary was nothing but her fear. By connecting to my privilege[50] I could do something different and meet Mary where she was rather than where I thought she ought to be. This also meant joining her in challenging some of the social circumstances affecting her rather than attempting to change Mary.

We can identify our privileges by noticing those aspects of our identity that have dominance in our society and/or give us access to sought-after resources, and then considering our normal activities of daily living that result from them. When we do this we realise that what ought to be rights actually turn out to be privileges.

When I teach psychology/psychotherapy trainees on working with difference in therapy I present some inequality statistics, invariably framed with respect to disadvantage. I write these statistics on the whiteboard and ask the group to reverse them and re-tell the story from the point of view of privilege. The following are examples of these reversed statistics.

- The income of the world's 500 richest people exceeds the collective income of the world's 416 million poorest people (UNDP, 2005).
- In 2003, 88 per cent of people with a degree in the UK were in full-time employment, compared to 50 per cent of people with no qualifications (Office for National Statistics, 2004a).
- In 2003, life expectancy for male professionals at birth in England and Wales was more than seven years higher than for unskilled workers (Office for National Statistics, 2004b).
- In Northern Ireland only 5 per cent of school leavers have no GCSEs or equivalents, compared to 92 per cent of the traveller community (Kenny, 1997; Charles, 2008).
- Diagnoses of schizophrenia are up to eight times lower among White English people than African Caribbean people in England and Wales (Harrison, 2002).
- In the UK only 12 per cent of straight men and 20 per cent of straight women have clinically recognised mental health problems, compared to 42 per cent of Gay men, 43 per cent of lesbians and 49 per cent of bisexual men and women (King et al., 2003).
- Heterosexual young people in England and Wales are six times less likely than Gay young people to commit suicide (King et al., 2008).
- White people in the UK are seven times less likely to be stopped and searched than Black people and half as likely as Asian people in the UK (Clinks, 2008).
- In London White people are 10 times less likely to be a victim of racist attack, seven times less likely to be a victim of homicide, 2.6 times less likely to suffer violent crime and 1.6 times less likely to be a victim of robbery than Black people (House of Commons Home Affairs Select Committee, 2007; Clinks, 2008).
- Only 13 per cent of adult men in the UK are in the bottom quintile of individual incomes, compared to more than a quarter (27 per cent) of adult women in the UK. Almost a third of UK men are in the top quintile of individual incomes compared to just 10 per cent of UK women (Trade Union Congress, 2008)
- The average British man's full-time pay is £14.98 an hour; the average British woman's full-time pay is £12.40 an hour (Trade Union Congress, 2008). The average British man will earn £330,000 more over the course of his life than the average British woman (Trade Union Congress, 2008)

When trainees are asked to re-tell the story from the point of view of privilege, a very interesting discussion ensues. The class starts to talk in terms of the things they take for granted that have been sold to them as inevitable and natural rather than privileges for the few denied to the many. One class member described how angry she felt that so often the press and general population portray poverty, particularly in the African continent, as the result of despotic tyrannical leaders, corruption and greed, despite the reality of gross global exploitation and injustice. Indeed, Sorenson (1991) has shown that famine is often blamed by the news media on internal factors, such as African governments, to conceal continuing structural inequalities and Western benefactors.

Another class member from Northern Ireland commented that just by virtue of not having a nomadic lifestyle he was assigned certain privileges and afforded certain rights that Travellers and Romani people were not. Travellers live with the daily threat of being refused access to community services such as shops, launderettes and pubs. The class talked about how much is known about the settled communities of the UK and Ireland and how little about the unique history, oral tradition, languages, customs and value systems of the Traveller community. The settled community does not have to justify and protect their way of life, identity and traditions in the way the Traveller and Romani community do.

A class member commented that heterosexual people do not worry about 'coming out' and what this means with respect to personal and emotional safety, feelings of belonging and feeling respected and valued by others. We talked about how it was only six years previously in the UK that it was no longer illegal for teachers to support Gay lifestyles by presenting them as having the same worth and status as heterosexual lifestyles (repeal of Section 28 in 2003), only five years previously that same-sex couples could register as civil partners with the same legal rights as married couples (Civil Partnership Act 2004) and two years previously that an act was passed in the UK that protects people from discrimination relating to sexuality, by any provider of services or goods Equality Act (Sexual Orientation) Regulations 2007.

Another person commented, 'Just by virtue of being White I am less likely to be stopped and searched, detained under the Mental Health Act, remanded in custody, be a victim of racist attack, homicide, violent crime and robbery. And yet Black people are often portrayed as perpetrators rather than victims.'

Guilt, shame and privilege

Schneider (1992) asserts that shame is not a disease but a mark of our humanity. However, we can experience shame in both creative (helpful) and reactive (unhelpful) ways. Jenkins (2009) argues that shame is unhelpful if it (a) is self-centred and (b) closes the individual down so that they do not challenge domination. Kimmel (2006) argues that 'guilt may be appropriate, even a necessary feeling – for a while. It does not freeze abjection but can motivate us to transform the circumstances that made us feel guilty in the first place, to make connections between our experience and others', and to become and remain accountable to the struggles for equality and justice around the world. Guilt can politicise us. Perhaps that is one reason why we resist it?' p. 69). The difference between reactive and creative guilt is that reactive guilt is based on self-centred needs (to be forgiven, released from responsibility, avoid or hide from difficult feelings) and creative guilt is 'an awakened sense of the reality of another' (Gaita, 1991, p. 52).

Similarly, Jenkins (2009) describes the problems that can arise when restorative justice is about an apology, which often accompanies an externally prescribed moral obligation on the part of the offended person or community to forgive. Reflecting on privilege should not be about our own preoccupations, but about moving towards the world of other people. This involves a process – rather than a one-off event – of expanding our understanding of our position and the position of others (including the possible feelings of hurt and harm we have contributed to).

Power and collaborative practice

Who controls meaning?

Shotter (1980) described joint action as the complex mixture of influences both from within us and from outside of us. The notion that meaning is created relationally means that one person alone cannot control meaning even if that person is called a therapist. Any meanings we have are never quite complete until met with the client's meaning. In therapy I try to use language that is a combination of curiosity and uncertainty ('I could be wrong, but I was wondering . . .', 'have I got that right or wrong?', 'what do you think?'). Without such verbal markers of uncertainty and invitations to respond and give feedback, the client may hear not simply one perspective out of many possibilities, but 'truth'.

The more open we are to the complexity of life, the more magical it becomes. There can be no magic and mystery if everything is known and under control. The complexity of life can never be fully defined. All we can do is explore it together again and again, at once becoming more familiar with it *and* noticing all the ways in which it is becoming more and more mysterious.

An important part of joint action and of becoming an 'us' is relational reflexivity, defined by Burnham (2005) as the mutual to-ing and fro-ing between the therapist and client in their attempt to make the relationship helpful to the client. Because relational reflexivity directly involves the client in deciding the direction of therapy, it enables a client to express resistance in a constructive fashion in which resistance serves a purpose. We can never really be sure a question will be useful until we ask it and elicit client feedback. So clients might be asked 'questions about questions', such as: 'Do I tend to ask you questions that are easy to answer or difficult?' 'Which questions are most helpful to you?' 'If I asked you questions that were too difficult to answer, how might you let me know?' (Burham, 2005).

Relational reflexivity is more than merely asking a client at the end of therapy how they found it; it involves consistently getting client feedback throughout the therapeutic process. It is important that clients have the power to request or initiate changes in the therapeutic relationship. Therapists might ask 'experience of experience' questions about how the client is experiencing therapy; such as: 'How is this conversation going for you?' 'Should we keep talking about this or would you be more interested in . . .?' I have also found it useful to ask: 'Are we talking about the right things? Are there things we should be talking about that we're not?' To ensure that I am not missing vital contributing factors in the wider context I might ask a question like: 'Are there factors outside our sessions that are affecting our work together, that are important for us to talk about here?' or 'Is there anything I really need to know that I haven't considered yet?'

As part of my regular practice I use Scott D. Miller and Barry L. Duncan's Outcome and Session Rating scales (Bringhurst, Watson, Miller & Duncan, 2006; Campbell & Hemsley, 2009), which are an easy, jargon-free way of eliciting client feedback about how they are feeling in themselves, in their relationships and in their lives; as well as how they experience the therapeutic relationship. Giving these forms to clients at the end of every therapy session seems to reinforce my message about the importance of client feedback to the therapeutic relationship, and gives clients the opportunity to demonstrate how they experience the session as a complement to ongoing conversations with me as the therapist.

Warming the context

It probably goes without saying that empathy and connectedness are important components of therapy. Bateson (1972) talked about 'warm ideas' (more inviting) having a greater chance of facilitating connection between the therapist and client than 'cold ideas'. In explaining how the context for therapy can be 'warmed up', Burnham (2005) suggested 'talking about talking'; that is, talking with the client about what it would be like to talk about certain issues before doing it. For example, he suggests that therapists ask clients about their relationship with praise and compliments, such as: 'If I were to appreciate something about you, how might I say it in ways that you could accept as genuine?'

I might for example 'warm the context' for challenging self-blame following disclosure of sexual abuse, by saying something like: 'I really want to challenge your belief that you are in any way responsible for what happened to you. But I don't know how that might sound or if it would be helpful right now for me to do that. Would you like me to stay with my desire to challenge your self-blame, or would you prefer me to respond to you in a different way?'

Relational responsivity

Cecchin, Lane and Ray (1994) describe an interventionist model as one in which a 'therapist organises an action, suggestion or prescription for the purpose of having a predictable result' (p. 13). Many approaches to psychological difficulties are founded on the notion that therapy can get clients to see or do things in particular ways. The more the language of intervention promises prediction of outcome, the more appealing the intervention becomes to policy makers, funders, commissioners and clients. Although we enter interactions with particular intentions we cannot determine the specific effects of our actions on others. When people interact, they inevitably influence each other, but not always in predictable ways.

Relational responsivity – responding to the actions and feelings of another – is based on the idea that there is not much that is more terrible for people than a lack of response (Seikkula, 2002). Rather than a single focus on outcome, relationally responsive approaches focus more on the moment-to-moment experience in therapy (Lowe, 2005). Narrative and systemic approaches can be used in an 'interventionist' rather than a purely responsive way, given their emphasis on trademark questions, set tasks between sessions and intervention based on clear direction and purpose. Liberation psychology can also be interventionist in this way.

The concept of responsivity adds to these approaches an intimacy and empathic joint action. Therapy that is responsive does not eradicate the possibility of resistance, but uses resistance to reflect on the relationship, while being fully within the relationship; not 'referentially or representationally . . . stepping out of their flow to think "about" them – but responsively, relationally, spontaneously and practically from within their ongoing flow' (Shotter & Katz, 1999, p. 155). When we are responsive we fully enter into and honour the experience of the client, which includes a willingness to question what we think we know and a commitment to continually learn more about what clients have to say about their experience.

Resonance

Resonance can be defined as complex arousing of emotion in another person by virtue of the emotions of a first (Shotter & Katz, 1999). Resonance reminds us of the fluidity between self and other that both separates and merges personal experiences, as well as the fact that identity is formed

in the relationship between self and other. A woman with learning difficulties (I will call her 'Sally'), who was part of a women's group I set up and
co-ran for survivors of sexual abuse, was supported in individual therapy
with me to write about her experiences in the form of a 'story' and asked
me to read it to the rest of the group. I invited her to read parts of it with
me. The following is an excerpt from post group interviews about us
reading this story together.

Sally: I couldn't read it on me own I don't think *(laughs)*. We done it
        between us, so it don't matter . . . Is it all right if I show Wendy [her
        social worker] that story?
TA: It's up to you really.
Sally: Remember it's your story as well.
TA: Well it's your story really, I just helped you to tell it.

After Sally's comments I wondered if she was right that clients' stories
become ours in some way because we help tell them, we hear them and take
them away with us. In the same way, when reading a poem, 'the image
offered us by the poem now becomes really our own. It becomes a new
being in our language, expressing us by making us what it expresses'
(Bachelard, 1992, p. xix). Resonance and responsivity refer to ways we are
changed by what we hear in therapy. The consequences and responsibilities
for the therapist who respects and connects to the client's reality are
enormous. We might ask ourselves what we will do differently because of
what we have heard. When we are relationally responsive to others we
allow ourselves to be ethically answerable to them. Therapy in this way
involves an opening of hearts with a willingness on the part of the therapist
to have theirs broken.

Responding to negative feedback

Responding to negative client feedback in responsive ways is one way that
we might address our unwitting abuse of power in therapy.

Despite my attempts at multi-partiality, in one session with husband and wife
Pervenah and Bez, Pervenah commented that although she felt I could be
empathic with her husband's tears she did not feel that I showed empathy for
her anger. This kind of selective empathy affected my ability to engage
Pervenah and restricted the possibility of multiple perspectives being shared

and reflected on. Palazzoli, Boscolo, Cecchin and Prata (1980) found that positively connoting the behaviour of one person might negatively connote the behaviours of other family members. This type of selective empathy can be replaced with 'systemic empathy' applied to more than one person in a system that connects to the strengths and resources of a system as a whole (Wilkinson, 1992).

The importance of responsivity when systemic empathy has not been achieved was highlighted when Mrs K, the older sister I saw with her younger brother, complained that the psychological report that I wrote might be read by some who had been cc-ed into it as suggesting that her brother (Mr F)'s difficulties resulted from his relational and social experiences and not his psychotic illness, which left Mrs K feeling blamed. I had unintentionally caused Mrs K distress. In my letter in response to Mrs K's complaint I apologised for my mistake, explained what I had learnt from her comments and how they had changed how I write reports. I explained that I now routinely show clients copies of my reports before sending them out or write the reports with clients so as to co-create meaning *with* them rather than *about* them. I also discuss with clients who will be an audience to the letter/report and how we might write parts with respect to how they might be read by different people. At other times I might pass reports back and forth between reflecting team members, gathering different perspectives about what to write and how to write it.

As a result of Mrs K's complaint I learnt the following.

- Words are very powerful and can 'bring forth' (Mendez, Coddou & Maturana, 1988) ways of being and feeling that are not helpful.
- Words in writing concretise an experience that is not solid, but shifts and moves depending on who is experiencing and/or telling it.
- Whereas my report featured descriptions of Mr F's strengths and Mrs K's strengths as separate resources, it may be important in reports to describe relational resources and not just balance empathy for different parts of a system.
- Stories that may fit for clients in the context of therapy where insights are shared between system members may change in their descriptions over time or change in their meaning depending on the audience outside of therapy. This is particularly important with respect to the number of professionals that might be involved in a client's care.
- When responding to a complaint it is often important to be responsive to it by sharing with the person making the complaint how I have been changed by what they have alerted me to, as well as what changes will be made in the real world.

Client preferences

Preferences for living are very important. Once I stopped to talk to a homeless man before giving him a bag of oranges, saying 'these are for you'. I said goodbye and walked off before he could look at what I had given him. Soon afterwards he ran up to me with the bag of oranges and said 'I don't eat oranges' and gave the bag back to me. This man's response seemed to communicate that whatever our social circumstances we all have preferences. The most responsive, humanising approach we can take to each other is to enquire into and respect people's preferences for living. Rather than my rude and disconnected approach with the bag of oranges, I should have asked him if he wanted what I was offering. Despite our good intentions it is not difficult to offend or dismiss each other if we do not ask about preferences.

Therapeutic approaches to resistance

It is true to say that domination could not sustain itself without concealing some if not most of its acts. It is equally true to say that domination works by concealing acts of resistance to it. Moane (2003) described the niches constructed by oppressed people that shelter them from oppression and provide opportunities for resistance. Global poverty remains one of the most devastating forms of suffering and oppressive forms of living, and yet people in poverty demonstrate remarkable solidarity and compassion. This is not to romanticise poverty, but to humanise people living in these circumstances by paying attention to a total range of their experiences.

If we depict liberation as a journey from a place of relatively uninformed inaction to sustained, informed and strategic action, we might see resistance only emerging in the context of 'critical consciousness' rather than experienced in everyday life. Alternatively we might shift focus from helping people towards critical consciousness to exploring what people already do in response to their circumstances. This in itself is likely to lead to further social action, as Freire (2006) pointed out: 'to every understanding, sooner or later an action corresponds' (p. 39). Similarly, systemic theory is predicated on the notion that there is always a circular relationship between meaning and action.

I will now explore therapeutic ways of highlighting resistance to social abuse, before describing ways of working with experiences in therapy that might be understood as forms of resistance. In doing so it is important to acknowledge that resistance in therapy may not be visible or overt but confined to the thoughts and feelings of the client that are not shared.

Resistance to social abuse

As Watts et al. (2003) point out, 'There is much more to the experience of oppressed people than their oppression. If this is the sole emphasis, we do

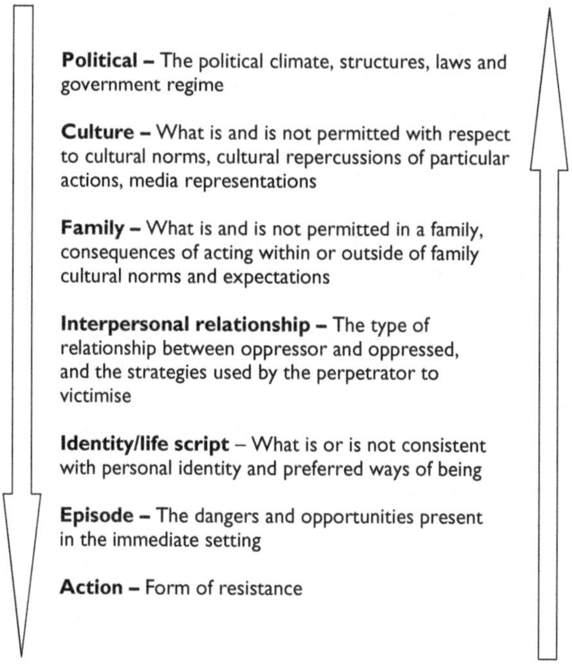

Political – The political climate, structures, laws and government regime

Culture – What is and is not permitted with respect to cultural norms, cultural repercussions of particular actions, media representations

Family – What is and is not permitted in a family, consequences of acting within or outside of family cultural norms and expectations

Interpersonal relationship – The type of relationship between oppressor and oppressed, and the strategies used by the perpetrator to victimise

Identity/life script – What is or is not consistent with personal identity and preferred ways of being

Episode – The dangers and opportunities present in the immediate setting

Action – Form of resistance

Figure 10.1 Levels of context influencing what form individual and collective resistance takes

little more than substitute one deficit orientation toward human beings for another' (p. 187). Due to the threat of retaliation people typically disguise or conceal their resistance (Wade, 1997) so that open defiance becomes the least common form of resistance (Scott, 1990). Reflecting on levels of social context is a useful way of understanding why resistance takes the form it does (Figure 10.1).

Wade (1997) contrasts therapeutic questions based on an 'effects-based' view that regards oppression as conditioning the minds of the oppressed to become accomplices in their own oppression, with questions based on a 'response-based' view, based on how people respond to their circumstances. It is not surprising that a focus on effects slots easily into the prevailing culture and deficit frameworks developed in the 'psy' professions; whereas a focus on responses means that the self emerges as a 'stance-taking entity' (Wade, 2005). Effects describe a one-way, passive and linear process, whereas resistance is a response that speaks of personal and collective agency. In this closed system – where the cause (for example childhood abuse) is sufficient to explain the effect (for example, depression) the social context, such as social responses to those who are victimised, can be easily ignored. When working with survivors of torture it is impossible to understand fully the emotional distress of refugee and asylum-seeking people without understanding the impact of an oppressive immigration system that creates poverty and destitution, questions the credibility of those victimised and insensitively moves people around in a hostile social context beset by anti-refugee sentiment.

Responses to oppression can take many forms. They may be physical, mental, emotional and/or spiritual. They may be open and direct but are most often disguised, indirect and/or confined to the privacy of the mind. Responses and resistance can be based on protecting oneself or caring for the dignity of others. Responses may be spontaneous, tactical, improvised, individual or collective (Todd & Wade, 2003).

Therapeutic conversation might explore the impact of the media as part of the cultural context influencing what form resistance takes. The overly heroic themes found in books, movies and television programmes shape people's expectations of themselves and others. Therapeutic conversations might deconstruct these ideas and explore the gaps and flaws in the images clients might have in their minds about how they should have responded (Beaudoin, 2005).

Given that resistance to oppression rarely stops or reduces oppression, securing complete liberation from oppression may be an inappropriate criterion for determining the usefulness of 'psy' interventions influenced by a liberation agenda. The significance of resistance to oppression cannot always be gauged by accomplishing an end to it, but should be based on what it signifies about the values of people resisting that pre-exist, or exist because of, the oppressive experience. Highlighting forms of resistance is also an important way of challenging oppression, given the strategies that exist to suppress and conceal overt and covert resistance (Renoux & Wade, 2008). Responses are inherently social and political in nature as they comment on the social world (Wade, 2005).

I shall now revisit the case of Victoria, introduced in Chapter 8.

By my shifting towards a point of view that Victoria's position that she was 'dirty' as a result of being raped made inherent sense to her, we began to have different conversations about how this idea came to be. Victoria and I began to explore her experiences using an analogy of someone breaking into her home, throwing rubbish all over the house and smearing excrement on the walls. We explored the ways in which an outsider walking into that home saying that it was not dirty would be highly invalidating of the experience of the person who had to live in it.

We built on this metaphor to explore how she might find a room to live in that was not covered in mess and gradually spread this lack of mess around the house. We also explored who needed to take responsibility for creating the mess, so that Victoria alone did not take full responsibility. We explored who she might trust to see this mess and help her clean it up. This enabled Victoria to experiment with a different perspective where 'feeling dirty' became an externalised notion of 'mess'.

It felt important for me to join her in her disgust and anger at her experience and the position of women in society, with respect to being victimised through rape and then cultural expectations that the woman should, or should not, feel damaged and impure. This enabled us to explore the relationship between emotional pain and injustice, rather than locating her distress and responsibility for healing purely within her. Victoria talked about 'this mess' as an important testimony to the significance of what was precious to her being violated by the act of rape (White, 2005a, 2005b). We were then able to see the intensity of her belief that she was 'dirty' as a reflection of her social, cultural, political context, as well as a reflection of the depth of her continued connection to the things that she valued – chastity, family, purity, belief in fairness, belief that being a good person pays off. Victoria's resistance to being told by me she was not dirty was a refusal to be separated from her values and to have her experience renamed *from the outside*. Only when I could enter into her experience (into her 'home') could we make sense of 'the mess' there *together*.

Victoria was able to explain that by wanting, even subtly, for her to feel that she was not dirty, I was, she felt, denying the significance of what she went through and implying that she had not really been raped, which replicated some of the experiences she had when testifying in court. As White (2005b) pointed out, ongoing distress can be an invitation to witnesses to stay outraged, as well as an important form of resistance. In further sessions we explored what her values called her to be in the world and Victoria described herself as a future parent, teacher and community member. She talked about wanting to go to teacher training college because it was only through education that real changes can happen in the world; rather than focusing on changing herself.

By exploring the abilities and values that pre-existed and existed beyond her experience of rape, Victoria began to feel able to reflect on the resources she could draw on to fulfil her dreams and pass on to her children. Victoria felt humanised by me when, rather than trying to talk her out of a given belief about herself, I began to listen out for what she gave value to and respond to that. A responsive approach to clients helps us to keep open to their cues about what is truly helpful and liberating.

Resistance in therapy

The previous example is a good illustration of how the unhelpful position of the therapist might lead to client resistance. We could argue that it is by inviting clients to critique therapy that we become better therapists, rather than placing emphasis on the learning we gain from each other within the profession (through training and reading). The following is a brief reflection on some client responses in therapy that may be viewed as forms of resistance that invite a deeper understanding of the client's experience. It is important to note that 'resistance' is my construction of the behaviour of clients and *not* a truth about the experience.

Ambivalence

In everyday language ambivalence is often viewed as the coexistence of conflicting attitudes or feelings towards a person, object or idea. This can lead to uncertainty or indecision. In psychoanalysis ambivalence is a term that was introduced by the psychoanalyst/psychiatrist Paul Eugen Bleuler in 1911 and referred to the ways in which one or other coexisting contradictory feelings is repressed, such as love for a person being consciously experienced and hate felt for the same person being indirectly or unconsciously expressed. The contradictory attitudes are thought to be interdependent and derive from a common source (Rycroft, 1995).

If we take the focus away from the client's internal world, ambivalence might be understood as the client's responses to the many contradictory and conflicting discourses and experiences swimming about in their context. For example, a therapist may be both warm and helpful and at times disconnected and intrusive. We might then talk with clients about ambivalence as an understandable response to the mixed experience of the therapist and the client's attempt to develop a meaningful relationship despite it.

Rejecting the therapist's praise

If approached in an expert-driven way, the aim of counselling and therapy might be to 'use therapeutic "weapons" in an attempt to render clients unable to resist the will of the therapist or the therapy' (Gurman, 1982, p. 8). If the main aim of a collaborative approach is to use strength-based questions and reflections to encourage clients to fit with the therapist's agenda, it might be rejected as unhelpful by the client and/or a denial of their difficulties. It might be important, as Burnham (2005) points out, to check out people's relationship to praise rather than assuming one response fits all. Praise and congratulations from the therapist may feel disrespectful of where a client is in their lives and how they see themselves. We live in a culture that does not encourage people to praise themselves, and clients may have experienced consistent attempts to undermine them. We might inadvertently join the oppressor by trying to get clients to have experiences that do not feel right to them and are not of their choosing. It might also be important to avoid sharing our thoughts about something from an invisible value system – that is without giving the client an idea of why we think as we do and where our ideas come from. Such transparency might be important even if what we are offering is acclaim.

Saying 'I don't know'

When clients respond to my questions with a number of 'I don't knows', I often ask them what type of 'I don't know' it is; for example, is it an *I don't want to answer that question* type of I don't know, or an *I don't understand the question* I don't know; or an *I feel tired, bored and disconnected* type of I don't know, and so on. Amanda Redstone and Mark Hayward call this exploring the "I don't know dictionary". Mark Hayward adds that this client response is not their failure to know but our failure to ask an adequate question.[51]

Not 'improving'

The therapy literature tends to focus on the association between outcome – that is, the client 'improving' – and the therapeutic relationship. Despite the usefulness of this approach, there is a danger of neglecting to look at how the lives of clients outside of therapy contribute to their ability to 'move on'. Reflections and connections made in therapy may be single events in the client's life, and single events are vulnerable to being undermined by ongoing oppression. We might need to be directed towards the relationships and community that can be an audience for the client's resources and preferences so that they can be nurtured by multiple people rather than a single voice. A client once said to me: 'your words soothe me for a bit then reality hits me again'.

Standing in front of, rather than next to, the client

Client resistance might be a communication that we are going too fast for them, standing in front of them in some way and/or barking up the wrong tree. The client may also be communicating their need for greater safety and agency in the process of therapy. Client resistance therefore may be a useful cue to slow down and check with them how they are experiencing the process.

Feeling offended

Shotter and Katz (1999) argued that 'only if "you" respond to "me" in a way sensitive to the "relations" between your and my actions, can "we" act together as "collective-we"; and if I sense you are not being sensitive in that way, then I feel immediately offended, ethically offended. I feel you lack respect for me in some way' (p. 152).

If we are curious about what resistance in therapy communicates we might explore the client's values, preferences and creativity. This might mean reflecting on:

- niches of resistance in the client's life outside therapy – and how these might be similar to the resistance we encounter in therapy
- experiences that are life-enhancing for the client – what might we be doing or saying that is at odds with the client's life-enhancing abilities?
- desired futures – what might we be creating together in therapy that is at odds with the client's own preferences?
- preferred ways for the client of coping with present difficulties.

Is surviving oppression an ability?

Although members of an oppressed group may experience life very differently from the dominant group, these perspectives are often not valued in wider society. The abilities inherent in these unique perspectives are often actively repressed by dominant groups. In addition, privileges come with some constraints. For example, there are constraints that come with the 'privileges' of heterosexuality such as strict gender-based expectations, roles and responsibilities. I am not suggesting that dominant society embrace minority cultural understandings wholesale; rather I propose that dominant groups could expand their view of the world based on the life experiences of those who are routinely oppressed, rather than viewing them as 'quaint reminders that some people are different' (Peterson, 2001, p. 222).

So what are the abilities one might develop as a result of being a member of an oppressed minority? Given that I am Black African I am going to reflect on this question from that perspective. Du Bois (1906/1994) argued that if subjugated people are to survive they must develop an understanding of those who attempt to dominate them. In this way oppressed people often understand the mechanisms of oppression and the ways they are deployed in mundane, everyday situations. This 'double consciousness' or second sight is the ability to see oneself through the perception of others. It involves the ability to see what mainstream society sees as well as to see from vantage points outside the mainstream, with access to both dominant worldviews and subjugated perspectives.

To understand anything about African history and social development is to understand that African knowledges constitute one of the most sophisticated worldviews that has been. Despite this I routinely come across racist views about the inferiority of Africa and African people. As a Black African therapist I often have to keep my professionalism in the face of inflammatory remarks made by colleagues and clients. It is rare for people to ask us how we survive discrimination and oppression and for these stories to act as stories of inspiration for others.

By virtue of who we are as marginalised people, our desire for a different society and our quest for equality inherently impacts on our approach to living. We are connected in a direct and substantive way to a deep quest for freedom. By virtue of our position in the world, our efforts to live meaningfully inevitably require a movement towards social transformation. Like other marginalised groups, Black people are useful consultants on alternatives to prevailing unjust social practices. It is actually those who are banished from history books who make history, as they are the ones who transform societies. Because we are invariably defined by deficit, the abilities that oppressed people acquire and develop as a result of their experiences are rarely acknowledged, understood or valued.

In the next three chapters I hope to bring the previously described ideas alive by exploring a collaborative and responsive approach to clinical practice with case examples of adults with a range of difficulties, based on Martín-Baró's three tasks of psychology.

1. *The recovery of historical memory.* Martín-Baró (1996) argued that the struggle to survive oppression could potentially force people into a near-and-now focus on the status quo which neglects the importance of the past and future. Dominant discourses often present reality as natural, as though the way things are is not bound by history, which makes it more difficult to derive lessons from past experience (Martín-Baró, 1996). As a result, many oppressive acts are expected to be accepted without question – for example the sexualisation of Black women and demonising of Black men. To recover historical memory means to discover through social, interpersonal and collective memory those elements of the past that prove useful in challenging oppression and facilitating liberation.
2. *De-ideologising everyday experience.* For Martín-Baró (1996), to 'de-ideologise' meant to witness, name and highlight abuse, oppression and discrimination. Prevailing discourses often deny significant aspects of social reality and instead construct a reality that has little bearing on people's everyday lives. 'It goes along . . . conforming to a fictional common sense that nurtures the structures of exploitation and conformist attitudes' (Martín-Baró, 1996, p. 31). To counter these fictions it is important to name and address people's experiences of oppression, in ways that are meaningful and respectful to them.
3. *Utilising the people's virtues.* Martín-Baró (1996) talked about the importance of bringing alive the virtues that enable people to survive and connect to what is valuable, significant and life-affirming. This might involve developing stories with clients about their principles,

hopes and dreams, as well as highlighting the meaningful relationships that help people to live creatively. Positive communities are essential in helping people hold onto their preferred identity and purposes for living, given that we experience ourselves more richly when we are connected through relationships.

Chapter 11

The recovery of historical memory

Du Bois argued that the methods used by our Black ancestors to fight slavery and oppression can be put to use in present struggles against racism. Before we can recover historical memory in a therapeutic context, we have to do something quite radical within the 'psy' field: to politicise the concept of memory. The recent global growth in the field of trauma work is indicative of the common understanding of trauma as a 'thing' that overwhelms the mind, significantly impacting on the mind's ability to remember and process information normally. This growing popularity focuses on technical approaches to reducing the 'symptoms' of trauma rather than firmly locating forms of distress and forms of resistance in their political, social, cultural and historical context. My aim is not to disprove any set of ideas but to explore how a focus on power, resistance and liberation might change some of the ways we come to understand and work with memory.

Trauma and memory

PTSD is considered to be a disorder of a person's perceptions of time, in which memories of the past intrude on the present as though there were no differences between events across time. This is based on a view of healthy and unhealthy memory, with healthy memory based on an individual's coherent, 'true' and rational narrative of the past. Because trauma is seen as a cause in and of itself, there is less need to comprehensively explore the people involved in traumatic events, as well as the wider social, political and cultural contexts the traumatic events take place in. Theorists may talk about 'exposure to trauma' being enough to render normal people disordered. In many books detailing the most popular approach to PTSD (cognitive behavioural therapy – CBT), descriptions of the individuals and systems that create or contribute in some way to the client's experience of trauma, by for example responding with disbelief, are almost entirely absent. Instead there is an emphasis on treating 'trauma' (e.g. Wilson, Friedman & Lindy, 2001; Yehuda, 2002; Taylor, 2004) and teaching 'victims' how to prevent re-victimisation (e.g. Kubany & Ralston, 2008).

Trauma is viewed simply as an 'etiological agent in the genesis of psycho-pathology' (van der Kolk, 2002, p. 127).

For many theorists the fact that trauma and its effects on memory are now recognised is a positive step for 'victims' of abuse, violence and oppression. As a result many forms and derivatives of PTSD have emerged in the hope that the same benefits will be given to their oppressed group:

- battered child syndrome (Kempe, Silverman, Steele, Droegemueller & Silver, 1962)[52]
- rape-trauma syndrome (Burgess & Holmstrom, 1974)
- child sexual abuse accommodation syndrome (Summit, 1983)
- post-sexual abuse syndrome (Breire, 1984)
- battered women syndrome (Walker, 1984, 1986)
- complex PTSD (van der Kolk et al., 1996; Herman, 1997)
- post-traumatic slave syndrome (DeGruy Leary, 2005)

These descriptions of disorder were felt to:

- legitimise responses to experiences of abuse and oppression
- highlight the seriousness of the impact of these experiences of abuse and oppression
- facilitate understanding of the difficulties experienced by victims and enable them to access 'treatment'
- create alternative and clinically useful ways of conceptualising the symptoms described in ICD-10 and DSM-IV, based on experiences of abuse and oppression.

It could be argued that the attention these terms attract for their cause is accompanied by a view of those who have been harmed as passive victims of their experiences who have succumbed psychologically to disorder and disturbance. This view is reinforced by the prevalence of 'psy' models of trauma that focus our attention inwards.

In a CBT understanding of memory the brain and mind are likened to computer hardware and software. Human beings are thought to process information about the world just as software programmes process and store information. The effects of trauma on memory are thought to result from a failure in processing. Therapeutic approaches therefore focus on attempting to guide the client to process traumatic memories in healthier ways (Bracken, 2002). CBT's focus on reducing symptoms in an 'evidenced' and 'scientific' way means that when clients fail to get better the focus might be on what the client is not doing – such as 'the client's readiness to change' and 'matching interventions to the patient's stages of change' (Murphy, Rosen, Thompson, Murray & Rainey, 2004, p. 78), rather than the adequacy of the intervention.

The effect of trauma on memory is conceptualised as a purely individual internal process located entirely within the confines of the individual. This is where minority world 'psy' expertise comes in with 'technical interventions' that encourage the processing of traumatic material (Summerfield, 2001; Bracken, 2002). The global popularity of technology and computer literacy make these explanations of emotional distress appear rational and easy both to understand and to execute. Complex difficulties are thus twinned with simple solutions. This framework, based on individualism, is thought to be universal across cultures. That other cultures outside of the minority world may have other frameworks of understanding is rarely considered.

It is cognitive psychology that is needed to help understand the ways in which experiences of oppression, abuse and violence impact on people's memories. However, this cognitive understanding is just one story out of many possible understandings. Even if taken at face value, cognitive integration of traumatic experiences will always happen in a social, cultural, socio-political context and as part of significant relationships that either help or hinder the process.

I am not arguing that people do not experience debilitating re-experiences that intrude on their lives; or that a processing approach to their difficulties may not be helpful, as it most definitely can be. My argument is that it is not helpful to view a part of the picture as though it were the whole, assume its universal relevance and ignore the interpersonal, cultural and political context it takes place in (for example when torturers tell those tortured that they will scar them emotionally and physically so that they 'will never forget'; or when political activists tell themselves and each other that they must 'never forget the struggle'; or when abusers tell children 'it never happened').

A relationally responsive approach to therapy suggests that outcome is not the only important consideration, but the process of what we do must be ethical. Is it ethical to attempt to encourage survivors of torture to talk through their traumatic experiences in detail when they have explicitly expressed a desire not to remember, because the cognitive processing model of trauma suggests that this might rid them of their intrusive experiences? In this situation do we need to 'improve treatment tolerability?' (Taylor, 2004, p. 5) or are there other ways of talking that are useful, respectful and responsive?

Trauma will impact on individuals and systems in different ways depending on context. For example, nightmares do not have the same significance in all cultures even though they are reported in every society. If trauma is viewed as a pathogenic 'thing' that disturbs the natural func-tioning of the mind, 'then it makes sense to probe the contents of the mind in an effort to fix the faulty information processing' (Bracken, 2002, p. 95). If on the other hand the restoration of meaning requires a focus on power, resistance and liberation, our approach looks very different. Instead of the focus being on what is happening inside the heads of 'victims', it could be on the political, social and cultural dimensions of trauma that impact on remembering.

A trainee came to supervision wanting support with helping Mirza, a woman with recurring nightmares who survived detention and torture in her country of origin and who witnessed her best cousin being raped and murdered. Mirza had a recurring nightmare of cousin shouting angrily at her 'why did this happen?' Mirza was deeply religious and believed the spirit of her cousin was haunting her. When a CBT formulation was offered, Mirza disconnected from the conversation.

In supervision we talked about the limits of a cognitive behavioural approach given that this was not how Mirza made sense of her difficulties. Supervision explored how to enquire about Mirza's meanings rather than centralising the cognitive behavioural one. The trainee talked with Mirza about her religious faith and Mirza decided she would talk to her pastor, who told her that her cousin's soul was 'roaming' and would eventually rest. This validated Mirza's sense that her cousin's spirit was finding it hard to rest because her death had not been normal or just. Indeed, Mirza saw it as morally important not to process the memory of her cousin's murder as a normal memory or to come to terms with it. For Mirza her cousin was reminding her 'this should not have happened'.

The trainee explored the values that had been violated by the government-sanctioned rape and murder of her cousin (family, the importance of protecting women from abuse, love for her cousin), the aims of the brutality Mirza and her cousin experienced (to silence their activism and disconnect Mirza from the full memory of her cousin) and Mirza's desire not to forget her cousin or what had happened to her. Mirza described how she blamed herself for her cousin's rape and murder and, together with the trainee, worked on redirecting responsibility to those who persecuted and violated them. The trainee explored what memory Mirza wanted to have of her cousin, as a form of resistance against the memory imposed on her by their oppressors. Mirza began to explore memories of her cousin that reconnected her to what she valued about their relationship.

Mirza began to consult her cousin when she wanted advice. She bought a CD of a musician they used to listen to together. She stopped having the recurring nightmare and began to have pleasant and innocuous dreams about her cousin. In one Mirza's cousin came to her home and they chatted for a while before her cousin said goodbye and flew out the window.

Rather than inadvertently undermining Mirza's cultural and religious resources by providing her with an explanation of her experiences that ignored her faith and political commitments, this trainee explored the territories of Mirza's life that were deeply important to her. As White (2004b) suggested: 'In the explorations of these other territories of life, people's stories of trauma and pain are not invalidated or displaced. However, people find that . . . they have another place in which to stand that makes it possible to give expression to their experiences of trauma without being defined purely by these experiences' (White, 2004b, pp. 60–61).

Power, resistance, liberation and memory

If we look through the lenses of power, resistance and liberation we might critique the ways in which our 'psy' theories pathologise those who experience oppression, ignore the social, cultural, political context of oppression and focus our attention on victims of abuse and oppression rather than those who enact these forms of violence.

Pathologising

One danger of an apolitical approach to memory difficulties resulting from oppressive experiences is that the person affected comes to believe that their responses are dysfunctional. Yet it is the ways we are abused by society and in relationship that are dysfunctional – not our responses to these experiences. The individual who experiences memory difficulties is thought to be trying to cope with a disrupted inner world rather than actively responding to various activities that promote and sustain an oppressive social world. In the apolitical approach the individual can only be helped by challenging their erroneous conclusions about the world. However, we could argue that the conclusions come to after experiences of abuse, violence and oppression are, for those affected, accurate rather than erroneous.

Ignores social, cultural and political context

If we focus on power, resistance and liberation we might explore what oppression continues to exist in the life of the client and requires that they continue to resist. For example, a woman sexually abused as a child may also be responding to the ongoing abuse, exploitation and oppression of women she experiences as an adult. What often gets left out of trauma discourse is the way in which social circumstances and political climates impact on whether people can direct their emotional and mental energy to the present and forward to the future. An asylum-seeking person may feel tied to the traumas of the past partly because they are living in limbo waiting to hear if they will be granted asylum in the UK, partly because they feel loyal to their community's experience of ongoing persecution, and because feeling unsafe in their present living circumstances replicates past experiences of danger.

Focus on victims

If it is the inner world of 'victims' that gets explored, we tend not to focus on the relational and social responses to the person who has been traumatised, the behaviour of the 'perpetrator' or their strategies of abuse. The perpetrator is largely absent from cognitive explanations for traumatic memory, other than creating the context for 'trauma'. As part of the exercise of power there is often an active attempt by perpetrators to shatter the individuals' assumptions about themselves and the world, and disrupt memory. In fact we could see an attack on memory as one of the major strategies of oppression in acts of violence and abuse.

Focus beyond victims

People who have experienced sexual violence typically report negative social responses to disclosing their experiences as well as active attempts to distort these memories in favour of the perpetrator. Violence is widely misrepresented in legal and mental health settings (Coates, 1997; Coates, Todd & Wade, 2000; Bavelas & Coates, 2001; O'Neill & Morgan, 2001; Coates & Wade, 2004), where language is used to distort memory by (a) concealing the violence by calling it something innocuous such as 'a domestic', (b) obscuring perpetrators' responsibility, (c) concealing victims' responses and resistance, and (d) blaming and pathologising those victimised.

The victimised person's acts of resistance to their experiences might be recast as problems to be treated (Wade, 1997; Todd & Wade, 2003). At times professionals use misleading terms and metaphors (Coates et al., 2000; Coates & Wade, 2007). For example, Nimisha Patel rightly pointed out to me that my use of the term 'persecutory rape', when writing asylum reports, obscured the ways in which all rape is persecutory.

Perpetrators of sexual abuse or domestic violence often try to ensure that their abuse remains unseen, unacknowledged and not remembered. As Herman (2001) points out, 'in order to escape accountability for his crimes, the perpetrator does everything in his power to promote forgetting' (p. 8). People who perpetrate abuse rely on the power they have to distort and manipulate the victimised person's reality. In addition, those who perpetrate abuse deliberately isolate those they abuse, in order to try and ensure that the victimised person's memories are made up of the perpetrator's distorted version of the victim and a version of reality that justifies abuse. Isolation disconnects the person from those who might challenge these versions of reality. The victimised person might also become separated from the importance of their resistance to abuse, with respect to what is meaningful to them (White, 2004b). Memory difficulties could be viewed as an attempt to create coherence in the face of active attempts by perpetrators to create chaos and confusion. By distorting the memories of 'victims', they are:

- less likely to report the abuse, oppression and violence
- more likely to blame themselves for their experiences
- more likely to experience intense and long-lasting distress
- more likely to receive a diagnosis of mental illness even after the abuse has ended (Coates et al., 2000; Coates & Wade, 2004).

If the aim of perpetration is to victimise, silence and distort people's memories, therapy might direct its focus to:

- highlighting the strategies of perpetration
- highlighting the resistance of those victimised
- supporting those victimised to reclaim their preferred memories (Wade, 2007; White, 2004a).

Donna was sexually abused by her uncle who terrorised her for most of her childhood and died when she was a teenager. Donna had a diagnosis of schizophrenia because when she was 'unwell' she felt 'mentally chaotic' as a result of recurring nightmares and flashbacks. We explored Donna's intrusive experiences and how she understood them. CMM levels of context served as a useful framework for exploring strategies of perpetration as the power of contextual forces and Donna's strategies of resistance as the power of implicative forces.

- With respect to *cultural context* we explored the negative ways the media and criminal justice system often responded to those sexually abused, why this was and what Donna thought about it.
- With respect to *family and relational context* we explored responses from significant people in Donna's life to her disclosure of abuse. For example, Donna's mother pretended she had not heard what Donna had said; whereas Donna's husband and best friend were supportive. We explored Donna's ethical position on the negative responses she received, what Donna would do differently if being disclosed to and what her alternative approach said about her. We reflected on the consequences of open resistance to these negative responses – such as her mother cutting Donna out of her life – in order to make sense of the form Donna's resistance took (a commitment to sustaining the relationships that were important to her).

- With respect to *relational context* we explored the ways in which Donna's uncle actively attempted to distort her sense of what was real and not real.
- Exploring Donna's *identity context* meant asking her what her experiences (of abuse and the mental health system) had her thinking and feeling about herself. It was also important to listen out for Donna's strategies of resistance and build on this story. We explored the origins of Donna's abilities, qualities and convictions (for example, Donna described a positive relationship with her drama teacher who supported Donna's skills in amateur dramatics, which enabled Donna to creatively escape the constraints of her family life by being someone else and experimenting with the fluidity of personal identity).

As Donna started to experience herself as more and more coherent and happy with herself she began to experience more frequent intrusive images of her uncle. We explored the relationship between Donna developing a positive sense of herself and the increasingly menacing presence of her uncle, having to become more and more present as the power to define Donna waned.

Rather than Donna's flashbacks indicating that she had a disorder and was becoming unwell, they were an indication of her growing strengths. Donna felt that the stronger and happier she was becoming, the harder her uncle had to work to take back the power he previously had over her. Donna felt stronger than her uncle for the first time, realising that she was living the life he said she would never have.

Reclaiming memory

As a result of the attack on memory that often comes with abuse, violence and oppression, people who experience emotional distress and psycho-social difficulties often experience life as single-storied, predominantly featuring hopelessness and despair (White, 2004b). Reclaiming memory is therefore an important part of resisting abuses of power. As White (2004b) argues, forgotten or silenced stories represent other territories of living, knowledge and action that could assist us to 'go on'. The aims of violence, oppression and abuse are often to fully colonise a person's memory. Asking therapeutic questions that connect clients to neglected and overshadowed events and actions of their lives can help them reclaim their identity.

Storytelling

How people respond to attacks on memory might lead to narratives of self that are intertwined, separated, interrupted or rigid (Roberts, 1999).

Intertwined stories

Intertwined stories refer to when events that occurred at one time are used to understand new circumstances. A story might also be intertwined because it is formed against or opposite another story – for example, 'I won't do what my parents did'. With intertwined stories what is happening in the present is lived in some ways as if it were happening in the past (Roberts, 1999). As one story resonates with another, meaning is passed between them. With intertwined stories the therapist might help clients respect the integrity of each story and let each story stand on its own, while exploring the differences between them, with 'difference questions'.[53]

> Sanjida and Bilkis, came to therapy because Sanjida felt responsible for Bilkis' depression. Couple therapy brought forth the intertwined story of Sanjida's childhood experiences of sexual abuse and her sexual relationship with her girlfriend Bilkis. Sanjida at times withdrew from Bilkis' sexual affection because of re-experiencing memories of being groomed for abuse. Bilkis felt rejected and depressed. Exploring this pattern seemed helpful for Bilkis as she had been living this intertwined story without knowing the script.
>
> I asked 'difference questions' to punctuate the differences between Sanjida's past and present life experiences ('How do these stories influence or affect each other? Is this influence helpful or not? What are the differences between Bilkis and your brother and the power you have to say what you want and need? How would your sexual experience with Bilkis be different if it did not trigger the memory of abuse?'). This helped to amplify the relationship that Sanjida and Bilkis wanted. By thickening the story of what made their relationship precious Sanjida began to embed this story in her bodily and sexual experience of Bilkis. Bilkis was able to give a different meaning to Sanjida's behaviour that did not leave her feeling rejected.
>
> As Sanjida built on her ability to talk about her needs and her boundaries, we drew on 'guided pleasure' techniques, where Sanjida took control of guiding Bilkis to where she wanted to be touched and what she did and did not like. We moved from thinking about Sanjida as an abuse survivor to discussing what the couple wanted from each other in their intimate relationship. This helped Sanjida to experience her body in a more sensual and empowering way, and she discovered that it is never too late to learn how to enjoy touch despite the trauma of abuse.

Distinct/separated stories

Rather than being overly connected, separated stories are not seen as linked at all, which means that clients lack access to levels of meaning that could be enabling. Connecting similar patterns in different stories may help people to better understand their responses and feel better able to respond in transforming ways. Glenda Fredman suggests asking 'similarity questions' to give clients 'the opportunity to tap meaning-making across different contexts' (Roberts, 1999, p. 15), such as:

> If you were to connect this story to another story in your life, what story might it be linked to? How would your current story be different if you made this connection? What might the effect be on your life if the current story continues to stand alone?
>
> (Roberts, 1999, p. 15)

With intertwined and separated/distinct stories, the therapist and client explore whether there is 'too much or too little resonance between them' (Roberts, 1999, p. 6). Later in this book I talk in more detail about separated stories with respect to the aims of torture and the experience of asylum seeking in the UK.

Interrupted stories

One of the by-products of war, torture and forced displacement is to disconnect people from their sources of joy, pride, belonging and identity. Such losses can mean that people lose contact with the locations, symbols, relationships and activities that generate life-affirming stories (Roberts, 1999). The therapist can help clients expand the social network that would help resurrect these interrupted stories as well as ask questions about how their story might have developed if it had not been interrupted. Example questions include:

Who could help you continue living this story so that it carries on into the life you have now? Why would this story continuing have been a threat to the oppressive regime? How does this story being interrupted suit the heterosexist agenda? If you were to kick-start this story again, how would you like it to be? What difference would it make in your life if this story continued?

Rigid stories

Roberts (1999) also talks about rigid stories, referring to descriptions of living where time seems to be frozen and stories are told the same way over and over again despite changes in context, time and relationships. However, we have to be careful when making judgements about the types of stories clients tell and reflect on our assumptions about what we think is more useful. A story that seems rigid to the therapist might say something about the cultural and interpersonal context the story survives in.

Exploring levels of context helps make sense of how stories come to appear from outside the experience as rigid and static. In addition to the power of social context, what we do with stories can either be liberating, enabling us to move on, or disabling, feeding into stuckness. We cannot know without talking to clients which approach to storytelling is most liberating.

Re-membering

When I found out my father has cancer I was devastated. My father has always been a consistently wonderful, warm and gentle presence in my life, and I have loved and valued him not just as my father but as a beautiful spirit in his own right. I did not think I would ever be able to get used to him not being in my life and I felt intensely sad for him, for me, for all who love him and the world. After the tragic news, whenever I asked my father how he was he smiled deeply and said he was good. I could not understand why he seemed so happy and relaxed, whereas he normally looked like he had things on his mind. My father, who has always been warm, seemed warmer, hugging me tight, telling me he loved me in every (frequent) phone call and smiling frequently.

While I was on a Buddhist retreat in the winter of 2009, listening to a talk on Buddhism by Jnanavaca, something profound happened. Jnanavaca talked about seeing an interview in front of a studio audience on YouTube between Byron Katie (Byron Kathleen Mitchell) an American speaker and author, and a man with cancer. This man talked about the suffering he felt when he thought about wanting his cancer to stop growing and being told by his doctors that it was in fact growing. With much compassion and warmth, Byron Katie asked this man what the opposite thought would be, to which he replied 'I want my cancer to continue growing'. Byron Katie asked this man to think of reasons why this thought would be true. Tearfully, the man answered, among other things 'because it's opening doors I would not have been able to open on my own . . . because it's opening my heart".[54]

I realised that despite the undeniable tragedy of cancer, my father's already large heart was opening further. Since then when I meditate, I think about my father; when I catch myself with my heart open, I think of both my parents, and the legacy they passed on to me. When my father is no longer on this earth I will remember him through my acts of loving kindness, as he lives on in me.

Martín-Baró (1996) talked about 'rescuing those aspects of identity which served yesterday, and will serve today' (Martín-Baró, 1996, p. 30). In this vein Michael White developed an approach to memory as potentially liberating rather than constraining. The idea of 're-membering' drew heavily on the work of anthropologist Barbara Myerhoff (1982, 1986) who worked with elderly Jewish people around their experiences of death and dying. Myerhoff concluded from her work that we experience ourselves more richly and feel more connected to what is important to us if we explore our identity in a community. Myerhoff's work was concerned with how we reconnect people to important people in their lives, often people who have died (Myerhoff, 1986).

Re-membering practices are based on ideas about identity, much more common in the majority world, as relational, public and social, which differ from the predominant view in the minority world of identity as internal to us and fixed. A relational and social view directs us towards the relationships that help create our identity, our 'club of life', and what our preferred club would look like (White, 1997). Re-membering conversations are not about passive recollection, but about purposive engagement with the significant figures of our history by re-creating the membership of our club of life. Membership refers to the valued relationships that we have had and the meanings we develop out of these relationships. When people die they do not stop having membership to the club of our life; we can keep our relationships with significant people who have died alive and consult them about the things they know about us and about life that may be useful (White, 1997).

Whereas some people earn their status in our lives, others achieve it through abusive and undermining practices. In therapy, clients can explore whose voices they want to be recognised in matters of their identity, and these can be made up of real people, characters in a book, lyrics of a song, artists or public figures (White, 1997), as well as who they do not want to inform how they see themselves. These conversations can also help people feel that cherished people are standing with them in their lives rather then feeling that they face difficulties alone.

After his main caregiver, his uncle Barry, died, Simon grew up in a children's home and experienced continued physical abuse. In our therapy sessions we explored the way this relationship magnified and evoked the qualities of his preferred self, such as his respect for women. I asked questions to thicken the story of his relationship with uncle Barry, such as: 'Why would uncle Barry not be surprised to hear you talk about women the way you do? How might uncle Barry have noticed these values in you? How did knowing uncle Barry change or shape your life?' Simon found these questions relatively easy to answer and did so with enthusiasm and tenderness. He talked about uncle Barry as planting a 'good' seed in him that made him good.

When it proved difficult for Simon to reflect on how he was valued by his uncle, we built on Simon's metaphor of having a seed 'planted' in him. The reflecting team asked what uncle Barry saw in Simon that made him know that the seed could be cultivated and would grow. For example: 'What were some of the things uncle Barry might have seen you doing that would have shown him that you held values and hopes that would enable the seed to take root?' As a result it became easier to ask questions such as: 'Can you talk about what it meant to uncle Barry to know you and have you in his life? If you were to see yourself through Barry's eyes, what would you most appreciate about yourself? Are there times when you have conversations with Barry? Does his voice help you at any time?'

Memory as testimony

On a social level it may not be sufficient just to remember if remembering does not lead to an interruption of injustice and violence and move societies towards peace. 'If there is no hope of justice, the helpless rage of victimised groups can fester, impervious to the passage of time. Demagogic political leaders well understand the power of this rage, and are only too willing to exploit it by offering to an aggrieved people the promise of collective revenge' (Herman, 2001, p. 242).

Similarly, Watkins and Shulman (2008) describe how Abdel Aziz al-Rantisi, the Palestinian founder of Hamas, explained before being assassinated by Israeli forces that Hamas was attempting to 'morally educate' Israelis into better understanding the Palestinian experience of Israeli occupation, by forcing them to actually experience violence themselves. Alternatively 'spaces of recollection [can] work against such cycles of violence, interrupting them and posing in their stead other processes through which empathy can be built' (Watkins & Shulman, 2008, p. 130) that do not reconstitute violence.

An example of ways in which remembering can be used to make changes in the social world is the writing of medico-legal reports in support of people seeking asylum. Medico-legal reports, as well as being a moral imperative, also document persecution, violence and torture. Writing such reports is best done as a collaborative process, which often means spending time going over and discussing what has been written, including the purpose of an emphasis on the effects on the client of their experiences rather than on their resilience. This involves discussing how such a report might honour both the vulnerability and the resourcefulness of a client within the confines of a legal system that sees signs of distress as evidence of torture. As much as possible I write these reports using the client's own words to describe their experiences and the impact on them.

From a cognitive processing point of view, retelling their stories of persecution might facilitate the integration of clients' fragmented memories, and from a psychodynamic point of view this process can support clients to re-establish meaning and integrity out of fragmented and painful internal experiences. From a liberation psychology perspective this testimony locates the source of psychological difficulties firmly within the social sphere. It produces a historic, public document that accuses oppressive regimes of human rights violations. The collaboration between therapist and client creates a united advocacy against political suppression. In addition, many cultures have healing rituals in which testimony is an essential part (Cienfuegos & Monelli, 1983; Agger & Jensen, 1990). This type of testimony has a clear social action agenda; it is meant to change something for the better.

Chapter 12

De-ideologising everyday experience

Naming oppression

From a liberation psychology point of view, prevailing discourses deny significant aspects of social reality. Martín-Baró (1996) argued that to de-ideologise was to witness and name oppression. Naming and talking about oppression is not an easy endeavour for those who experience it. Those who speak the truth of their experience risk further assaults on their experience of reality ('that's not how it really is', 'you're making something out of nothing', 'not everything is about race/gender/sexuality' – probably not if you are White, male and heterosexual).

When someone who experiences oppression accuses a socially dominant person of abuse or oppression – particularly if these acts are by and large tolerated in society – they risk being accused of over-reaction, paranoia and even madness. Yet to name something experienced as abusive as abuse puts it out there in the world, in the interaction between people, taking it out of the inner experience of the person who is the target of it. The energy that comes from other people's prejudice belongs to them and not the people it seeks to oppress. Lee (2005) and Cross (1994) put it this way: 'I can think of no greater challenge than for us to begin the conversations we have often thought but seldom had' (Lee, 2005, p. 114). '"Naming" in itself is powerful and political. To name child abuse, sexual harassment, violence, enables these things to be spoken of. To leave them unnamed is to silence the voice of those oppressed by these actions' (Cross, 1994, p. 9).

Naming homophobia

Hazel was a working-class white British woman in her forties who had known she was Gay since she was 13 years old. She grew up in London with her younger brother, grandmother and mother. Hazel was divorced with a 10-year-old daughter. Hazel explained in therapy that as she grew up she had no awareness of Gay culture or history. She had been with her present partner, Angela, for four years. A year after meeting Angela, Hazel went to Brighton Pride as the civil partnership law had just been passed and met a number of lesbian couples who had been together for decades. When Hazel got home she asked Angela to be her civil partner. Hazel talked about finally having a validating story about being Gay that made connections with a larger community.

A few weeks after proposing to her partner, Hazel reported that she was feeling depressed and linked this to what she described as internalised homophobia.[55] When I asked her what this meant, she gave examples of being out with Angela and being conscious of not showing her physical affection. I asked Hazel why she referred to this as internalised homophobia, and she explained that she sometimes felt as though her relationship was not as valid and important because she was with a woman and not a man. This led her to engage in behaviours and to have thoughts that she later felt ashamed of and that caused difficulties in her relationship with Angela.

Hazel described herself with respect to a negative psychological entity residing within her. For Hazel her belief that she was suffering from internalised homophobia added to her sense that she was flawed, inadequate and other than what she should be. Hazel described Angela as 'liberated' and therefore believed that she would eventually get sick of Hazel's inadequacies and choose to be in a relationship with someone more comfortable with herself. This reinforced Hazel's emotional withdrawal and Angela's confusion about why Hazel 'blew hot and cold'. I shared my belief with Hazel that it was not intrinsic to being Gay to feel bad about it, and therefore it might be useful to look at what was happening in these moments and where certain ideas and feelings were coming from.

Whenever I hear a term beginning with the description 'internalised' I am curious about it (and, if I'm honest, rather critical). I do not think it is an actual entity, and so I wonder how experience gets to be described and thought of in this way. When clients talk about internalised homophobia it is important for me to acknowledge my heterosexual privilege while also being curious about the term and its meaning.

Externalising homophobia

Fisher (2005), influenced by Foucault, talked about power holding out a promise. He says: '[Foucault] argued that practices of power get a grip on us not merely through offering repression and pain, but rather because power also promises us "productivity, knowledge and discourse" (1976/ 2003). I like this thought about the promise of power. I like to think it is helpful in my life to be suspicious about power operating through promise' (Fisher, 2005, p. 13). Given that oppressive discourses might hold out a promise and reward people who participate in them based on what they accord value to, we could view 'internalised oppression' very differently and interrogate strategies of oppression more fully.

For example, some heterosexual women talk about 'playing dumb' or limiting themselves to dating men who earn more than them, because they believe that men would be too intimidated if their girlfriends were smarter or higher earners. The promise of romantic love and commitment might be enough to pull some women towards behaving in ways that reinforce the idea that they are inferior to men. It may not be accurate to say that these women have 'internalised' sexist ideas, but it is clear that they have responded to oppressive ideas outside of them in ways that may enable them to acquire some of the things they value. I would add that oppressive strategies also hold out a promise about the ways in which people can avoid negative experiences (for example, 'If you are Black and you want to be accepted by the dominant culture, try and look and behave as much like that culture dictates as possible').

When I asked Hazel what she meant by the term 'internalised homophobia' she gave a textbook answer, saying that it describes when Gay and bisexual people internalise the negative beliefs and feelings held about them. I acknowledged that what was very real for Hazel was that anti-Gay rhetoric had found a place in her thinking, such that she felt that she had come to dislike aspects of herself. I shared my dilemma with Hazel that I wanted to respect her experience while also being concerned about the term. I asked Hazel if she wanted to hear my concerns or if she wanted me to stay with how she was feeling. Hazel said that she wanted to stay with her understanding of her 'problem' but explore its impact on her experience. We explored the constraints and opportunities afforded to her in referring to homophobia as internal, and then explored if there were other ways of making sense of this experience that did not internalise the oppression she experienced.

Hazel and I went through what she described as her internal homophobic statements and we used a daisy model to explore where those ideas and beliefs came from; whose voice they represented and what maintained their presence in her life (Figure 12.1). All these enquiries came up with the same conclusion: It was homophobia that was the culprit, not an internal deficit; and it became clearer that homophobia is everywhere in the social world. As a result Hazel seemed more able to challenge homophobia as an external discourse and not pathology within her.

Although the homophobia Hazel experienced was deeply rooted in society, its impact was also felt in her interpersonal and private experience. The effect of Hazel referring to homophobia in terms of social discourse rather than self-abuse was that she could take an agentic position on it.

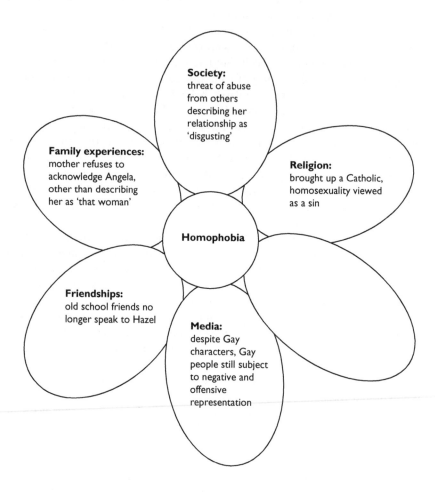

Figure 12.1 Daisy model exploration of homophobia – Where do ideas come from?

Hazel began to have conversations with Angela about this, and they learnt to tolerate their difference while joining together on issues they shared. The following session Hazel told me that she had written a letter of complaint with Angela about the homophobic content of a comedy show they had gone to. Hazel said to me: 'it is situations like that that make it harder for me to be out in public'.

Locating homophobia in social context

When we enter into the idea that oppressive discourses are around us all the time we can externalise them in ways that do not locate these ideas within the essence of people who enact them. Rather than absorbing homophobia into our beings, homophobia can be viewed as ideas we draw on in creating our emotional responses, building our beliefs and trying to coordinate with others within a homophobic society. Russell (2007) suggests that we can talk about 'homophobic learning' that we are *all* invited into and can *all* challenge.

Given that homophobia is an inevitable outcome of living in a homophobic society and that everyone participates in it in some way, how is the distinction between homophobia and internalised homophobia helpful? Russell (2007) argues that the only difference is that a person who is heterosexual tends to relate to homophobic discourse as a narrative that refers to 'other' people. They are more likely therefore to harm others, while homophobic discourse may not be personally harmful to themselves – other than limiting their connections with varied humanity – and can actually help them gain access to privilege and power.

Rather than drawing on concepts and ideas based on self-blame for homophobic learning, we can talk in therapy about how we are all potential candidates for enacting the homophobia that is rife in society. This makes both the therapist and the client take responsibility for what they are enacting. For example, I asked Hazel to challenge me when she felt that I was making unhelpful assumptions and taking positions that did not fit with her.

Entertaining ideal scenarios

One of the ways in which Hazel and I explored homophobia was to talk about how things would be for her in the present if homophobia in the world did not exist. We redid the daisy model to see what the different voices might be saying if the idea did not exist that heterosexuality was the only natural and valid route to emotional fulfilment and sexual expression within an intimate relationship (Figure 12.2).

Asking how things ideally would have been, should be, or might be did not disregard how things were at present but served to make visible the

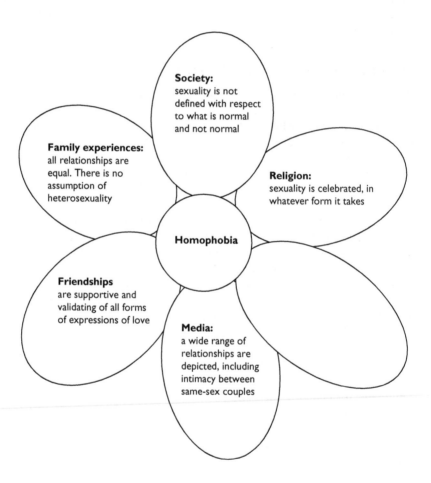

Figure 12.2 Daisy model exploration of ideal scenario: A liberated society

social and historical context of homophobia. Hazel realised that although the absorption of oppressive ideas may be automatic, their enactment or expression did not have to be. By exploring exceptions to the story of Hazel having 'internalised homophobia', Hazel reflected that she was contributing positively to the social world around her by enabling certain freedoms to be possible for her daughter that had not been open to Hazel as a child.

Interrupting the impact of self-blame and self-judgement enabled Hazel to examine the ways she participated in the very discourses she wanted to challenge. It was also important to explore the ways in which as a couple they interrupted homophobia in their public and private spaces. This was not a linear and uncomplicated process for Hazel – becoming more 'authentic' meant she was confronted with more and more prejudice. Hazel commented that the fact that some of her ideas about homosexuality felt automatic did not mean they came from within her: they were manifestations of the continued pervasiveness of homophobia in the social world.

Bisexuality and psychotherapy

Homophobic society simultaneously perpetuates the idea that anything but heterosexuality is bad and the idea that we must settle on one of only two dichotomous sexual orientations – either homosexual or heterosexual. Therefore if a person is not explicitly 'homosexual' they must be 'heterosexual'. People who identify as bisexual might experience misunderstanding from Gay people as well as heterosexual people. Bisexuality might not be viewed as a legitimate experience but as a transitional identity, on the way to the 'correct' destination, whether that is Gay or heterosexual. The fact that transition might be the experience of bisexuality for some Gay and heterosexual people does not mean that this is universally what bisexuality is about for all those who identify with it. The sexual identity dichotomy also perpetuates the idea that bisexuals are either in denial or maladjusted.

People who identify as bisexual might also straddle different communities – for example being a bisexual man or woman in a relationship perceived as heterosexual. Outwardly the bisexual person in a heterosexual relationship may be perceived as living out the ideals of heterosexist society, thereby silencing an important part of the identity and experiences of the bisexual person. It may be very important for bisexual clients to be able to explore freely the incongruence between perceived heterosexuality and actual bisexual feelings and desires, as an important part of resisting a view of sexuality as limited, distinct and static.

Yolanda was a bisexual woman in a heterosexual relationship, referred to therapy for help with depression and self-harm, and had seen me for three sessions before she told me she wanted to see a Gay therapist. I understood this request as wanting the totality of her experience to be validated, but arrogantly felt confused about why Yolanda did not think I would be able to provide that.

My clinical supervisors Glenda Fredman and Sharon Bond helped me to think about this request with respect to the systemic idea of 'abilities'. As well as having abilities as a psychologist and therapist, Yolanda was looking for someone with abilities related to the experience of being a Gay or bisexual woman. As a result I acknowledged the similarities and differences between us; the limits to my 'abilities' and the fact that all clients had a right to question therapists about their abilities.

Yolanda decided to keep seeing me, and despite my lack of ability we had conversations about people in her life she wanted to talk to who only knew her in heterosexual relationships, about having been in Gay relationships. Although this would not have been the same type of conversation that she could have had with a Gay therapist, Yolanda was able to have a conversation that she had not thought she would be able to have.

Responsibility of the therapist

Cornel West argues: 'It seems to me to talk about the history of hetero-sexism and the history of homophobia is to talk about ways in which various institutions and persons have promoted unjustified suffering and unmerited pain' (West, 1999, p. 20). An approach based on the idea that we all participate in the transmission of homophobic ideas and have the potential to challenge it points the therapist towards their responsibility as a member of the global community to uphold a commitment to challenging all forms of domination and oppression.

Every time I let homophobia rear its ugly head – such as assuming everyone is heterosexual or laughing at homophobic jokes – I am con-tributing to its existence in the world. Every time I interrupt it I am contributing to challenging it (even if this means that I am viewed as having no sense of humour because I am choosy about what I find funny).

Naming racism

'Race' and racism

'Race' is a social construct. What we view as racial differences do not in fact map on to actual biological differences between people (Fernando, Ndegwa & Wilson, 1998). Scientifically, 'as a way of categorising people, race is based upon a delusion' (Banton & Harwood, 1975, p.8). Although the myth of race as a scientific category has been thoroughly debunked 'race' as a social reality continues with much vigour (Fernando et al., 1998). Given that we exercise power by drawing on discourses, racism involves drawing on racist discourses and enacting them in relationship. Racism is often treated as a possession or some sort of internal, static quality; such as when people respond to challenges to their use of racist discourse with 'but I am not racist'. The fact that racism is not a permanent personality characteristic leaves open the potential of doing something different – of acting from a position of antiracism, of challenging racist discourse, of reflecting on taken for granted assumptions and responses, regardless of previous actions.

Racist ideology has permeated every sector of society for centuries and continues to do so in ever more insidious ways. When racism is framed largely with respect to access to employment and other opportunities, it becomes easier for other manifestations to be ignored, and for the presence of Black people, for example in certain professional positions, to be viewed as evidence of the eradication of racism. hooks (1993) writes that 'the vast majority of Black people, particularly those of us from non-privileged class backgrounds, have developed survival strategies based on imagining the worst and planning how to cope with it' (p. 62).

In my experience, 'imagining the worst' is not about imagining what is not there, but is born out of the experience that 'the worst' tends to happen. Given the insidious nature of racism, it is more likely to be tolerated and even encouraged than challenged. Unlike other forms of abuse (such as sexual abuse), when racism is the abuse bystanders routinely side with those causing harm rather than those being harmed. In fact 'victims' of racist abuse are more likely to be further attacked (for example accused of not having a sense of humour, of having a chip on their shoulder, or of being mad/disconnected from reality). If not attacked, those victimised by racism are frequently invited to rescue both the perpetrator and the bystander(s) from their own anxiety and difficult feelings about their involvement in abuse – for example, the person who has made a racist comment might say 'I hope you did not take offence at what I said. I hope you can see it in the spirit it was meant.'

Naming racism experienced by clients

Black women naming racism together

As a Black woman I frequently see myself portrayed in the media and social discourse as tolerable, 'mad' or 'bad'. We are 'tolerable' because we are perceived as strong, maternal, obedient and passive. We are 'mad' and 'bad' because we are viewed as angry, ignorant, irresponsible, overly sexual, emasculating, aggressive and loud. Black women are also portrayed as 'good for one thing only' and therefore not girlfriend or long-term partner material. The other representation in the media is that of the 'de-raced Black woman'; that is, the Black woman who is 'really just a woman' – a white woman in brown skin. *This* woman can have complexity, can generate sympathy and interest in ways that the 'raced Black woman' cannot; because the de-raced Black woman is not really Black.

Black women are not valued as diverse, or valued for the skills and abilities we acquire in order to survive a misogynistic, racist, classist and homophobic society. The difficulties Black women face rarely make public interest unless they are viewed as impacting on the rest of society – such as the stereotype of Black women in single-headed families thought to be responsible for delinquency and violent crime. The painful and difficult experiences Black women face often remain invisible. In this context therapy with other Black women who validate, connect with and witness those difficulties and the ingenious ways they are resisted can be immensely powerful.

Talking about the effects of prejudice and oppression is just as important as exploring the ways people resist. If we do not learn from clients about their actual experiences of oppression, we cannot fully appreciate their abilities in resisting them. Premature praise or highlighting how strong someone has had to be might feel disingenuous if what the person has had to survive is not fully understood. There are, of course, many difficult experiences faced by Black women such as sexual abuse, domestic violence and bereavement; however, for Black women these traumas exist in the context of misogyny and racism, which are themselves forms of violence and abuse.

Racism as repetitive abuse

It goes without saying that skin colour is a major organising factor in the world today, and yet Black people are expected to live in a world made for White people and be happy with it. Overlooking or minimising racism as a form of abuse constitutes a form of abuse in itself. Bryant-Davis and Ocampo (2005) draw parallels between racism and experiences that are acknowledged as abusive, such as rape and domestic violence. They argue that conceptualising racism as abuse may help therapists to evaluate their responses to disclosure of racist abuse compared to hearing about other abuses. The responses of others to our experiences of abuse are very important. It is well known that respectful and empathic interpersonal responses help those victimised by abuse to recover from their experiences in the short and long terms (Coates & Wade, 2004).

Karumanchery (2003) and DeGruy Leary (2005) have also explored the notion of racism-based trauma. In particular, DeGruy Leary (2005) talks about the continued impact of slavery as unfinished history in the lives of Black and White people in the US. It is testimony to the lack of understanding in mainstream White society about the pervasive and deeply impacting nature of racism as a form of abuse that theorists and survivors themselves often have to draw parallels with 'acknowledged traumas' (Bryant-Davis & Ocampo, 2005). In order to highlight deep pain we often need to show evidence of actual (psychic) wounds in the form of symptoms (see Bryant-Davis & Ocampo, 2005 and DeGruy Leary, 2005 for examples of this).

It may be difficult for those who do not experience it to understand why racism is traumatic. When I went to a conference on 'de-medicalising misery' in London in 2006, one of the speakers who spoke eloquently about the link between trauma and 'psychosis' failed to mention racism as a trauma. When racism was mentioned by an audience member the speaker said that she did not know what the link between racism and 'psychosis' was even though she knew there was one.

It is my experience that at best mainstream society views racism as an inconvenience for Black people and at worst something that too much fuss is made about. In the case of racist trauma Black people have come to expect very little from the White people who may witness it. In the British Television show *The Apprentice* (2009) one of the contestants, Debra, told Yasmina (who went on to win the show) that she was deeply offended by Yasmina's suggestion that having two brown people on advertising posters was one too many. These forms of protest are rare and, more often than not, do not get supported by mainstream society.

A focus on the trauma of racism leads more naturally to an effects-based approach to understanding the impact of racism rather than the various forms of resistance that have enabled individuals, families and communities to survive racism for centuries. I am also aware of the danger of such an approach to racism leading to misguided intervention strategies designed to address trauma (in the form of 'racism stress management'), rather than the racism causing distress. On the other hand, if we deny the existence and impact of racism as abuse then we are relieved from the responsibility of having to address it and respond to it ethically.

Drawing parallels between racism and other forms of abuse might also help us understand the strategies of racism that attempt to repress resistance. Bryant-Davis and Ocampo (2005) argue that there are parallel motivations for perpetrators of racism and perpetrators of rape to propagate dehumanising myths about those whom they victimise in order to justify their abusive behaviour, their power and their privilege. In the same way that the sexual assault of women is justified with discourses about her behaviour, character and appearance, racism is either justified or denied if its target is viewed as arrogant (that is, does not know his or her place), is angry, is sexist, is a high achiever and so on. A lecturer who came to talk about forensic psychology when I was training to be a clinical psychologist said about a Black client who complained of racism: 'something about him meant that he brought this racism on himself'. The racism was his responsibility and was self-induced. Similarly I have witnessed racist attitudes expressed towards a Black male client excused by referring to his sexist attitudes. A man who is sexist does not deserve racism any more than a mother who physically assaults her son deserves to be raped. Physical assault and rape are equally indefensible. Sexism and racism are equally indefensible.

There are also societal parallels between racism and other forms of abuse in that 'victims are disbelieved, blamed and are taxed with the burden of proof' (Bryant-Davis & Ocampo, 2005, p. 490). 'If the survivor is not to blame, then society must face the psychologically overwhelming reality that life is full of injustices. Believing that racism and sexual assault are not prevalent and those who claim to encounter them must be crazy or somehow culpable is easier' (Bryant-Davis & Ocampo, 2005, p. 490). Instead of dealing with the abuse of racism itself, society focuses on the person who has broken the rule of silence (Bryant-Davis & Ocampo, 2005) or on justifying the actions of the perpetrator ('he's just a product of his generation').

There is a danger that when we make excuses for the person perpetuating abuse, we (a) align ourselves with the abuser and (b) respond to witnessing abuse as though we have no responsibility to address it. Justice is not just about what might be beneficial for the survivor. People who perpetuate racism and who do not face justice or challenge have their delusions of superiority reinforced and their actions are justified.

Eve was a young woman in her 20s of Ghanaian origin with a diagnosis of schizophrenia. I saw her in therapy with a Black woman systemic therapist, Ntake, in the reflecting team. Eve commented that it was great to have Black women in therapy as she felt she could talk about being a 'Black woman . . . rather than talking either about being Black or being a woman'.

When Eve was experiencing emotional 'chaos' and 'confusion' (her words for her experience) she covered her face in white chalk and talked about being rescued from 'earthly evil' by Jesus. As Black women in therapy with her, Eve felt that we approached her 'psychotic speech' as meaningful and rational, rather than nonsensical, with respect to her experiences of racism and her religious and cultural ideas about the nature of 'good' and 'evil', as well as the ways in which these intersected, such that she was surrounded by subtle yet piercing associations between blackness and badness, with the weight of history behind them.

When Eve was not feeling this chaos she was able to explain that what the doctors called 'psychosis' was for her an exaggerated state of isolation in which her thoughts about her experiences, which had few validating voices to connect with, became more and more monologous and frightening.

Paradoxically, the more Eve was viewed as psychotic the more she felt negated and silenced by others, making the possibility of joint meaning-making and dialogue even less likely. Eve then felt more and more emotionally disconnected from the world.

Therapy was a space for Eve to find new ways of being in dialogue with herself and others that did not invalidate her experiences. Rather than accentuating Eve's sense of disconnection from the world (by responding to her as 'mad', and therefore not like everyone else) we attempted to attenuate it. As three Black African women we talked about experiences that were potentially silenced in other contexts, such as the ways in which racism and sexism formed the context for Eve feeling unattractive and needing to make her face white with chalk. Eve described the power of being able to relax the vigilance she often felt in a White male world.

We talked about the ways in which skin colour, hair texture, hair length, body shape, facial features have all been distorted by the constant flow of White European images of beauty. White skin privilege, spirituality and sexuality were not taboos, but topics for discussion and deconstruction. It was also incredibly important for me as a lead therapist to have Ntake in the reflecting team, as it freed me up to explore these issues authentically.

We talked about how Black people learn early on that bringing up racism is so costly, so dangerous that we often self-censor, minimising our experiences or denying our reality. Eve also talked about feeling that traumatic experiences involving other Black people seemed easier for her White psychiatrist to hear about than her experiences of racism. I was able to open up a conversation about how she might equally feel reticent talking to us about her anger towards her family and other Black people whom she felt rejected by.

Given that we felt that we could identify to some extent with Eve's experience, it was important that we did not bring our experience into the room at the expense of Eve's unique experience. Instead we tried to use our personal experiences to enable Eve to tell her unique story.

The fact that as Black women Ntake and I were prepared to hear, validate and explore Eve's experiences does not mean that we had to be Black in order to do so. Lee (2005) suggests that all therapists reflect on whether therapy is a safe place for disclosing racist experiences by asking themselves questions such as:

- Does anyone ever disclose racist experiences to me? If not, why?
- Do I ever have in-depth conversations in my personal life with people who might have experienced racism?

- What happens to me when people I know disclose racism? How do I feel and how do I respond? Does it make a difference who is disclosing? Does it matter where the disclosure happens and who else is there?
- What responses do I want to have to people who disclose racism to me? What needs to happen to increase the likelihood of these responses emerging?
- Do my responses have depth? Do my responses validate the other person's experience?
- How do my responses seem to be received?
- If I enquire and people I know do not describe racism, what are the many reasons why this might be? For example, Lee comments: 'at the moment of disclosure, the already injured client is fearful of re-injury, shame, minimisation, invalidation and devaluation. Clients have expressed to me how they experience more acute fear in retelling their stories than they did when the victimisation occurred' (Lee, 2005, p. 110).

Satou was a Black woman in her forties with four small children. She was referred for 'anger management' as she was felt by her new employers, in a male-dominated working environment, to be 'inappropriately angry all the time'. When we explored what this meant, Satou explained that she had not physically assaulted or verbally insulted anyone, but was felt to be 'angry' because she 'did not stand for nonsense' and spoke up if she or anyone else was being unfairly treated. Satou seemed to be describing assertiveness. She felt that her history of psycho-social difficulties meant that her employers experienced her assertiveness as signs of mental illness, and as a Black woman her self-expression was often viewed as 'angry'.

In therapy we talked about the complexities of being an assertive Black woman in a society where:

(a) If you are a woman, to keep your feelings in, to not show anger and to not make challenges are seen as virtues; women are expected to keep a low profile and not compete with men.
(b) Black people are expected not to show any level of open assertiveness or competitiveness except in sports; otherwise they might be viewed as aggressive or arrogant.
(c) Black people should be 'seen and not heard' – equality and diversity policies invariably reflect this with their continued obsession with audits and quotas rather than listening with any real intent to Black people's experiences.
(d) There is 'gender silence' (Crenshaw, 1992) for Black women who feel loyalty to the story of racial solidarity at the expense of their experience of gender-based discrimination.

We talked about how these factors combine to make assertiveness, voice, loyalty and pride complex interacting issues. We reflected on the subtle attepmts to keep Black women in their place, and make them feel as though they should value humility and invisibility over confidence and honesty. While White middle-class men at work made statements as though they were fact and talked about things as though they did not expect to be challenged, Satou felt that any confidence she showed tended to be treated as unacceptable.

Therapy gave space to legitimising Satou's assertiveness in the face of injustice and describing the differences between anger and hatred, with respect to anger as a short-lasting emotional response and hatred as a longer lasting sentiment. When I asked what might make angry feelings move toward hatred, Satou poignantly explained: 'I think that happens when people don't hear your legitimate anger. Hatred is when you've given up . . . given up hope of being understood; of connection. But I haven't given that up.' This enabled us to explore the type of connections Satou wanted to make and the role of her self-expression in either facilitating those connections or stifling them.

Satou reflected on the usefulness of being assertive and realised that her anger was something she wanted to reserve for when it had a desired effect and not when the effect on others was not desired – for example, closing down their thinking, making them feel ashamed and defensive or hurt. Anger was important to Satou because it told her that something was wrong, or that someone had been wronged; therefore anger connected Satou to her values, principles and commitments. Once she had refined what anger meant to her, what it was for, Satou was able to reassess what she wanted to get anger to do for her and what she did not want to recruit anger to do. Satou said: 'Anger can become a habit and actually it is supposed to be about what's most important to me.'

There are obvious differences and interacting factors between racism, rape and domestic violence as forms of abuse. For example, racism often leaves no physical scars or visible evidence and is much harder to prove; rape or violence may be motivated by racism; racism is ubiquitous and occurs all the time throughout one's life. Whereas one may escape child sexual abuse when reaching adulthood or leave an abusive relationship, Black people cannot escape racism. There is no corner of the globe where one is immune from its effects and influence. I would argue that feeling angry is an understandable response to this type of violation and yet survivors of racism and other forms of abuse are often judged harshly for expressing anger, and as a result may be further isolated and blamed.

When I do consultations with staff teams and they tell me about a client 'claiming they are a victim of racism', I always say that it is important to take these accusations seriously and respond as though racism is a serious issue. It is incredibly important to 'respect the energy it takes for the client to hold these stories for long periods of time before there is a safe space to disclose them' (Lee, 2005, p. 109).

Ben, a Black middle-class office worker in his fifties separated from his partner and 16-year-old daughter, talked about his hurt that despite being friendly, dressing professionally, being clever and articulate, he continued to experience racism. Ben talked about working hard all his life to try to make other people trust his common decency. Ben's experience was that many White people he met had few if any Black friends, and the encounters they had with Black people were so brief that the conclusions they came to when they met him were imbued with racist assumptions.

We talked about unspoken rules about how to avoid racism that did not work, and Ben described his admiration for those who 'throw the rule book out altogether' and do their own thing. Ben talked about the pride and envy he felt when we saw young Black men walking with a confident swagger and with their hair natural, sometimes with a natural hair comb in it. We named these forms of self-expression forms of resistance. We talked about the number of times we heard confident young Black males described as 'cocky' or 'arrogant'.

Ben felt that he had resistance beaten out of him as a child by parents who did not want him to 'get into trouble' as they knew all too well what often happens to Black boys who express themselves freely. Ben said movingly 'I am not depressed. I am tired. When I learn how to follow my own rules maybe I'll feel more awake.' I wondered if being tired was a rejection of the injustices he experienced, such as 'people looking and not seeing you'.

Anger as a story

Anger has been associated with the experience of injustice and the attribution of responsibility and blame to others. Anger can also enable a person to retain a sense of power and control in the face of abuse and oppression. However, anger can be viewed as more than just an expression from the inside – it can be viewed as a relational social event. Hence we might ask clients questions that link their stories about their emotions to their relationships (Fredman, 2004).

Emotions link to our beliefs, ethics and moral logic. What we name something directs how we make sense of it and what we do with it. There are many ideas around about what anger is and what should be done with it. For example, Buddhists might see anger as an unskilful emotion leading to unskilful acts. Rather than trying not to be angry, the positive energy of mindfulness and compassion can take care of the flames of anger (for example see Nhật Hạnh, 2001).[56]

Some feminists see anger expression in women as a healthy and legitimate response to oppression that should be encouraged (Cox, Stabb & Bruckner, 1999). These are simply stories about an emotional experience we call anger. The stories people draw on to understand their experiences will have constraining and/or liberating effects on how they make sense and coordinate with others.

We can use CMM levels of context questions to explore the stories people have about anger (and to reflect on our own), where these stories come from as well as what gets opened up and closed down as a result of these stories. Exploring CMM levels of context enables us to reflect on emotions as actions created between people that invite others to respond in particular ways, not just emerging from inside our bodies but learnt in cultures with rules about what they are, what they are called and appropriate situations to do them in (Fredman, 2004; Pearce, 2007). As Fredman (2004) points out 'exploring the story of a person's experience with feelings through the different contexts of that person's life helps us create richer understandings of his or her emotions' (Fredman, 2004, p. 38).

Naming racism experienced by therapist

During my training as a clinical psychologist, working with difference was always talked about from the point of view of a White middle-class heterosexual norm (Afuape, 2004). After my training I had no templates to help me cope with or respond to racist comments from clients. As well as hearing racist comments about Black African people, I also heard racist statements about other ethnic minority groups. Before I was able to talk about these experiences in supervision, I felt paralysed, partly because I did not know if the ways I had learnt to respond to racism in the world outside of therapy were appropriate or therapeutic within therapy. Given that I had no blueprints to guide action, saying nothing seemed the only option open to me. Absorbing harmful statements in therapy and seemingly accepting them in passive silence takes its toll. I was caught in a double bind: on one hand I did not feel I could say anything; on the other hand not saying anything left me feeling I had silently colluded in my own oppression, which was deeply shaming.

I decided to train as a systemic psychotherapist believing that I would have some tools available to me to think about social difference in therapy. In addition, I was fortunate enough to have invaluable clinical supervision with Nimisha Patel, Aruna Mahtani and Sharon Bond, in which I was able to think about what it meant to be Black women therapists and to have numerous conversations about the pain of racism with women who deeply understood this experience and validated it. In addition I had clinical supervision with a White woman clinical psychologist and systemic psycho-therapist called Glenda Fredman who supervised me on my clinical work in adult mental health. My ability to talk about prejudice with clients was facilitated by conversations in supervision with Glenda, who never invali-dated my experiences of racism in therapy by saying 'perhaps he's that way with you because you look young' or 'it is probably more to do with your gender than race', or other such comments that would have supplanted my experience of racism with another reality. Glenda acknowledged that many possibilities were likely to be factors at once in my interaction with White clients without negating the importance of skin colour.

Glenda seemed very aware of the veracious existence of racism and the fact that there is often room for two or more issues to coexist. She seemed to understand intuitively the price I paid being silent in the face of racism and helped me construct an empowering story of my resistance that replaced a story of shame and passive resignation. I was able to reflect on the extent to which my silence was a manifestation of my desire not to harm the client and the extent to which I had learnt to protect White people from their enactment of racism. As Ken Hardy says:

> To avoid being seen by Whites as troublemakers, we suppress the part of ourselves that feels hurt and outraged by the racism around us, instead developing an 'institutional self' – an accommodating façade of calm professionalism calculated to be non-threatening to Whites. To survive in the White world, [Black people] learn to become 'good, effective, mainstream minorities' or what I call GEMM. I have found that when I am in my GEMM-mode, Whites approve of me and wonder, 'Why can't all black people be like Ken?'
>
> (Hardy, 1993, p. 52)

Glenda acknowledged and amplified the ethics that lived alongside my silence and hurt. She named this juxtaposition a skill – being able to feel hurt and stuck AND respond with respect and curiosity. In supervision we explored what enabled me to connect to this ability, as well as who in my life shared it or knew I possessed it. In exploring this, Glenda drew on the voices of my cultural community, asking what my mother, father, sisters, brother, friends and ancestors would say, and how their voices could act as a resource for me when experiencing racism in therapy.

As well as giving me the space in supervision to name racism, Glenda highlighted my skills in a situation where I felt my abilities were under attack; that is, my skills in being able to 'hold the emotion of the moment and not rush to put the client in her or his place with the power imbued to us as therapists' (Lee, 2005, p. 111). I was able to explore safely the ways in which my most difficult therapy experiences could be opportunities for mutual growth and learning with clients.

Having these conversations in supervision supported my ability to have these conversations in therapy with clients. As Pearce (2007) argues, 'avoiding disagreements shuts us off from the positive effects that dialogue can have on our evolution as selves and in relationships' (p. 216). How we coordinate with others who take different positions from us is important. Rather than silent, I learnt how to be both challenging and connected. Jonathan R. Flojo (2005), talking about experiencing racism in therapy, asks the question: 'Am I inches or miles apart from my client?' (Rasheed Ali et al., 2005, p. 127). Actually I feel I can be both at the same time.

When Ted, a 53-year-old White professional man, met me in therapy to get help with 'a lack of pleasure in anything' and severe panic attacks, one of the very first things he said to me was: 'You're not what I expected'. He then told me that when he received my letter and saw my name he asked himself what someone who is African can offer him. Ted talked about growing up in a small town outside London and having virtually no contact with Black people. He asked me what my qualifications were and enquired about how I managed to do so well in my life. Ted made comments about fraud executed 'by those greedy Nigerians'. As Ted became more comfortable with me he started to share his 'dislike' of Black people and Black culture because it is 'so aggressive'. I found myself feeling more and more frustrated as I tried to defend myself and other Black people from his attack.

In supervision I reflected on:

- how a White middle-class professional man in his early fifties felt about coming to see a young Black working-class woman to talk about his most painful experiences
- how he might try to feel powerful in a disempowering position
- how I might try to feel powerful when positioned as inferior and ineffective.

I wondered if Ted was attempting to regain power by connecting to racist discourses. This enabled me to reflect on how to abstain from a defensive position and have conversations in therapy that felt safe for us both to have. By sharing our expectations and my asking him to define how we proceed, we were able to have honest discussions about how he initially viewed me and how to work towards a relationship of trust and safety. We were also able to explore his fear of being let down and his fear of being inadequate. The following are examples of the types of question it became safe for me to ask Ted.

- I was thinking about talking about something you said that seems important to me as a Black woman, but may not be to you. Is it okay if I ask you about that? What would make it safe to talk about?

- Some people may hear that comment as prejudiced. What are your thoughts about the potential for that comment to be heard in that way?
- I know what I think about that as a Black woman and of course you are a White man, so it's important for me to not make assumptions. So I may ask you what your unique understanding is.
- Is it okay if I ask you how you came to understand some of the things you believe that strike me as a Black woman but may not strike you as a White man?
- Do you have many opportunities to have conversations about these issues with Black women? From time to time I might make it explicit that I am talking from the position of a Black woman. What would that be like for you? Would it be helpful?
- As a Black woman I may hear some of the things you say differently to how you hear them. I may also want to comment on things you say from my perspective as a Black woman. What would that be like for you, and how can I do it respectfully? How would I do it disrespectfully?[57]

Naming the oppression of those in authority

The Home Office

When I first saw consultant clinical psychologist Nimisha Patel, at the Medical Foundation for the Care of Victims of Torture, present the 'aims of torture' in a 2005 workshop I was struck by how similar the list was to the experience of seeking asylum in the UK. It became a useful reflection to make in therapy with asylum-seeking clients. Making these comparisons seemed to help clients make sense of why they often felt that their experiences in the UK were just as bad – if not worse – than what they suffered in their countries of origin. We treated the aims of torture and seeking asylum in the UK as 'separated stories' that are not presented as linked at all, despite psychological parallels. We connected similar patterns, by exploring how seeking asylum might replicate the aims of torture (e.g. 'psychological and physical debility', 'loss of control', 'maximising helplessness and powerlessness').

The power of experts

Anoushka was a 53-year-old Asian working-class woman, who grew up in South Wales and was married with three children. Anoushka was overweight, had a number of serious medical conditions, and wanted to work on how she could register with a general practitioner, which she had not been able to do for many years. I asked how Anoushka learnt new behaviours – whether she preferred to understand the reason behind things first or go straight into action mode, trying out new behaviours. Anoushka said that she had an idea why she was scared of doctors and wanted to explore this before trying something practical.

Anoushka grew up in care and the home she lived in came under investigation when one of the workers was arrested for sexually abusing children. Although Anoushka told the police that nothing happened to her, the police insisted that she have a very intrusive examination by a male doctor. Anoushka felt violated and not believed. When Anoushka was a teenager she was sent for a psychiatric assessment and saw three male psychiatrists who she felt also did not listen to her, talked about her as though she was not there, and then told her that she had people phobia. In another experience Anoushka had to have a painful procedure done in hospital. She was told by the doctor that she should signal when the pain got too much and he would stop. Despite agreeing what the signal would be, when she asked the doctor to stop as he had promised he did not stop until he decided to. Anoushka described how these experiences reinforced the racism and sexism she encountered and the message that as an Asian woman her experiences and preferences did not matter.

I asked if I could share my thoughts and if Anoushka would let me know if I was off the mark. I reflected that it sounded as though Anoushka was very aware of her boundaries, was able to articulate them clearly when given the chance, and needed other people to respect them. Anoushka responded: 'Yeah that's right. That's exactly it.' I said that I was not surprised that she did not like going to the doctor's given her multiple experiences of not being heard. I went on to say: 'We all have power, especially in the helping profession and mental health system. We have a lot of power and we may not be aware of how our power impacts on others. So what I think I am hearing is that you want people to be aware of the power they have and the impact on you as a patient and person and respect your boundaries so that your protective strategies do not have to kick in. And that includes me, because there may be times when I don't respect the power I have and you feel I have not listened to you properly.' Anoushka said: 'Thank you for saying that. I don't have people phobia; I just need people to listen to me.'

I asked Anoushka: 'Where did you get the idea that professionals should listen to you and that you could fire them if they don't?' Anoushka told me that when she was a child she told her social worker that she felt as though adults did not care about her opinion and that all her life things had been done to her without her consent. The social worker told Anoushka that having choices and being heard were very important and that Anoushka had the right to expect those things. It was not long before Anoushka was able to utilise the abilities we explored in therapy to devise a plan of action, and eventually she was able to register with a female GP.

Chapter 13

Utilising the people's virtues

Creating community

Martín-Baró (1996) talked about the importance of bringing alive the virtues that enable people to connect to what is meaningful to them. This might involve developing stories about values, principles, hopes and dreams. New stories may be so unfamiliar to clients that they find it hard to withstand the constant assault from long-standing forms of oppression. A client's community might be essential in helping them hold onto their preferences. We might create community in therapy by enquiring about the people in the client's life who might appreciate and stand behind their efforts to develop in the ways that they prefer, through letter writing or invitations for members of the client's significant system to join them in therapy.

> The link between identity and community is illustrated beautifully by the Nigerian tradition of asking significant people to give a newborn child a name (I have six names). These names say something about the child's potential with respect to positive relational qualities and it is up to all in the child's life to help them fulfil their potential, particularly those who name the child.
>
> Given this cultural link between identity and our relationships with others, I have been drawn to therapeutic approaches that are social and communal in addition to private and confidential. These social approaches involve the participation of significant people in the lives of the client inside and outside of therapy.

My interest in community was reinforced by being brought up by my older siblings, aunts, uncles and cousins as well as my parents. In addition, my parents often looked after other children in our wider family and community. Nancy Chodorow (1978) and Patricia Hill Collins (1995) suggest that collective child-rearing generates very different understandings of self than does the nuclear family with mother as primary or sole caregiver.

Chodorow (1978) contends that 'studies of more collective child rearing situations suggest that children develop more sense of solidarity and commitment to the group, less individualism and competitiveness, [and] are less liable to form intense, exclusive adult relationships, than children reared in western nuclear families' (p. 217). She also argues that exclusive parenting potentially harms both mother and baby and that both benefit from situations where 'love and relationship are not a scarce resource controlled and manipulated by one person only' (Chodorow, 1978, p. 217).

Given my experiences of community as family, I certainly hold to the view expressed by Collins (1995) that 'vesting one person with full responsibility for mothering a child may not be wise or possible' p. 120). The minority world view of children as the sole 'property' of their biological parents is challenged by seeing other people in a community as equally responsible for child-rearing and identity development. Similarly we could challenge the traditional 'psy' view that individuals are ultimately responsible for their own emotional wellbeing.

Peterson (2001) argues that in the minority world community is normally defined with respect to similarity among members (e.g. the Black community, the Gay community, the deaf community). However, when I have given workshops on 'developing community in therapy' a plentiful variety of reflections have been made by learners about what constitutes community.

For some it is linked to geographical area; for others it is an image or concept that gets conjured up in our minds that links together different aspects of ourselves. For some community is where you live; for others it is where you grew up; for others there is no such thing as community, only a universe of living beings.

For some community is transition and movement rather than a static place; for others community is locus of relatedness, identity and belonging, based on a network of people who matter but may not live in the same place. For some community is a place imposed on you; for others community is a choice.

For some community is a political gathering of resisters against marginalisation; for others community stifles individuality, creativity and freedom. For some community represents a place to escape from; for others a place to retreat to.

For some community comprises the people who live or work close by; for others community is an active attempt to maintain a sense of relatedness across distance. For some community conjures up images of small-minded thinking and narrow concerns; for others community has connotations of solidarity and collective responsibility. Of course community might be any or all of these.

Welch (1999) proposes a model of community based not on similarity but on contiguity – nearness and contact. Welch argues that community need not be limited to those we share important characteristics with, because we can have important relationships with those who are different from us, which requires 'learning to see the world through multiple lenses' (Welch, 1999, p. xv). Conversations in therapy can build community by reflecting on relationships that are highly validating of what people give value to. Proximity in this case is not determined by the physical closeness of others, but by how close the contribution of others to our identity fits with our preferred selves. Oppression and abuse can be very successful in minimising or making invisible relationships past and present that are enabling, whereas therapeutic conversation can support the client to stand with significant others, dead or alive, around preferred aspects of identity.

An Iraqi refugee, Sardar, was described by the psychiatrist who referred him as clinically and chronically depressed. He had been in various forms of therapy over six years and nothing seemed to help him. Initially with me, Sardar was non-responsive, looked upset and often replied to questions with 'I don't know'. Sardar was most vocal when we talked about the political and social situation in Iraq and the emotional impact on him of the continued destruction of his country. Sardar said that what his psychiatrist described as depression was actually his inability to live in a world that allowed this mass murder to take place.

Sardar felt that previous professional contact conceptualised depression as a self-centred preoccupation with a failure to attain personal fulfilment. In actuality Sardar's sadness was linked to his deep sense of social responsibility and being able to feel in the deepest part of him the continued pain of others he felt connected to.

We explored a number of issues:

- How does he move towards a positive future when there is so much violence and pain in his country, and he has lost so much that is important to him?
- How does he create a new identity that both is based on and moves away from an old identity?

We talked about Sardar's feelings as a form of 'protesting' and we explored who in his life might understand his protest. Sardar talked about his friends in the UK and how their friendship challenged the voice of hopelessness, most often when they shared laughter as well as protest. Sardar's friends were holding his hope for him until he was able to return to it himself (Madigan, 2007). We talked about the aim of oppression to disconnect people from their collective, social and political selves and turn all of their experiences into private struggles.

> We came up with the idea of writing to Sardar's friends and asking them if they would write back to us, with some thoughts on ways they could join Sardar in his struggle to continue to protest the wrongs done to him, his family and his community. I also asked them Madigan's question: 'If you could imagine that hope could be rediscovered in Sardar's life, what present qualities in him would give it staying power?' Sardar, who was not expecting his friends to write back, was visibly moved and invigorated when he read their replies.

Martín-Baró (1996) was critical of European and American psychology's emphasis on individualism and hedonism, based on a model of a free-standing autonomous bounded individual whose single most important goal is personal happiness and satisfaction. This individualised construction of self would be hard pressed to explain revolutionary suicide (e.g. Huey Newton, Bobby Sands), sacrifice, commitment to community, collective struggle, solidarity and collective distress linked to social injustice.

Madigan (2007) came up with the idea of 'therapeutic letter writing campaigns' as an attempt to create a community of concern (Madigan & Epston, 1995) 'to assist in the re-remembering of unique aspects of lives . . . restrained by cultural, professional and problem discourse' (Madigan, 2007, p. 107). These letters can help create communities of resistance and liberation. The community becomes a viable site of resistance to support the vulnerability of an individual trying to live a new and empowering story in a powerful world.

> Eleni, a middle-class woman of Cypriot origin, rarely felt loved growing up. Her mother left home when Eleni was six years old, and she was physically and sexually abused by many of the members of her family. When Eleni was old enough she left home, met her partner David – an African Caribbean man of West Indian origin – and had three children with him. David himself had run away from home when he was 15 years old, which meant that Eleni and their three children were his only family.
>
> Eleni talked about how much she missed the community she felt in her family and extended network, despite the abusive experiences. She was worried that her children would suffer as a result of being disconnected from their wider family. As Eleni talked about missing her 'roots' (her family of origin), I wondered about the story of Eleni's 'shoots' (the family of her own creation) and what difference it would make to be defined by the resources and abilities inherent in her shoots, rather than her roots. I wondered if Eleni had created a new family tree and grown her own ecology, which she felt

needed a community to water, prune and nurture it. Eleni began to talk about seeing herself as the creator of a new, liberating chapter in her family's history, her culture's history and the global historical story of the abuse of women.

Eleni and David's daughter, Isis, was doing well in school and was described as confident and popular. To develop the story of Eleni's 'shoots' I asked questions like:

- What are some of the abilities and interests Isis has that you appreciate?
- What makes Isis unique? What are your hopes and dreams for her?
- How have you and David contributed to Isis' positive sense of her identity?
- What aspect of your daughter makes you feel like you are a good parent?

As Eleni began to develop both intimacy with Isis and community with the people she lived and worked with, she realised that her resistance to the abuse in her family of origin did not have to mean isolation. Isis brought with her a community of friends, mothers of friends, teachers and other families.

It was important to explore the impact of Eleni's movement towards her preferred self on her relationship with David, who was becoming more and more distant. In couple sessions David was able to describe feeling marginalised. David grew up in a family where he felt there were 'too many people around and not enough intimacy'. Whereas Eleni valued community, David valued intimacy and closeness in isolation. We explored how gender stories gave David few acceptable roles that would enable him to engage more in his shoots. These conversations helped Eleni and David understand each other more.

Challenging the client's abuse of power

Utilising people's values might also mean connecting to the ethical potential of those who have harmed others. Working with the oppressed also means working ethically with those who are oppressive, as there is often not a neat dividing line between the two. This requires being able to think about power in complex ways, such as in the case of men who have abused members of their families. According to Jenkins, men from less privileged backgrounds are more likely to come to services for men who have abused their partners or children; not because they are more likely to engage in such behaviour, but because they are more likely to be arrested, prosecuted and sent to court-mandated treatment programmes (Jenkins, 1994, 2009). Social privilege often goes hand in hand with a high degree of credibility (Jenkins, 1994).

Men who have abused or are abusing others are easily regarded as limited or deficient and in need of correction and education once their impulsively violent nature is controlled and modified. Jenkins (2009) reminds us that even when people are violent and abusive they may still have an ethical system that points to preferred ways of being as well as a desire for connection, love and respect. By critiquing essentialism, which sees men and women as essentially a particular way that is not likely to change significantly, therapy might provide spaces to perform and enact counter-hegemonic ways of thinking and being – that is, ways that do not support and replicate dominant values (Nylund & Nylund, 2003).

The practices of power that inform and produce dominant masculinity and abusive behaviour have a cultural history. They are not invented by those individuals who enact them. Although individuals cannot be held responsible for the origins of these practices, they must always be held accountable and responsible for their enactment (Jenkins, 2009). In the same vein, those of us in the 'psy' profession must be held responsible for our enactments of dominant practices that might be experienced by clients as abusive.

Given that many men who are sent to prison for domestic violence are from disadvantaged backgrounds (Jenkins, 2009), their own experiences of disadvantage might be rendered invisible to others. While the violence might be noticed and addressed, protest or resistance against experiences of oppression can be overlooked or ignored by those with greater privilege. A sense of injustice might then become a defensive avoidance of responsibility for abusive and violent behaviour. Jenkins (2009) argues that through futile and destructive forms of resistance these men can become further marginalised and increasingly detached from their own ethics (Wexler, 1992).

Understandably, the 'psy' professional might be concerned that acknowledging the violent person's past experiences of victimisation and oppression might give them ammunition to excuse their present behaviour. This might lead us to expect people who have been abusive to take responsibility for their actions, without acknowledging that no-one may have taken responsibility for their past experiences of abuse or injustice. It is important therefore to explore how we can acknowledge and address a person's experience of disadvantage, marginalisation or abuse, without sacrificing a focus on responsibility for their own abusive actions. Anything that sounds like blaming those victimised should be interrupted and the person who has abused others reminded that responsibility for harm *always* stays with the person who has caused the harm.

The concept of strong irony is important here, in helping us take a both/and position. On one hand we condemn abuse and insist the person who has abused take responsibility for it; on the other hand we look out for any values that suggest that there is more to the person who has abused than their violence and that might inform an ethical position that shifts them from a self-centred to an other-centred focus. Men who act from a sense of exaggerated entitlement may not have thought very much about the experience of those harmed (Jenkins, 2009). The therapist collaborates with the man in collating an ethical inventory that will become a reference point to assist him to act in non-abusive ways, as well as to challenge acts that are incongruent with his ethics.

I have been heavily influenced by Jenkins's approach. This is not to say that every man at any time is equally motivated or inclined to move in ethical directions, as this would require facing, and bearing shame and the responses of, those who have been abused. What I value most about this approach is that it is the person or persons harmed that are made accountable to, therefore the person who has harmed reflects on the needs and wishes of others, rather than their own.

For example, the abusive male wanting to apologise might put pressure on the person he has harmed to relinquish their anger and hurt feelings. Ideas about forgiveness and compassion might make those harmed feel obliged to minimise or downplay their experiences of harm and emotional responses to it. Apologies are ideally given with no expectation or require-ment for forgiveness, and the person who has abused should be prepared to accept whatever are the needs of the person harmed (Jenkins, 2009).[58]

Valbona was a 43-year-old Albanian woman from Kosovo who was gang-raped by soldiers. In our sessions she said she often felt she wanted revenge. We talked about the similarities and differences between revenge and justice, and I gave her details of the human rights organisation *Redress* which assists survivors of torture to achieve personal, specific and practical justice and reparation. At the end of one session Valbona said that she was reading something that talked about forgiveness and how this helps the person who forgives have peace of mind. Valbona wanted to know what I thought.

I said that I thought Valbona absolutely deserved peace of mind and however she found that was important for her but that I did not think that she owed those who hurt her anything that she did not want to give. Valbona nodded and said it was an important distinction. We were able to talk about the abused person's entitlement to make their own judgements about whether or not to relinquish feelings, forgive or reconcile.

Representing people who abuse as monsters allows us to believe that abuse and violence are the aberrant iniquitous behaviours of a deviant population or rogue individuals; therefore we do not have to apply the same ethics to those we dehumanise as we do to everyone else. Dehumanisation means that abusive *behaviours* get conflated with bad/evil/irredeemable *people* and the social contexts of abuse along with our social responsibilities are obscured. CMM forces us to look outwards to the relationships and social structures that people live within, that they at once shape and are shaped by. It forces us to think about power, resistance and liberation with respect to collective responsibility, community and social action. It forces us to face up to the ways in which abusive actions get created in mainstream culture, rather than in the minds of crazy or wicked individuals. If we tell ourselves that some people are just bad, then we do not have to acknowledge how ingrained acts of abuse, violence, exploitation and oppression are in society.

Much research into domestic violence explicitly or implicitly excuses men who enact this violence by reverting to biological, sexual, evolutionary or genetic explanations (for example Counts, Brown & Campbell, 1999; Dutton, 2006). Levels of context analysis of violence requires that we neither demonise individuals nor excuse the abusive behaviour of individuals, but link individual and collective violence to individual and collective responsibility.

Developing resistance

As discussed previously, developing resistance is an important part of utilising people's virtues. Resistance arising from therapy can be thought about from different positions:

- the resistance of the client
- the resistance of the therapist
- the resistance of the therapist and client together against oppressive discourses.

These forms of resistance can be conceptualised with respect to:

- resistance as creativity.

I will now elaborate on this, using case examples to highlight how the concept of resistance in therapy might be enabling for clients and therapists.

The resistance of the client: The therapist's unhelpful emotional posture

Resistance can be viewed as client power or counter-power. Client power is often viewed as a negative energy in therapy that manipulates us, distracts us, pulls us in unhelpful directions and burns us out. Burnout is often attributed to prolonged exposure to clients' suffering, rather than to the wider systems and organisations we work in; and thus clients are seen as filled with a destructive form of power we need protection from.

The following is an example of the ways in which clients might resist being met with an unhelpful emotional posture in therapy. In particular I explore what might happen if we witness injustice without outrage, as opposed to – as Ché Guevara is quoted as saying – 'trembling with indignation at every injustice'.

Emotional postures refer to the way we ready ourselves to receive or express various emotions, with respect to 'mental activity such as shifts in attention and physical shifts such as changes in heart rate' (Griffith & Griffith, 1994, p. 46). For example, if my emotional posture is distant I may not be well placed to receive an emotional experience from a client who may then choose not to communicate their feelings. Griffith and Griffith (1994) argue that 'emotional postures can either open or close possibilities for therapeutic dialogue' (p. 66). They distinguish emotional postures of tranquillity and mobilisation and examine the ways in which each opens or closes possibilities for positive therapeutic dialogue.

Postures of tranquillity include states of listening, wondering, reflecting, affirming, understanding, and trusting. In emotional postures of tranquillity, attention is focused inwards, vigilance to threat is low, and there is openness to new information. Emotional postures of mobilisation, on the other hand, involve the physiological 'fight or flight' response and include states of guardedness, hyperarousal, shaming, blaming, defending, justifying, controlling and distancing (Griffith & Griffith, 1994). Vigilance is high and attention is focused outwards in an effort to predict and control others' behaviour. The assumption that Griffith and Griffith (1994) make is that when people are primed to fight or flee they are not well positioned to take in information or engage in creative problem-solving.

My understanding of the distinction Griffith and Griffith (1994) make is that in postures of mobilisation we are reactive and our actions are based more on our own needs than on those of the other person. In postures of tranquillity we are reflective and reflexive, with our responses based on the needs and experiences of the other person. Their analysis is based on the 'fight-or-flight' response to stress model that has dominated research into stress responses. However, Taylor et al. (2000) argue that most research exploring stress responses has been conducted on males, particularly male rats. When women have been researched the predominant response to stress has been to tend-and-befriend, rather than fight-or-flight[59] (Taylor et al., 2000). Without essentialising male and female responses to complex social situations, the point that is important to make is that it is easy for one framework of understanding to be seen as universal, regardless of gender, culture, time and social circumstances, and yet the meaning we attach to events and our responses to our circumstances are varied and complex

One way of thinking about client resistance is to reflect on the emotional withdrawal or anger that might be generated if we meet a client's experience of injustice, oppression and abuse with tranquillity. I often work with the assumption that when someone is getting more and more angry, staying calm defuses the anger. But another assumption that I have learnt to draw on is that joining with the intensity of someone's anger might enable them to feel heard and let go of their angry feelings more readily. Although the intention behind an emotional posture of tranquillity might be to look after the injured person, it might be experienced by the injured person as the therapist's attempt to get them to cope with the intolerable. On the other hand we might view a posture of mobilisation as a responsive approach to the injustice of another, if it is in the form of social action, acknowledging that something must change and sharing outrage.

When clients are in imminent danger, where hypervigilance, fear and anger are understandable responses to grave social abuses, being met with a posture of tranquillity might make their struggle a solitary and private one. Ina (2001) refers to 'taking an involved stance' to contrast the ways a neutral position aligns oneself with the oppressor. This does not mean taking on the role of rescuer, which reinforces hierarchy. It is a 'standing with' in whatever form that takes. Clients who are understandably angry and fearful about their situation might present with a posture of mobilisation and be misunderstood as manipulative, demanding or not utilising therapy appropriately.

Leila was a woman in her forties from Turkey seeking asylum in the UK after experiences of physical and sexual torture in her country of origin. In the first session Leila was extremely distressed. I tried to meet her distress with calm sensitivity and genuine care, but this only seemed to make her feel worse and she appeared to be angry with me at the end of our session. It later became apparent that her most immediate concern was that I demonstrate my ability to validate her pain and join her in a condemnation of the injustices she had experienced.

Leila appeared less distressed and became more vocal when I started to show genuine anger and outrage about her experience. She said that it was important for her that I was able to tolerate her rage about being disbelieved by the Home Office and the cruel comments made by the adjudicator. We talked about being believed as an important tie to reality and a condemnation of the wrong done to her. We explored how knowledge of trauma and torture can shatter assumptions about a benevolent world and lead to further abuses by the listener, particularly if the listener does not like the world the survivor asks them to share. In doing this a quote from Judith Lewis Herman proved useful:

> It is very tempting to take the side of the perpetrator. All the perpetrator asks is that the bystander do nothing. He appeals to

the universal desire to see, hear and speak no evil. The victim, on the contrary, asks the bystander to share the burden of pain. The victim demands action, engagement, and remembering.

(Herman, 2001, pp. 7–8)

Leila said she wanted to write a letter to the adjudicator, even if this letter could never be sent. We decided to write this letter together, Leila from the point of view of having experienced the injustice and my parts of the letter as a witness to this abuse. I also wrote a separate letter to Leila describing my admiration of her. We spoke to Leila's solicitor about how she could make a complaint about the adjudicator's comments. Leila's 'mental health improved'; she eventually received her asylum and began training mental health professionals about working with asylum-seeking people.

The resistance of the therapist: Power in wider systems

Simone was a single White woman of Italian heritage in her thirties with a diagnosis of psychotic depression. She grew up the eldest of three sisters in the East End of London with her parents, who argued so much that they eventually separated. Simone always felt put in the middle of their relationship with her needs coming second to their disagreements. When her marriage broke down, Simone felt depressed and isolated and began to believe that her friends and family were trying to poison her. Her psychiatrist, Dr Peter, gave her antipsychotic medication which helped Simone feel more stable.

I first met Simone on a psychiatric ward where she had recently had electroconvulsive therapy (ECT), and was told by Dr Peter that she should have more. Simone told me that she had mixed feelings, because although she did not want to have more ECT she trusted Dr Peter's opinion that it would be good for her. The thought of having ECT made Simone feel safer and more afraid at the same time. On one hand, she hoped that ECT would get rid of her 'paranoia' once and for all. On the other hand she was worried that having to have ECT meant that she was mad. In addition, Simone did not like what ECT did to her memory and concentration.

It seemed important to help Simone create a story about her ECT that did not reinforce a sense of her as bad or mad and that could be incorporated into her story of herself moving in a preferred direction. We talked about being in hospital allowing her a temporary place to stand and hold the problem at arm's length for a while, which permitted her time to regain some energy and perspective. When Simone asked me what I thought about more ECT I explained my dilemma with respect to not wanting to present opinions that might be opposing the opinions of Dr Peter and therefore putting her between two discourses from two people she respects equally (the position she was put in as a child between her warring parents). I wondered whether it would be more respectful to explore her views more, and I asked Simone what she preferred.

Simone said that she had found my respectful position very helpful, but that now she wanted me to share my actual opinion with her. Before doing so I explored whether Simone would view my ideas as expert fact or just one other opinion among many; as well as how she thought my opinion on ECT would help her. Simone thanked me for giving my opinion (which was that I was not in favour of ECT as an approach to psychological distress, although I was aware some people have claimed to have benefited from it) and explained that she felt she now had permission to refuse to have any more.

We explored what Dr Peter was seeing, and what I was missing, that made him feel that more ECT would be helpful. We also explored what changes in the person she was becoming Dr Peter might have been missing, with respect to what Simone wanted Dr Peter to know about her.

The resistance of the therapist and client together: Working with other discourses

While Simone and I often co-created therapeutic stories about the links between her experiences and emotional difficulties, Dr Peter often languaged her experiences using medical discourse such as 'mental illness'. In addition, Dr Peter at times questioned my approach to therapy with Simone and made alternative suggestions. Simone felt confident about Dr Peter's beliefs, given his authority and certainty. I noticed that if I even subtly challenged his perspective, Simone was positioned by me as his defender. When I took the position of curiosity and spoke in terms of grades of experience rather than either/or dualities, Simone did not feel she needed to defend either position, and instead chose her own.

I found William Madsen's (1999) ideas about externalising psychiatric discourses, rather than viewing them as invented by those who perform them, extremely helpful. In trying to better understand Dr Peter's perspective I thought about his professional and personal context with respect to CMM levels of context and conversations we had when we met for meetings (Figure 13.1). Dr Peter grew up in South Africa in a middle-class family where both parents were doctors. He resisted their desire for him to become a surgeon and came to the UK to train as a psychiatrist. In addition Dr Peter had participated in a scheme in the UK in which first-year clinical medical students saw a patient for psychotherapy, supervised by a psychoanalytic psychotherapist. This was in addition to the psychotherapy training he received as a senior house officer (SHO) for the first six months of his rotation, as part of his basic specialist training in psychiatry.

Dr Peter   **Taiwo**

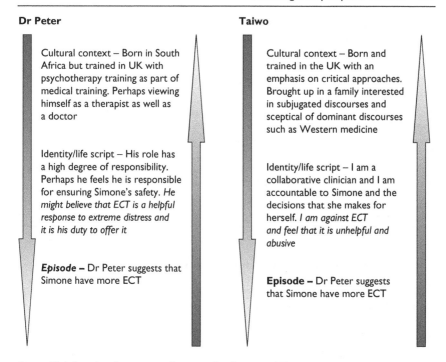

Cultural context – Born in South
Africa but trained in UK with
psychotherapy training as part of
medical training. Perhaps viewing
himself as a therapist as well as
a doctor

Cultural context – Born and
trained in the UK with an
emphasis on critical approaches.
Brought up in a family interested
in subjugated discourses and
sceptical of dominant discourses
such as Western medicine

Identity/life script – His role has
a high degree of responsibility.
Perhaps he feels he is responsible
for ensuring Simone's safety. *He*
might believe that ECT is a helpful
response to extreme distress and
it is his duty to offer it

Identity/life script – I am a
collaborative clinician and I am
accountable to Simone and the
decisions that she makes for
herself. *I am against ECT*
and feel that it is unhelpful and
abusive

Episode – Dr Peter suggests that
Simone have more ECT

Episode – Dr Peter suggests
that Simone have more ECT

Figure 13.1 Levels of context influencing Dr Peter and Taiwo

Dr Peter felt he was a progressive psychiatrist with an understanding of psychotherapy.

Madsen (1999) talks about three types of juxtaposed professional discourses that emerge in medical settings and pull clinicians to respond to emotional distress in particular ways: deficits and possibilities; professional expertise and collaboration; protection and accountability. Reflecting on the different 'pulls' each of these discourses creates helped me to better understand the challenges, expectations and pressures on myself and Dr Peter (Table 13.1).

Deficits and possibilities

A discourse of deficits seemed to pull Dr Peter into identifying problems, discovering their causes, and then intervening to cure or ameliorate them. In addition, an emphasis on deficits in the mental health system receives significantly more institutional and societal support than an emphasis on possibilities (Madsen, 2007). For Simone there were times when she felt reassured and validated by Dr Peter's expert position, whereas my emphasis on possibilities at times felt like minimising her distress.

Table 13.1 Discourses potentially impacting on Dr Peter and Taiwo's
approach with respect to levels of context

	Dr Peter	Taiwo
Ethical responsibility	Prevent risk and protect Simone	Collaborative working
Focus of approach with Simone	Reflect on aspects of Simone's experience that increase her risk of distress and harm	Focus on possibilities and moving towards Simone's preferences
Assumption about Simone's needs	Draw on professional expertise and take control of situation	Encourage Simone to share her own beliefs
Intended outcome	Simone feels better	Simone feels better

Professional expertise and collaboration

The medical model seemed to position Dr Peter as an expert who assessed
clients, developed treatment plans, and implemented interventions designed
to bring patients in line with appropriate functioning. This privileging of
professional knowledge over client wisdom is supported by a culture where
certainty and expertise are given more credence than curiosity and collaboration (Madsen, 2007).

Protection and accountability

Dr Peter seemed to be guided mainly by a discourse of protection (professional responsibility *for* clients) in his work with Simone, while I was
acting from a discourse of accountability (professional responsibility *to*
clients) that assumed Simone was the best judge of what was right for her
(Madsen, 2007). Having conversations with Dr Peter about the contexts
influencing his practice enabled us to foreground the voice of protection
and reflect with Simone on its opportunities and constraints.

Both Dr Peter and I were committed to supporting Simone as best as we
could; but we emphasised different issues. For Dr Peter the most important
level of context was his ethical responsibility to prevent risk and protect
Simone from harm. For me my highest context was my ethical responsibility to work collaboratively with Simone.

Dr Peter and I were able to highlight the ways in which we were both
privileging our relationship with Simone in our desire to help her feel less
distressed. It was our ethical responsibility that guided us. However, different levels of context as well as aspects of the GRAACCCEESS that differed
between us (working-class Black female, middle-class White male) influenced our approach to our relationship with Simone and each other. Given

the different concerns we privileged in working with Simone, Dr Peter and I had the potential to clash. Given our shared intended outcome there were also possibilities for mutual respect and coordination. Rather than working from the premise that there are good discourses and bad ones (bad discourses being ones that other professionals have), Madsen's (2007) approach helped me to appreciate how different levels of context influence the emergence of different discourses, pulling us towards certain practices and away from others. Being curious about other people's underlying values allowed me to connect to the principles that were similar to mine and work from there.

> Dr Peter and I being able to better coordinate opened up different conversational opportunities in therapy with Simone, who explained that when she was in crisis she needed someone who could tell her what to do and she wanted something very different when she was in a safer position. This led me to ask Simone in our meeting with Dr Peter what type of support she wanted at different times and who might be best placed to provide it. Having this conversation in front of Dr Peter meant openly acknowledging that his perspective was valued as well as highlighting the way Simone's needs changed. This shifted the potentially oppositional discourses between Dr Peter and me from 'Who is (morally/objectively) right?' to 'What does Simone need at different times?'

In order to coordinate with other professionals in mental health systems, we might need to meet their discourses rather than dismiss them. This can be done at the same time as being critical of the assumptions implicit in them. For example, when asked in a consultation how to respond to professionals who refer to self-harming adolescents as 'attention seeking', I suggested asking the question: 'What might the adolescent be trying to get us to attend to?'

Implicit in this question is an assumption that young people deserve to be known, without the other person's position being dismissed. A collaborative approach does not necessitate being in agreement with a client, a colleague or a diagnosis. A dialogical perspective enables us, despite disagreement, to see differing positions as a starting point for conversation.

Deconstructing 'madness'

Psychiatric diagnoses limit the explanation of emotional distress to the level of the individual, potentially restricting what is understood and avenues for action. Even if we are able to conceive of depression and anxiety as resulting from social conditions we tend to view more complex emotional distress as resulting from 'true madness' or 'mental illness'. The more unusual, challenging to relationships and disruptive a person's feelings, thoughts and actions are, the more likely internal sources are sought to explain them. The person becomes less a person – becomes mad, bad or even evil. People with psychiatric diagnoses experience stigma and discrimination as a result (Reed & Baker, 1996; Barker et al., 1999; Read, 2001), given that diagnoses concretise identities for people that are limiting. For example, I have been asked by women with a diagnosis of schizophrenia: 'How can I have children if I am schizophrenic?'

Diagnostic labels give the impression that professionals are all working on the same entity or thing. Although some people report benefits from being diagnosed, this only makes sense if we reflect on the cultural, social and political context psychiatric diagnosing happens in. A psychiatric diagnosis might make forms of distress that might otherwise go unnoticed more visible,. We might therefore wonder:

- What is the purpose of a diagnosis? What questions are believed to be answered by diagnosis? What information is thought to be gained?
- What do we want a diagnosis to communicate and to whom?
- What does diagnosis suggest we should do with the problem?
- How does diagnosis invite us to act, in helpful and unhelpful ways?

Donna felt that the distress she felt as a result of flashbacks of childhood abuse was only taken seriously by her mother when Donna was diagnosed with a psychiatric disorder, which gave her distress legitimacy and enabled Donna and her mother to talk about it, without talking about abuse. On one hand Donna felt that her diagnosis gave her permission to have difficulties. On the other hand Donna felt constrained by the psychiatric label which she felt reinforced the idea that she was the problem.

Rather than the diagnosis being a description that told the whole story of Donna's experience, in therapy we became curious about what else was inside the word 'schizophrenia' (Andersen, 1995; Fredman, 2004). Because Donna described the psychiatric diagnosis given to her as a key part of her identity, we used the daisy model to explore her identity in relation to her mother, her partner, her father, her uncle, and her sisters. We discussed the meaning of each relationship; the story they each told about her; as well as what her preferred versions of herself were, at different times, in different relationships and in different contexts. With respect to her preferred self, we explored which relationships she wanted to foreground. We explored what meaning the diagnosis had for each person involved in her life, and if the meaning was respectful and opened up possibilities or if it created more problems for her.

When she first came to see me, Donna saw her 'flashes of memory' as 90 per cent due to mental illness and 10 per cent because of past experiences of abuse. As therapy progressed, different ideas were elicited that gave a richer description of Donna's experiences. The richer Donna's description of her experiences, the less concrete and fixed her sense of herself became, and Donna began to describe her difficulties as 50 per cent due to her past experiences and 50 per cent due to 'madness'.

We talked about what enabled this shift, what this shift meant to Donna with respect to moving towards her preferred way of living and being, as well as where she wanted to take this movement. Donna said that she wanted to get to a place where she felt 'just 10 per cent mad'.

I learnt from Donna that psychiatric diagnoses should not stop us having conversations that are dialogical, in which the diagnosis has an opportunity to change as a result of the conversation. This moves psychiatric diagnoses from the realm of private experience and expert discourse towards the client and therapist involved in a mutual discovery processes. Accepting the diagnosis 'schizophrenia' did not prevent Donna from expressing agency regarding the nature of her experience, her preferred self and her ability to influence her life in a preferred direction.

Questions linked to this dissolving of her problems were:

- If your psychiatrist saw these changes happening in front of him, how might he describe you differently?
- Would you prefer to update him on some of those changes or just keep yourself anchored in them?

This shift enabled Donna to move from having to take an either/or position of 'I have a mental illness'/'I don't have a mental illness' to: 'What type of conversation about my difficulties will most help me to move ever closer to my preferred self and preferred life?' A view of emotional distress that emphasises power, resistance and liberation does not see diagnoses as fixed entities, given that difficulties always have the potential to shift and dissolve over time.

When I first saw Sarah she was very distressed because she thought she had gone mad. When she arrived in the UK having fled Cameroon she started hearing voices telling her that they were going to kill her. Sarah heard other voices; in particular she often spoke to the spirit of her dead sister and experienced this as incredibly supportive. We explored how to make her sister's voice stronger and the persecuting voice weaker, and thus gain access to conversations that made her feel good about herself. In turn Sarah started developing opportunities to carry out valued social activities that introduced her to the world of others rather than a preoccupation with inner dialogues.

Sarah started attending a local Black African women's group, and as she began to feel more connected and confident she reported seeing her dead sister less often. Sarah said: 'Maybe she does not think I am so alone now'. We wondered together if her sister was not appearing so much because Sarah was feeling more socially connected, and seeing the spirit of her sister in other Black women.

Resistance as creativity

Resistance can be thought of as a type of poesis; that is, creative freedom from tradition that can be beautiful, express difference and challenge convention. To paraphrase Confucius (Chinese teacher, philosopher and political theorist, 551–479 BC), creativity produces a kind of pleasure that human nature cannot do without. In fact creativity might be the most important human resource of all, as it textures everyday life.

As Maya Angelou said, 'You can't use up creativity. The more you use, the more you have.' As well as the desperation, frustration and struggle that can accompany resistance, there might also be a pleasurable energy that goes with resisting attempts to suppress the human spirit and proclaiming our difference.

In answer to the question, 'Could you tell me about some of the ways that uncle Barry invited you into his life to join him in what was important to him?', Simon (introduced in Chapter 11) told us that uncle Barry took him to football matches and introduced him to art and literature. Simon felt growing up that there was not a world for him to exist in happily, except the world created by his books. Simon's dream as a child was to be a writer.

In therapy we explored what uncle Barry wanted Simon to do to keep Simon connected to him and what uncle Barry saw Simon doing that showed him they were still connected, even after death. Whenever he read a book, wrote a short story or went to a play, Simon felt uncle Barry close to him.

Creativity is the energy that brings forth life, and life is stagnant without it. Creativity is the art of seeing the world in new yet familiar ways and enables us to have unique views on how life is and how life could be. Creativity reaches deep into the core of us, as it is difficult to be creative on the surface of living. To be truly creative is to work beyond what we know. However, in the process of creating something outside of ourselves, we draw on ourselves and further add to the ongoing creation of who we are.

Hence, creativity fills any space with possibility. With respect to the therapeutic process, McNamee (2000) argues that suspending the discourse of fact and engaging instead in improvisation (working without a plan) turns therapy into a creative activity between client and therapist.

Chapter 14

Drawing the practices together

Systemic and narrative theory and practice remind us we are always in relationship to others and part of a wider context. Helping to co-create new narratives for clients (stories told) can open up possibilities for action (stories lived). Collaborating in the telling and retelling of the client's story is done in such a way that each retelling becomes a more empowering experience. The GRAACCCEESS and CMM levels of context highlight the influence of power and resistance in layered realities.

Some bold claims about the issue of power being addressed have been made by proponents of systemic therapy. However, no therapy is immune from the impact of power and resistance. Therefore it seems imperative that the first responsibility of any therapy is to deconstruct itself 'as a site of intellectual privilege and power' (Larner, 1999, p. 43). Rather than collapsing critiques into the frameworks of systemic therapy, as though it is something that is done naturally and automatically as part of its practice, it is important to subject it, and all therapies, to continual critique while we engage in it. In that way a collaborative therapy is based on what we as therapists actually do, rather than what we believe we do, or ought to do.

Power

I have attempted to show that power is integral to the lives of all of us and forms aspects of all our ongoing interactions. Power is therefore not something we can ignore or eradicate; we have to do something with it. Power cannot be removed, but can be linked to ethics, responsibility and responsivity. We all have the potential to do harm by disrespecting the experiences, preferences and wishes of others. We might even do harm with a sense of entitlement and justification. As Jenkins points out, 'there is only a fine line between responsible therapy and therapeutic abuse which is "justified" in the service of a noble cause' (Jenkins, 1994, p. 17).

Justifications of abuse might be expressed by a man who has assaulted his partner because he perceives that she has acted dishonourably and requires correction. Justifications of abusive power are often used to gain support for war and the invasion of other countries. In each case the ends are seen to justify the means.

Despite the inherent power imbalance in therapy it is possible to reflect with clients on ways that it might be more dynamic, more mutual, more respectful, more transparent and more useful. All of us are involved in a complex process which involves activities that are complicit with dominant cultural interests as well as some that are resistant and produce creative alternatives. That we are never restricted to or fixed in any particular state of identity is potentially liberating.

I have tried to argue that differentiating between traditional and collaborative therapies has the potential to idealise certain forms of therapy as egalitarian and power-free, masking the working of power in all therapies. Instead, counselling and therapy need to integrate power and resistance into their practice, rather than claiming to have overcome them. This can be done by holding the tension between power (recognising the power inherent in our position) and resistance (finding creative ways of moving away from it).

Resistance

People always resist experiences of oppression and abuse, and bringing these responses from the periphery to the centre of counselling, therapy and psychology has the potential to be liberating. When clients are able to notice all the actions that constitute resistance to abuse, oppression and prejudice, and how congruent these actions are with their values, they are more likely to experience themselves as competent and capable individuals.

I am aware that my description of resistance has lumped together various acts that could be understood differently. It is also important to point out that resistance is *my* term for another person's behaviour. The purpose of using this term is not to claim I have some expert view of reality that informs me that a client is resisting, but to inform my responses to the ways clients attempt to influence the process of therapy.

There is a danger that terms such as 'resistance' and 'client-power' can be thought about in ways that are far removed from the spirit in which they are intended in this book. As therapists we sometimes talk about clients brandishing power in ways that are exploitative and/or attacking of the therapist or system around them. We say things like, 'It sounds like this client has a lot of power because they've got you anxious about them and unable to properly challenge them' and 'This client is very powerful. Look how many professionals they have got involved in their care.' Descriptions like these imply that the power of the client is potentially dangerous and in need of control or eradication, rather than positive, necessary and enabling. Alternatively, we can locate any behaviour that emerges in the therapeutic relationship in its interpersonal and wider social, cultural and historical context.

Taking action against oppression can take creative forms other than political activism. This necessitates a much broader understanding of the role we all play in change at the micro, meso, and macro levels of society. Much of the ways in which we traditionally conceptualise clients' problems and how we might contribute to their liberation centres on attempts to provide them with new skills and resources for action. If we look close enough, with our hearts as well as our heads, we might notice the ingenious and creative ways that people resist power over them that exist pre-therapy.

When viewing therapy through the lenses of power, resistance and liberation it may not be helpful to frame progress as evolving to a higher level of political consciousness. Resistance should not be judged as effective only if it stops oppression and abuse. Acts of resistance that might appear inconsequential have the potential to provide foundation for further action. In these 'small' acts are often unarticulated protests that yield even more power if given the space to be told and heard.

Nor can resistance be reduced to an expression of strength, as it might be experienced by people as generated by fear, desperation and powerlessness. Resistance is often painful, risky and exposing. It is also liberating, life-affirming and generous in its potential to inspire hope. Resistance connects us to our values and identity, but is 'no substitute for a life of equality and respect' (Wade, 1997, p. 31).

It is usually much easier to say 'yes' to someone, and focus on what you like about what they are doing, than to say 'no' and tell them you are not happy with something. Oppressed people often have to hold on to their feelings of anger and hurt and suffer the consequences of these, while those who contribute to those feelings, whether intentionally or unintentionally, are absolved of responsibility. Rather than the 'psy' professional becoming disheartened or defensive in the face of resistance, the relationship might feel more genuine as a result.

When we view resistance in counselling and therapy as something useful, to be encouraged, the whole nature of therapy changes. I certainly agree with the idea that 'we facilitate the greatest change in our clinical work when we focus on learning from our clients rather than believing that they are learning from us' (Wright, 1990, p. 484). When ways of resisting are met with honesty, transparency and respect and an invitation is extended to work on the issues raised together, the relationship might take on a depth and sincerity that is liberating.

Liberation

With any form of communication there can be a difference between what is received and what is intended, therefore any given theory or approach is open to interpretation and can be understood by the practitioner in varying ways. It is not surprising therefore that there are different ways of understanding liberation psychology and how it might inform counselling and therapy. One way is to focus on what Paulo Freire and Martín-Baró referred to as *conscientización* with respect to educating people towards their political development. Another approach might be to focus on justice in therapy in a way that invites therapists to confront those who oppress and cause harm.

The approach I prefer would focus on ways we can accompany oppressed people, working with them to develop collaborative relationships that recognise power inequities. For this reason, bringing the focus on collaboration in narrative therapy together with liberation psychology approaches allows me to view liberation psychology ideas as resources for transformation rather than a tool that will bring it about. There are no specific techniques to determine which ways of talking are therapeutic and which are not, and certainly no ways of approaching therapy that will ensure a given outcome. Collaboration means going with the process and client preferences rather than a pre-set agenda.

The therapeutic process can be many experiences weaving in and out of each other at the same time, with hopes to soothe, to deconstruct, to reconstruct, to accept, to challenge, to enable, to transgress, to explore, to be tranquil, to be mobilised, and so on. The question of what is therapeutic, and most likely to lead to liberation, should remain open and indeterminate. Just like conversation, we can never be certain where it will go. We can, however, attend to how power gets played out and to whose benefit. We can be attentive to the process of relating and engage in exploration that encourages multiple stories, multiple possibilities, and thus the potential for personal, interpersonal and social liberation.

Liberation psychology reminds us to reflect on the activities inside and outside of therapy that will propel the 'psy' field towards upholding the ethics of justice, compassion and transformation. A focus on social context means that therapy is not viewed as the only possible beneficial context. Therapy by no means holds a monopoly on helpful meaning-making. For Hazel, going to Pride and meeting other lesbian couples was very liberating. Government legislation that enabled civil partnerships and adoption rights contributed heavily to Hazel's sense of justice with respect to the increased options open to her, in ways that therapy could not.

I believe that to be fully moved by another's experience we need to find ways of fully entering into the many levels of it – not just the personal level but all levels of experience and meaning. The coordinated management of meaning and social GRAACCCEESS can facilitate our shift away from easy snap judgements or final conclusions towards exploring levels of context and meaning. They also provide a framework for challenging those contexts that restrict our abilities to move towards our preferences.

This book has focused mainly on restorative justice – restoring what was invalidated – rather than justice in the form of redress, which addresses more directly the macro or structural levels of oppression, such as in radical community psychology and political activism. This does not take away from the importance of fully integrating a liberatory ethic into therapeutic practice, which requires transgressing the strict boundaries erected between psychological, political, sociological, historical, and cultural discourses. This means framing our theories and practice in terms of power, hegemony, colonialism, resistance, emancipation, oppression, deprivation, structural violence and privilege. Such a focus is more likely to lead us towards a concerted effort to change the causes of distress than towards a focus on evidence-based practice and technological approaches to treating the effects of trauma. My hope is that liberation will not become another empty discourse in the 'psy' literature, but rather a belief system, an attitude and a relational and political stance.

In summary

I shared my own personal experience that oppression is not just a site of domination but a place of resistance. Herbert Aptheker argued that 'resistance not acquiescence is the core of history' (quoted in Craton, 1986). Whenever someone experiences abuse, oppression or violence they resist their experiences in some way. Hence, power and resistance are two sides of the same coin.

Power in therapy

Power is inevitable in all relationships and therefore cannot be removed; instead its presence is concealed. Power attempts to transform the actions/views of others, while others may resist. Power is not necessarily domination. Domination does not preclude the possibility of resistance, but the possibility of resistance having a legitimate impact on therapy processes and outcome, leading to an authoritarian imposition of meaning from therapist/counsellor to client(s) (Guilfoyle, 2003; 2005).

Paradox: It is impossible to escape power, but our responsibility is to move towards doing so.

Resistance can be viewed as 'counter-power', and client resistance as an opportunity to learn from the client. An ethical therapy does not require the absence of power but the legitimate acceptance of resistance.

Resistance, like power, is complex. It can be creative and expansive – opening up possibilities and embracing difference – or restrictive and destructive – closing down options.

Resistance in therapy

- The resistance of the client to power in all its forms
- The resistance of the therapist
- The joint resistance of the therapist and client working together against oppressive discourses in wider society

A therapy using the lenses of power, resistance and liberation:

- is based on resistance as creativity
- breaks the heart.

Part IV

Final reflections on theory and practice

Chapter 15

Resistance as creativity

Like Bateson's approach to power, de Shazer thought of resistance as negative as it made therapists think of therapy in terms of force, turning the therapist and client into opponents fighting against each other (de Shazer, 1984). Rather than thinking about resistance with respect to those metaphors, creativity can be viewed as a form of resistance and resistance as a way of living creatively. Creativity as an alternative metaphor for resistance might mean we are less inclined to kill off the need for resistance in our lives and in the therapeutic relationship. Instead we are invited with this new metaphor to view resistance as part of life's creative energy and therefore the creative energy of therapy. Resistance can be viewed as emergent liberatory behaviour as it is based on hopes of how things should be.

I will now reflect on the relationship between creativity and resistance from my personal perspective as a Black African woman, explore different ways resistance can emerge in our lives and make links with examples of resistance as creativity in therapy, with respect to:

* celebrating our difference
* connecting to potential, mystery and hope
* what we do with constraints
* protesting experiences of violence, abuse and oppression.

Creativity as resistance

In African cultures artistic expression is traditionally associated with community, mythology and healing. Music and dance paint the soul with joy and tears, based on experiences of connection and loss. African cultures have drawn on the power of creativity to resist exploitation and oppression as well as to call on the power of ancestral spirits and faith. In addition, resistance to oppression has led to greater access to cultural means of self-expression and collective expression. For me growing up, music, dance and art were important forms of self-expression, belonging, life-affirming pleasure and social/political resistance. I was particularly drawn to counter-cultural forms of creativity such as punk, rap and street art.

Female singers fascinate me because of the ways in which they symbolise the creative power of resistance and resistance as creativity. As a Black woman, being heard is important to me, and being visible can be experienced as a form of oppression, with respect to being seen as either a sexual object or a token Black presence. As Reinharz (1994) aptly describes, sight is a relatively passive human sense, whereas voice is by its nature active and therefore more powerful than merely being seen. Although the female singer can be objectified as a visual object of our gaze, her voice has the potential to overwhelm and captivate her audience. Everything else is eclipsed.

The female voice (Billie Holiday, Nina Simone, Jill Scott, Esperanza Spalding, Janis Joplin, P.J. Harvey, Eryka Badu, Ella Fitzgerald, Bat for Lashes, Sarah Vaughan, Odetta, Aretha Franklin, and Dianne Reeves – to name some of my favourites) mesmerises us with sounds that drown us with feeling, as an active force in the world. Not a victim of life but a willing creator, we hear her voice as creativity and freedom, as if the feelings she expresses have 'escaped from a body that the mind can no longer control' (Frith, 1995, p. 2), that the world does not have full power over.

Whatever the singer is in that moment of listening, she is also much more. The experience in the room is that a woman has been able to transcend what it means to be female and transcend what it means to be an individual. At the same time, the listener experiences themselves as more, while absorbed in the singer's pain, joy and beauty as well as their own. Black music – soul, gospel, rhythm and blues, blues, jazz, rap, hip hop – has always been a force of resistance against the demented logic of racism.

Angela Davis in *Blues Legacies and Black Feminism* (1998) makes distinctions between direct social protest, which was often argued to be absent from blues music, and the inherent political power of Black music. She argues:

> 'Protest' implies the existence of formal political channels through which dissent can be collectively expressed. In this context protest would suggest some strategic goal such as bringing black women domestic workers into organised trade unions. But such a historical possibility did not exist at the time. Protest when expressed through aesthetic forms, is rarely a direct call to action. Nevertheless, critical aesthetic representation of a social problem must be understood as constituting powerful social and political acts . . . a form of contestation of oppressive conditions, even when it lacks a dimension of organized political protest.
>
> (Davis, 1998, p. 101)

Creativity is a powerful metaphor for the various ways of resisting oppression open to humanity, such as: celebrating our difference; connecting to our potential, to mystery and to hope; what we do with constraints, rather than what constraints do to us; and the ways we protest our experiences of violence, abuse and oppression.

Celebrating our difference

Despite the fact that we are all different from each other, some groups of people become defined as 'different' as part of strategies of oppression. As a result, to be 'different' becomes something to avoid or feel ashamed of. In response, celebrating 'difference', having fun with 'difference' and actively attempting to *achieve* our 'difference'[60] are forms of creative resistance.

Creative ways of doing 'difference' describe how we transcend traditional boundaries, revel in rich and varied forms of life, and bring into being that which has not yet been.

The people described in the cases below were introduced in Chapter 12, except where otherwise stated.

Eve commented on the power of having Black women in therapy and the space that was created to reflect on being Black and being a woman. We talked about the difficulties facing Black women, as well as the values and qualities that came with being Black women. Eve talked about the 'gratitude' she felt for her 'Black womanness', for giving her an experience of life full of 'struggle, full of wisdom and full of aesthetic enjoyment'. Eve commented that the world needed her brand of beauty, passion and insight. Eve named her daughter Yaa Asantewaa after a powerful Ghanaian female warrior, which connected her to the preferences, hopes and values that Eve wanted to pass down to her daughter.[61]

A year after meeting Angela, Hazel went to Brighton Pride as the civil partnership law had just been passed, and met a number of lesbian couples who had been together for decades. She talked to them about the resilience, courage and love they harnessed in order to build solid connections while under overt and covert forms of attack. These alternative stories about being Gay made connections with a larger community, and to experiences of persecution, intimacy and joy.

Yolanda highlighted the importance of having her 'difference' understood and respected when she asked me if she could see a Gay therapist. Yolanda was looking for abilities related to the experience of being a Gay woman and found an ability to engage positively with difference in therapy.

Connection to potential, mystery and hope

Life is like energy found at the tips of things, where potential resides. It is an energy that reminds us that we are always becoming and never fully reach our destination. Creativity, growth and mystery lie in the space between a chrysalis and a butterfly as well as the space between hole and whole. Creativity therefore is both individual expression and participation in something greater than individual experience. Creativity is an important component of liberation because liberation inevitably requires vision of a better cultural, ethical and political order. Like liberation, creativity requires and feeds hope.

What is considered creative can be conservative as it is often defined by powerful ideologies, institutions and industries; and yet it can be innovative in that we have individual tastes and personal connections to that which has been created. For instance, much of mainstream society mocks aspects of Black youth culture (such as afros sporting afro combs, jeans below the waist) that others, like me, view as creative forms of resistance. Despite dominant society's ability to dictate what form creativity *should* take, no one can dictate what form creativity actually takes given that it appeals directly to our senses, with respect to physical, emotional and spiritual pleasure. Pleasure in the context of oppression is interference, interruption and hope.

Sardar's sadness was a form of protesting the experiences of trauma and injustice he suffered. Sardar began to explore the ways in which experiencing pleasure in the form of laughter was also a form of resistance against the aims of his oppressors to disconnect him from everything that was meaningful to him.

Eleni valued community and feared that disconnecting from her abusive family of origin (her roots) would negatively impact on the lives of her children (her shoots). Eleni was able to reflect on the community she was creating for and with her children. By growing her own ecology and diverging from the abuse trajectory of her family of origin, Eleni began to value the resistance of herself, her children and the future history of women who would benefit from her stance against abuse.

Simon re-membered his uncle Barry who introduced him to art and literature. Being absorbed in these forms of creativity connected Simon to a world of beauty and possibility that came to represent the liberating power of uncle Barry's continued presence in his life.

What we do with constraints

When I think of jazz scat singing – improvised melodies and rhythms using the voice as an instrument in place of an instrumental solo – I am reminded of the creativity that emerges when we run out of options and choices. Although scatting was originally a substitute for words when a singer forgot his/her lines (Cross, 1993), it has developed into an ingenious, technically challenging and exciting form of beauty. Creativity is thus what we do with life, in the face of what life does to us.

> Victoria (introduced in Chapter 8) resisted my attempts to impose on her an identity and description of her as 'not dirty'. Victoria's resistance encouraged me to reflect on my own personal, professional and political biases towards wanting to challenge her view of herself as well as to find ways of being more useful to Victoria in order to support her to experience liberation of her own kind. Victoria's own version of liberation was not to deny what life had done to her, but to connect to the way she could create life, by having a baby and being a teacher.
>
> Sanjida and Bilkis went from having an intertwined story (Roberts, 1999) that meant that Sanjida associated sexual contact with Bilkis with childhood sexual abuse, to discussing what they wanted from each other in their sexual and intimate relationship. As a result they were able to create their own meaningful sexual life together and Sanjida was able to experience her body in more sensual ways.
>
> Initially, Anoushka resisted registering with a GP because she refused to be in a position of not being listened to by a person in authority. Despite this, Anoushka was able to devise a plan that honoured what she gave value to and enabled her to register on her terms.
>
> Leila expressed greater levels of distress when she was confronted by my posture of tranquillity in the face of her outrage about the injustices and violations she suffered. It was as though Leila was saying 'I have been wronged and I want to do something with that, not feet better about it'.

Protesting experiences of violence, abuse and oppression

Creativity has always been used throughout history to protest forms of oppression. Renoux and Wade (2008) argue that 'Adults express their resistance to violence by refusing to be content, lying awake at night, withdrawing their interest and affection, becoming unpredictable, refusing to speak openly, becoming intensely vigilant, and acting with extreme caution. Children express resistance through nightmares, showing fear, refusing to obey abrasive adults, displaying disinterest, dwelling on the danger at home during maths class, and worrying themselves sick' (p. 3). These forms of resistance are often viewed as symptoms of emotional disorder or ways in which people act out emotional distress, rather than agentic responses to abuse that point directly to a person's desire for liberation.

Donna (introduced in Chapter 11) often had frightening flashbacks of the uncle who sexually abused her, and yet was able to 'shut him in a box' when she needed to. Talking about her psychotic experiences as forms of protest gave them an opportunity to change from making her feel 90 per cent 'mad' to 50 per cent 'mad'. Accepting her psychiatric diagnosis did not prevent Donna from expressing personal agency regarding the nature of her experience, her preferred self and her ability to influence her life in a preferred direction.

Satou reflected on her experience of being an assertive Black woman in a work context that pathologised her resistance to prejudice. Satou both valued her assertiveness and wanted to hone her relationship to anger with respect to her values and the potential for her responses to move her either towards or away from her preferred self.

Stories of resistance are often stories of confusion and pain. Ben described feeling 'tired' in a life where as a Black man he experienced oppression but was told he had depression. He commented 'the doctor says "you are depressed" and I heard "you require deep rest"'[62]

Creativity and relationships

As described earlier in the book, creativity both reaches deep within the core of us and intricately connects us to others. To be truly creative we have to go beyond what we directly know. This means that creativity has the potential to be genuine 'openness to otherness', that is, a commitment to reach into the world of the other and understand experience beyond the limits of our understanding. Resistance stops being creative when it no longer links to social relationships, social context and social responsibility. Resistance potentially harms others or disrupts coordination between people if it replicates or reinforces other forms of domination. For example, Terence's brother Robert resisted his experiences of gendered racism (discrimination aimed at him for being Black and male) by clinging so tightly to his heterosexual privilege that he fed into Terence's experiences of homophobia.

Resistance against dehumanisation and oppression is highly destructive when it manifests itself as abusive behaviour towards family members or others in more disadvantaged or vulnerable positions. Through desperate attempts to become somebody, resistance can take the form of violence, cruelty and an exaggerated sense of power and entitlement that moves people further and further away from ethical and compassionate behaviour (Wexler, 1992; Jenkins, 2009). It is my argument that it is important to challenge these abusive forms of resistance, as well as to remember the creative *potential* of resistance. It is not surprising that what is considered creative or destructive resistance differs depending on our experiences and values, the positions we take and the perspectives we have. However, therapeutic conversations that use resistance creatively and see forms of resistance as creative are potentially powerful.

Creativity is a useful metaphor for resistance because it speaks to places in our experience that are not dominated by oppression and reminds us that creative alternatives to present conditions always exist. Creativity describes reality as fluid, constantly moving and under construction. Creativity enables us to play with the power inherent in therapy, while understanding that we cannot eradicate it. It involves a collaborative engagement in improvisation and responsivity that honours the total humanity of everyone.

Chapter 16

Therapy that breaks the heart

Therapy may engage the heart of the therapist if based on their passions, assumptions and interests, or engage the heart of the client as a space to talk freely and feel heard. Therapeutic conversations that foreground the dynamics of power, resistance and liberation potentially energise the space between client and therapist where hearts connect.

Therapy breaks the heart when we keep open to all the ways we can abuse our power and are moved to address them. Therapy breaks our heart when we stay open to being told by clients we are not helpful, are wrong, are doing the wrong thing or contributing to their distress. Harm, violation and disrespect may not be the objective or intent of our actions and yet they may be the consequence. This book has been about asking ourselves how we strive to remain vigilant and accountable for the ongoing potential to abuse power in our own practices in the name of liberation.

A liberated heart – beyond technique

The dominant paradigm in mental health is a technical paradigm: the idea that psycho-social difficulties are primarily challenges of a technical nature. In this paradigm, values and ethics, meanings and contexts, relationships and power are secondary to techniques. Summerfield argues that the focus on the intrapsychic ignores the political implications of traumatic experiences, by making distress a technical rather than a political issue. Technical problems then require technical solutions that can be presented as politically neutral (Summerfield, 1998).

Guidelines such as those produced by the National Institute of Clinical Excellence (NICE) in the UK work to determine what the priorities of the 'psy' field are, where energy should be focused and how our practice is to be evaluated, using 'evidence'. Martín-Baró noted that 'an exclusive focus on those things that have been demonstrated by psychological science – with all its omissions and prejudices – ignores possibilities that have not been thus demonstrated, and thereby consecrates the existing order as natural' (1996, p. 21).

This focus on the technical is also seen in service frameworks. While there is usually a statement somewhere in all our policy documents about values and respect, the central focus is technical, to do with team organisation, structures, protocols and service models. In an attempt to do something different, when I managed a systemic consultation service I developed a recovery strategy that shifted the focus on service management towards values, principles and ethics in providing services for people in distress. My translation of recovery principles into a management strategy was an attempt to move beyond a technical focus to a socio-political one.

I have been drawn to the models and frameworks discussed in this book because of how they have deeply challenged and unsettled me, in ways that make me critical of what I do and the social context I do it in. As a result I believe that when we start to hear ourselves talking about other people as though they have one dimension, are less than human or destined to be always that which they have so far been, we are closing down on rigid conclusions about complex and fluid experiences. Theories that encourage us to tell stories about other people that are richer, more human and less dismissive enable us to contribute to a more liberatory context for all people. Systemic, narrative, and liberation psychology approaches encourage us to be curious about the limitless realms of possibility open to us all, despite the power of abuse, oppression and violence. Our values and principles point to who we are and fuel our resilience in the face of adversity, the way weeds come through cracks in concrete.

A focus on the heart of therapy means that to promote respect we have to be respectful, and acknowledge our own potential to abuse, whatever our theoretical orientation. My belief is that we cannot truly be liberated without knowing how to move on *in relationship with each other*. We cannot understand power and resistance without thinking about relational context. We cannot think about what liberation is without reflecting on the relational restraints and consequences of that liberation, as well as our responsibilities in creating a society where all can feel liberated.

A responsive heart – how we are changed by what we hear

If – as I believe – we are interrelated and interconnected, then one person feeling humiliated or dehumanised impacts on and affects us all. Violence, social exclusion, prejudice, humiliation, greed and selfishness are just some of the experiences that help create the context where abuse and oppression can thrive. It is not uncommon for those who listen closely to victims of abuse, violence and oppression to experience themselves being verbally attacked, dismissed as exaggerating or seen as extreme in their own commitments or beliefs. It is all too easy to greet evidence of widespread abuse with disbelief, or to view a person's unshakable belief in the potential for compassion in *everyone* as naïve. Even if revelations about abuse in society can no longer be ignored and are greeted with outrage, this response can quickly turn into forgetting; a type of forgetting that justifies a 'them' (abusive people) and 'us' (normal people) attitude.

I feel it is my responsibility as a 'psy' professional who hears stories of abuse and oppression not just to be moved by it, but to be moved to action. I wrote this book to put into writing my *challenge to myself*, to continue to critique myself, and be driven by values that did not originate in me. My aim is to push myself not to revert to individual solutions behind closed doors that do not respect the person in context, but to bring power, resistance and liberation from the margins to the centre of therapy.

A collective heart – social activism

Increasingly professionals working in the 'psy' professions are joining together and forming groups to act socially and challenge some of the social injustices that impact on lives and give rise to distress. I have not given examples of empowerment projects I have set up that demonstrate my activist credentials, as I have not yet had an opportunity to get involved in authentically community-based social action. I do however describe ways in which therapy might be one of many social settings in which clients connect to being activists in their own right, in their own lives. Everyday acts of resistance always create a foundation for more revolutionary social acts. Perhaps the more we engage in therapy that breaks our hearts, the closer we move towards a revolutionary 'psy' profession and mental health system.

I hope that despite my passion and commitment I have written this book as a comma rather than a full stop. There is still much that is unanswered and unfinished about reflecting on these issues. I hope reading this book encourages 'psy' professionals to continue to reflect on power, resistance and liberation in counselling and therapy and experiment with them. In Epston's (1999) terms this book might be considered creativity (knowledge in the making) rather than creation (completed knowledge).

Appendix

As Fredman (2006) points out, the term 'systemic' has 'many meanings that have changed and evolved over time according to historical and political contexts' (p. 4). When I use it I am referring to a social constructionist approach to therapy that differs in some ways in epistemology (philosophical foundation) from traditional forms of family therapy, such as strategic and structural.

Some key features of social constructionism

Social constructionism moved from the idea of objectivity, and the positivistic view of 'things' possessing intrinsic qualities, to an understanding of the world as socially created. Constructivism is a stage between positivism and social constructionism and is described in more detail in Table A.1.

Social constructionism is a philosophical stance about how we understand the world and human processes. A social constructionist perspective takes a critical stance towards taken-for-granted knowledge, because the ways we commonly understand the world are historically and culturally specific. From this view reality is co-created in daily interaction with each other and our environment (Burr, 2003). Table A.1 compares and contrasts positivism, constructivism and social constructionism with respect to their positions on reality, knowledge and language.

Social constructionism in clinical practice

The social constructionist position in therapy has lead to a focus on self-reflexivity (reflecting on our own assumptions, values and biases), attention to wider social and cultural contexts, the impact of power and difference on the lives of clients and experience in therapy; as well as the focus of systemic therapy being *human systems*, which includes teams, groups, communities, professions, cultures and individuals in relation to social context, rather than just family systems.

Table A.1 Contrasting positivism, constructivism and social constructionism
on reality, knowledge and language

	Reality	Knowledge	Language
Positivism	Sees *reality* as having an objective quality that refers to something with a real essence.	Knowledge is defined as an accurate and verifiable correspondence to things as they essentially are. Uses reliability and replicability to make methods and results more predictable, accurate and reliable.	Views *language* as a tool for representing the world.
Constructivism	Sees *reality* as internal perception produced by an individual's cognitive processes.	*Knowledge* is either something we believe or something we call what we do. We are biological entities involved in a cognitive process, thus knowledge is developed within an individual.	Views *language* as the manifestation of the structure of the human mind.
Social constructionism	Shifts focus from the individual to the interaction between people and the social setting. A move from knowledge to ethics.	Human thought and perception are inherently social and interactive, and can never originate privately. Thought is not proof of the individual mind but proof of the social world.	Believes that how we describe the world actually dictates how we experience it. *Language* therefore is imbued with power.

Key principles of this therapeutic approach include:

- collaborative, non-judgemental, non-pathologising conversations that enable clients to recognise and mobilise their own strengths, resources and expertise
- multiple perspectives rather than universal truth(s)
- a position of curiosity
- reflecting on our own assumptions and making these explicit
- a focus on social injustice
- an understanding that what we evoke in systems depends on our selection process, our assumptions and prejudices.

Reflecting teams and reflecting processes

Social constructionist systemic therapy advocates for the use of reflecting teams (Andersen, 1987, 1991, 1992), of two or more people other than the therapist in the therapy room, who listen to the therapeutic conversation and when asked make reflections to each other about what they have heard. A reflecting team, because of differences in race, gender, class, culture and life experiences, has greater potential than the individual therapist to offer a wide range of perspectives that might be helpful to the client (Selvini & Selvini Palazzoli, 1991). Research indicates that reflecting teams can enable individuals who are stuck to move forward (Moran, Brownlee, Gallant & Meyers, 1995) because increased perspectives and listening to the reflecting team enable clients to reflect on their problems in new ways.

Although reflecting processes emphasise dialogue and transparency, it is disappointing that Andersen's (1997) description of the usefulness of reflecting processes did not reflect on power. Instead Andersen (1997) described 'heterarchy' (that is, governing through the other, the opposite of hierarchy, which involves governing from the top down), 'democratic relationship' or an 'even relationship' in the reflecting process.

Although I can echo Andersen's (1997) desire to create therapeutic contexts that respect participants as having equally important contributions, I would say that equally important does not mean equally powerful. For instance, the issue of power within reflecting teams is rarely discussed in the literature, and yet differences in the team might lead to certain issues being silenced or different team members being heard or listened to differently.

Notes

1 Statistics are discourses of power because science is synonymous with knowledge and knowledge with power. This power is thought to enable control, prediction and manipulation.
2 In order to make my point I have drawn on dichotomous language, splitting human experience into that which is governed by the head and that which is governed by the heart. Although I am aware that they are not real distinctions that exist in the world, they are never-the-less distinctions that have been socially created and therefore influence how we engage with and understand ourselves.
3 My father later told me that he suffered racist bullying by a man where he worked who resented him being more qualified than him and holding a better position. Despite this venomous racism my father continued to drive him to and from work because he promised this man's wife after this man's heart attack, that he would. My mother confirms that my father and this man later became friends. I'm not quite sure how this happened, but apparently it did.
4 All case examples are made up but based heavily on my clinical work. The outcome of the case examples are based on outcomes I have witnessed, so as not to present fictional outcomes that are potentially unrealistic. To ensure confidentiality I describe therapy sessions giving brief and general information and provide sample questions rather than verbatim conversations.
5 I put heterosexual in inverted commas here because this is a term that I am given by society by virtue of my sexual and love experiences to date. It is not a term I would choose for myself, or a term I assume will necessarily define my experiences in the future. My choice would be to not label or categorise something as fluid, intimate and mysterious as sexuality. If I was forced to categorise myself as anything, it would be as 'queer', i.e. not categorisable.
6 To me pro-Gay equals pro-human; that is, I support a worldview that is as much pro-Gay as it is pro-heterosexual.
7 Audre Lorde defined homophobia as 'a terror surrounding feelings of love for a member of the same sex and thereby a hatred of those feelings in others' and heterosexism as 'a belief in the inherent superiority of one form of loving over all others and thereby the right to dominance' (Lorde, 2010, p. 276).
8 Afrocentrism emphasises the distinctive identity and contributions of African cultures to world history and culture. Eurocentrism – a focus on European world civilisation and history – led to the neglect and denial of the contributions of African people.
9 Members of US Black Liberation and resistance movements, targeted, falsely framed for murder and imprisoned by the US government and FBI in the 1970s.

10 There are many types of Rosicrucian. My father is a member of the Ancient Mystical Order Rosæ Crucis (AMORC) which is a worldwide mystical, philosophical, educational and humanitarian organisation devoted to the investigation, study and practical application of natural and spiritual laws. They study many mystics (such as Islamic, Hindu, Greek and Egyptian mystics) including the Buddha.

11 So much of Western psychological and psychotherapeutic theory rests on the importance of self-love, which originates from the undivided attention and love of the primary caregiver (almost always the mother). I have come to the conclusion, which fits for me, that instead of being guided by this perspective in an attempt to learn to 'love myself better' (which has not worked to date), I feel more fulfilled and connected when I merely notice myself loving. This was the gift my mother gave me, that connects me to her and her love in a profound way.

12 For example Alice Miller (1997) gives an ahistorical explanation of racism, arguing that the root cause is the racist person's personal history of abuse and not having worked through their own feelings of victimisation.

13 'Psy' professions are those that deal with supporting people's psychological needs, such as psychiatry, psychology, psychotherapy and counselling (Rose, 1985).

14 Although clinicians can refer to different approaches when they talk about working systemically, when I mention systemic therapy I am referring to social constructionist systemic therapy. I describe social constructionism in more detail in the Appendix. Systemic therapy has replaced family therapy as a term to highlight the ways that this type of therapy works with any system and relationship, including, but not exclusive to, the family – such as groups, organisations, schools, work contexts, communities, couple relationships, individuals in relation to social context, and so on.

15 Like Ani (1994) I refer to European culture as minority world culture since Europeans and the cultures they have created represent a minority in global terms; and those of Africa, Asia, the Far East, the Middle East and Latin America as majority world cultures, since they make up the majority of the world (Afuape, 2006).

16 Stonewall's 2007 survey of young Gay, lesbian and bisexual people at secondary school found that homophobic bullying is endemic in Britain's schools. Ninety-eight per cent of young Gay, lesbian and bisexual pupils heard homophobic language as commonplace and 65 per cent of young Gay, lesbian and bisexual pupils experienced direct bullying. Thirty-five per cent did not feel safe or accepted in school and 35 per cent reported that adults were responsible for homophobic incidents in their schools. Of those who have been bullied, 92 per cent experienced verbal abuse, 58 per cent were ignored and isolated, 41 per cent were physically assaulted, 30 per cent experienced vandalism and theft of their property, 17 per cent experienced death threats and 12 per cent were sexually assaulted. Fifty-eight per cent of young Gay, lesbian and bisexual pupils who experienced bullying never reported it, given that if they told a teacher, 62 per cent of the time nothing was done (Hunt & Jensen, 2007).

17 I once went to a vigil in the Gay village in Manchester on National AIDS day, in which the speaker asked the mainly White audience to think about the people in the world suffering from AIDS-related illnesses. As we closed our eyes he went through the continents in the world we should extend our compassion to – 'Europe, Asia, America, Australia' – he missed out Africa, the continent most affected by HIV and AIDS.

18 I refer to corporeal/corporal power to mean the experience of power and powerless as experienced through the body.

19 Gregory Bateson (1904–1980) was a British anthropologist, social scientist, linguist and cyberneticist whose work influenced many fields of study from family therapy, anthropology and communication theory to social sciences, linguistics and cybernetics. He is famously noted for writing *Steps to an Ecology of Mind* in 1972 and *Mind and Nature* in 1979.

20 In the 1970s domestic violence was more socially accepted in male-dominated cultures, justified in customs and traditions and condoned by law (Harne & Radford, 2008, p. 1). Until recently the criminal justice system saw its task as limiting the amount of force a man could use against his wife, rather than recognising spousal abuse as a crime (Berry, 1998). The United Nations' recognition of domestic violence as a human rights abuse in the 1990s (Committee on the Elimination of Discrimination Against Women, 1992; Fourth World Conference on Women, 1995) has meant that domestic violence has now achieved a much greater profile in terms of law and policy development in many countries. In the UK recent changes at local and national levels have been far-reaching and domestic violence is now high on the agenda of many professionals, practitioners and policy-makers (Harne & Radford, 2008). There has also been an increased criminalisation of perpetrators of domestic violence, with respect to gradual changes in police policy and practice, as well as recent legal changes to improve prosecution and conviction rates indicating a shift in government policy and social attitudes.

21 Although I focus here on adults who experience (or have experienced) 'psychosis' – as well as survivors of torture/war – I hope that the reader will apply these ideas more generally.

22 The *Thesaurus of Psychological Terms* states that religiosity 'is associated with religious organizations and religious personnel' (Walker, 1991, p. 184) whereas spirituality refers to the 'degree of involvement or state of awareness or devotion to a higher being or life philosophy. Not always related to conventional religious beliefs' (Walker, 1991, p. 208). Some forms of spirituality are not based on a belief in an external divine or transcendent force (e.g., humanistic–phenomenological spirituality) (Elkins, Hedstrom, Hughes, Leaf & Saunders, 1988).

23 Transpersonal psychology started off within humanistic psychology and studies the transpersonal or spiritual aspects of human experience; it is concerned with the study of 'unitive, spiritual, and transcendent states of consciousness' (Lajoie & Shapiro, 1992, p. 91) and 'draws upon ancient mystical knowledge that comes from multiple traditions' (Caplan, 2009, p. 231).

24 Spiritual emergencies are forms of distress associated with spiritual practices and experiences. Spiritual *emergence* refers to 'a gradual unfoldment of spiritual potential with minimal disruption in psychological/social/occupational functioning', whereas in spiritual *emergency* there is significant disruption in psychological/social/occupational functioning (Lukoff, Lu & Turner, 1996, p. 238).

25 Psychoreligious problems are experiences related to beliefs and practices of an organised religious or spiritual institution that a person finds troubling or distressing (Lukoff, 1998).

26 ICD-10: the European psychiatric classification system has yet to do the same.

27 People in different cultures describe experiences in different ways. What might be considered an indication of 'mental illness' in the minority world may be viewed as acceptable and positive in some countries in the majority world

(Kagawa-Singer & Chung, 1994; Kitayama & Markus, 1994; Markus & Kitayama, 1994a, 1994b). Psychiatric diagnoses are minority world labels that describe certain types of behaviour from a Western perspective and based on particular assumptions about health and ill-heath (BPS, 2001). As a result, psychiatric medication is the most common intervention offered to people with 'psychotic' experiences. However, two-thirds of people who have medication regularly are likely to experience a recurrence of their psychotic experience within two years. Medication can also have serious side-effects. If people who have had psycho-social difficulties live in non-oppressive, calm and relaxed atmospheres, their problems are less likely to return (Breggin, 1983, 1990, 1991; Romme & Escher, 1993; BPS, 2001). The widespread belief that genes can cause specific behaviour has been challenged by many psychologists, psychiatrists and critical biogeneticists (e.g. Rose, Kamin & Lewontin, 1990) and the idea that 'psychosis' is caused by an unknown disease entity with a soon-to-be-discovered biogenetic cause has been thoroughly debunked (Boyle, 1990; Rose, Kamin & Lewontin, 1990; Sarbin, 1990, 1991). Critical analysis of biogenetic research into 'psychosis' reveals a pattern of inconclusive findings, non-replication of earlier findings and confusion of correlation with causality (Fisher & Greenberg, 1989; Boyle, 1990). 'Evidence' for a genetic element to 'psychosis' comes mainly from studies that compare identical and non-identical twins and from adoption studies. However, Wright (1997) showed that the link between genes and traits is far more complicated than behavioural geneticists assume. Even if twins share genes, a given genetic trait may not be shared. The significance of Wright's research is the suggestion that twins might actually be a highly special case, and thus not comparable to singletons, which throws into question the very use of twin studies in genetic research (Burne, 1997). There are numerous problems in trying to disentangle genetic inheritance from social factors. In the studies related to 'schizophrenia' doubts have been raised about methods of determining the genetic similarity of twins, the length of time adopted children had spent with their families of origin, and the mental health status of some of the adoptive families (Boyle, 1990; Rose, Kamin & Lewontin, 1990). Some reviewers have identified more serious flaws that cast doubt on the validity of such data, which are based on making diagnoses from third-party reports and using dubious methods for calculating the frequency with which siblings share diagnoses (Boyle, 1990; Rose, Kamin & Lewontin, 1990). In the main, research into genetics, brain chemistry, the physical environment and brain structure has not led to clear conclusions about physical causes (BPS, 2001).

28 In my experience clients may hold many different explanations at once (e.g. biochemical, social and spiritual), which viewed from a mind-body dualistic medical perspective may seem contradictory but which for the client is meaningful and coherent.

29 People are often tortured, then released back into their communities, then captured and tortured again, as a warning to others in the community.

30 'First national people' refers to indigenous people.

31 'Even the most blatantly racist discourse routinely features denials or at least mitigation of racism' (Van Dijk, 1992, p. 89).

32 I refer to subjugated knowledges as a whole set of knowledges that have been disqualified and dismissed by dominant culture as primitive or invalidated by science.

33 When Albert Memmi grew up as a Jewish person in Tunisia it was colonised by the French. Memmi published *The colonizer and the colonized* in 1957 and according to Moane (1999) Memmi identified with both the colonised (the

Tunisians) and the coloniser (the French) because many Jewish people in the predominantly Muslim country 'attempted to assimilate as French' (Moane, 1999, p.75). As a result Memmi felt attuned to 'both sides' and reflected on the destructive impact of colonialism on both the colonised and the coloniser (Moane, 1999).

34 'Double consciousness' is a term coined by W.E.B. Du Bois, used to describe an individual whose identity is divided into several parts that are not well held together. Du Bois was referring specifically to the ways in which African Americans view themselves both through their own eyes and through the eyes of the society that oppresses them; that is, 'measuring one's soul by the tape of a world that looks on in amused contempt and pity' (Du Bois, 1906, p. 3). In an attempt to assimilate, African Americans developed a 'twoness – an American, a Negro: two souls, two thoughts, two unreconciled strivings; two warring ideals in one dark body' (Du Bois, 1906, p.3).

35 Socialisation is the process by which we are educated into the fundamental assumptions that make sense of our experiences, and always includes explicit and implicit value systems, beliefs, attitudes and ways of perceiving and understanding (Gilbert, 2006).

36 Instead of referring to the colonised and the coloniser as two distinct groups of people, Taiwo (1999), an academic of law, art and philosophy, refers to 'two moments in the colonial whole' (p. 157). I like this description as it refers to a process in which positions taken are not necessarily fixed, rather than distinct categories.

37 For example, I can feel highly resistant towards the sexist notion that women were put on earth to be physically beautiful and attractive to men, while also at times feeling deeply insecure about not being attractive.

38 Dr Cartwright was a surgeon and psychologist who was summoned to a Louisiana plantation in 1851 to investigate the cause of the high percentage of slave runaways (Cartwright, 1851). After weeks of study he wrote a long report which concluded that the slaves who ran away were suffering from a mental disease he called drapetomania, which literally meant the mania for running away. Resistance to the 'norm' of slavery was viewed as pathological.

39 'Culture circle' is a term borrowed from Paulo Freire and described by Almeida, Dolan-Del Vecchio & Parker (2008) as 'heterogenous helping communities involving members of families who seek treatment, volunteer helpers from the community who work with families, and a team of therapists' (p. 15).

40 *Stories lived* are the actions we perform with others in our lives; *stories told* are the explanatory narratives that people use to make sense of their lives.

41 Sometimes it is not the content of talk that is important but what we are creating and doing with our talk. For example, are we connecting or rejecting?

42 Sen (1999b) argues that for individuals, capabilities are 'the substantive freedoms he or she enjoys to lead the kind of life he or she has reason to value' (p. 87).

43 Alison Roper-Hall (1998) proposed an acronym of *social GRACES* 'to promote thinking and questions about potentially important influences in clients' lives and problems' (p.192). For Roper-Hall (1998), GRACES stood for G – gender; R – race, religion; A – age, abilities (physical and intellectual); C – class, creed, colour, culture; E – ethnicity; S – sexuality. I have seen many versions of this acronym that have extended over the years. I have settled on GRAACCCEESS, which removes 'race' and includes caste, colour (skin), economics, education and spirituality (although at a training event in 2008 a learner said that they felt health was missing, which might make the acronym CHEESSEERRAAG – cheese rag!).

44 An interconnected system of emotional and instrumental support over time, chosen by the recipient, that acts as a family, particularly when biological family members have been rejecting (Weston, 1991; Jay-Green & Mitchell, 2008).

45 As discussed earlier, we can use our bodies to connect in a non-verbal way to what clients are experiencing.

46 'Chav' originates from the Romany word for 'friend'. Other terms such as the highly offensive 'pikey' or 'gyppo', referring to Travellers – the latter being a pejorative of 'gypsy' – were earlier used to describe the white underclass (Preston, 2009).

47 This type of both/and (an 'it is' and 'it isn't') approach, which suggests that 'yes, racism exists but Black people are too sensitive about racism and see it where it does not exist', serves the dual purpose of allowing the holder of this belief to appear ethically sensitive to the existence of racism while also denying any personal responsibility for understanding and challenging its many complex forms. White privilege means having the choice to challenge whiteness in some contexts while enacting power, invoking privileges and reinforcing the status quo in others.

48 Reflecting on privilege is not the same as the 'thank God I'm not in that situation' or the 'I am a better person for having witnessed your deprivation' mentality.

49 What happens when two people are running together, and one is running with the wind at their back, the other with the wind at their front? Are they running in the same direction? How do they talk about their different experiences together?

50 Mary was away from her country and family in a foreign and often hostile country, and was going back to a hostel on her own in an isolated area, a place of residence that was dirty and rat infested, with few friends around her. I was not going home to that.

51 Described on the Institute of Narrative Therapy Level 1 Narrative Therapy training March and April 2009.

52 Syndromes are groups of symptoms that collectively indicate or characterise a disease, psychological disorder or other abnormal condition.

53 Glenda Fredman, personal communication, 2005.

54 Hear the Jnanavaca talk in full at www.lbc.org.uk/talks.htm entitled 'Is Buddhism a religion?'

55 Term coined by Weinberg (1972).

56 Thích Nhất Hạnh argues that we can use the energy of mindfulness and compassion 'to recognise and embrace the energy of anger . . . this is not an act of suppressing our anger. Mindfulness is you and anger is also you, so you shouldn't transform yourself into a battlefield, one side fighting the other. You should not believe that mindfulness is good and correct, while anger is evil and wrong . . . you only need to recognise that anger is a negative energy and that mindfulness is a positive one. Then you can use the positive energy in order to take care of the negative one' (Nhất Hạnh, 2001, p. 68).

57 The assumption that being Black only creates problems or barriers in therapy – or is only useful when working with other Black people – highlights the racist view of 'the other' as inherently flawed and inferior. As well as encountering experiences where clients have responded to my skin colour in negative ways, much of the time my skin colour seems to facilitate the therapeutic process by, for example, facilitating conversations about power and difference. I have discussed this in more detail elsewhere (Afuape, 2004).

58 I am reminded of the Buddhist story of Aṅgulimāla (Pāli for 'garland of

fingers'), who was depicted in the Suttas as a ruthless killer who is redeemed by conversion to Buddhism. This story seemed to epitomise my belief in the universal potential of all human beings to do good as well as the importance of respecting those we have harmed. Aṅgulimāla's story is written in the Buddhist texts Thera-gāthā (Thag) and Aṅgulimāla Sutta in the Majjhimain the Pāli canon.

Aṅgulimāla was born Ahiṁsaka, meaning 'harmless', and was sent to study under a well-known Brahim guru. The other students, jealous that Ahiṁsaka was the best pupil, sought to turn the master against him by making him think that Ahiṁsaka had seduced his wife and believed himself to be superior to him. The master in response told Aṅgulimāla that he must provide him with 1,000 fingers, each from a different victim, thinking that Ahiṁsaka would be killed in the process. Cast out of the guru's house with this demand, Ahiṁsaka began murdering pilgrims, traders and passers-by. He became notorious for his ferocity and mercilessness, as he wore the fingers of his victims around his neck to keep count – hence his new name, 'Aṅgulimāla'. The king of Kosala vowed to hunt him down. Fearing for his life, his mother went to find her son and warn him. The Buddha perceived with his divine eye that Aṅgulimāla had slain 999 victims and was desperate for his 1000th and would kill his mother on meeting her. The Buddha decided to intercept Aṅgulimāla. On meeting the Buddha Aṅgulimāla tried to kill the Buddha but could not catch up to him, despite running as fast as he could and the Buddha moving very slowly. Aṅgulimāla shouted at the Buddha to stop and Aṅgulimāla was told by the Buddha that he had stopped: stopped harming living creatures, as should Aṅgulimāla. As a result Aṅgulimāla became a Buddhist monk (Ñāṇamoli & Bodhi, 1995; Gombrich, 2006).

What is interesting about this story is that the villagers do not miraculously on meeting Aṅgulimāla forget his murderous ways and understand that he is reformed, such that his original name has become befitting of him. Although some people were sure of Aṅgulimāla's transformation and supported him, others could not forget that he was responsible for the death of their loved ones and threw stones at him. When he asked the Buddha what to do about these attacks, the Buddha told him to 'bear it' (Ñāṇamoli & Bodhi, 1995, p. 715). Despite being a reformed character, Aṅgulimāla was encouraged not to seek forgiveness, but to meet the responses of those he had harmed with acceptance and compassion.

59   The dominant model of human responses to stress or threat has been the fight-or-flight response, which argues that animals, including human beings, respond to threat by either confronting the source of the threat with aggression or fleeing literally or through avoidant behaviour. Taylor, Klein, Lewis, Gruenewald, Gurung & Updegraff (2000) research suggests that this analysis of stress is incomplete and androcentric, given that most of the research has excluded women. They argue that in the face of stress or threat, another response might be to affiliate with others and seek social support (Taylor, Klein, Lewis, Gruenewald, Gurung & Updegraff, 2000).

60   One of my best friends, Shahid Gani, once told me that he had spent his whole life 'trying to achieve' his difference. I thought this was a beautiful phrase and have used it ever since.

61   Yaa Asantewaa was Queen Mother of Ejisu, a state in the Asante Confederacy, which is now part of modern-day Ghana. She was also the leader of the Ashanti rebellion against British colonialism in 1900, which is known as the War of the Golden Stool. Yaa Asantewaa remains a much-loved figure in Asanti and

Ghanaian history for the courage she showed in confronting injustice. In 1960 the Yaa Asantewaa Girls' Secondary School was established at Kumasi with funds from the Ghana Educational Trust, and in 2000 a week-long centenary celebration was held in Ghana to acknowledge her accomplishments.

62 Many thanks to Gillian Hughes for sharing with me an insightful conversation she had with the late systemic therapist Maxwell Madondo Mudakiri regarding depression as a need for deep rest.

References

Adetimole, F., Afuape, T. & Vara, R. (2005). The impact of racism on the experience of training on a clinical psychology course: Reflections from three Black trainees. *Clinical Psychology*, 49, 11–19.

Afuape, T. (2004). Challenge to obscuring difference: Being a black woman psychologist using self in therapy. *Journal of Critical Psychology, Counselling and Psychotherapy*, 4(3), 164–176.

Afuape, T. (2006). Subjugating nature and 'the Other': Deconstructing dominant themes in Minority world culture and their implications for Western psychology. *Journal of Critical Psychology, Counselling and Psychotherapy*, 6(4), 238–255.

Agger, I. & Jensen, J.B. (1990). Testimony as ritual and evidence in psychotherapy for political refugees. *Journal of Traumatic Stress*, 3, 115–130.

Albee, G.W. (1992). Powerlessness, politics, and prevention: The community mental health approach. In S. Staub and P. Green (Eds.), *Psychology and social responsibility: Facing global challenges*. New York, NY: New York University Press.

Allman, L.S., De La Roche, O., Elkins, D.N. & Weathers, R.S. (1992). Psycho-therapists' attitudes towards clients reporting mystical experiences. *Psychotherapy*, 29, 564–569.

Almeida, R.V., Dolan-Del Vecchio, K. & Parker, L. (2007). Foundation concepts for social justice-based therapy: Critical consciousness, accountability, and empowerment. In E. Aldarondo (Ed.), *Advancing social justice through clinical practice*. London, UK: Lawrence Erlbaum Associates.

Almeida, R.V., Dolan-Del Vecchio, K. & Parker, L. (2008). *Transformative family therapy: Just families in a just society*. Boston, MA: Pearson Education.

Alschuler, L.R. (2006). *The psychopolitics of liberation: Political consciousness from a Jungian perspective*. New York, NY: Palgrave Macmillan.

American Psychiatric Association. (1994). *Diagnostic and statistical manual of mental disorders* (4th ed.). Washington, DC: APA.

American Psychiatric Association. (2000). *Diagnostic and statistical manual of mental disorders* (4th ed., text revision). Washington, DC: APA.

American Psychological Association. (2005). *Policy statement on evidence-based practice in psychology*. Washington, DC: American Psychological Association.

Amy, M. (2004). Measuring the clouds: A conversation with Jan Fabre. *Sculpture*, 23(2), 40–45.

Andersen, T. (1987). The reflecting team: Dialogue and meta-dialogue in clinical work. *Family Process*, 26(4), 415–428.

Andersen, T. (1991). *The reflecting team: Dialogues and dialogues about the dialogues.* New York, NY: Norton.

Andersen, T. (1992). Reflections on reflecting with families. In S. McNamee and K.J. Gergen (Eds.), *Therapy as social construction.* Thousand Oaks, CA: Sage.

Andersen, T. (1995). Reflecting processes; acts of informing and forming: You can borrow my eyes, but you must not take them away from me! In S. Friedman (Ed.), *The reflecting team in action: Collaborative practice in family therapy.* New York, NY: Guilford Press.

Andersen, T. (1997). Researching client–therapist relationships: A collaborative study for informing therapy. *Journal of Systemic Therapies*, 16(2), 125–133.

Anderson, H. (2001). Postmodern collaborative and person-centred therapies: What would Carl Rogers say? *Journal of Family Therapy*, 23(4), 339–360.

Anderson, H. & Goolishian, H. (1990). Beyond cybernetics: Comments on Atkinson and Heath's "Further thoughts on second-order family therapy". *Family Process*, 29(2), 157–163.

Ani, M. (1994). *Yurugu: An African-centred critique of European cultural thought and behaviour.* Trenton, NJ: Africa World Press.

Aptheker, H. (1969). *American negro slave revolts.* New York, NY: International Publishers.

Aptheker, H. (1986). Resistance and Afro-American history: Some notes on contemporary historiography and suggestions for further research. In G.Y. Okihiro (Ed.), *In resistance: Studies in African, Caribbean and Afro-American History.* US: Amherst, MA: University of Massachusetts Press.

Assagioli, R. (1989). Self-realization and psychological disturbances. In S. Grof and C. Grof (Eds.), *Spiritual emergency: When personal transformation becomes a crisis.* Los Angeles, CA: Jeremy P Tarcher.

Ayto, J. (1990). *Dictionary of word origins.* New York, NY: Arcade Publishing.

Azibo, D. (1990). *Liberation psychology.* Atlanta, GA: Clarity Press.

Azibo, D. (1994). The kindred fields of black liberation theology and liberation psychology: A critical essay on their conceptual base and destiny. *Journal of Black Psychology*, 20(3), 334–356.

Babacan, H. & Gopalkrishnan, N. (2001). Community work partnerships in a global context. *Community Development Journal*, 36(1), 3–17.

Bachelard, G. (1992). *The poetics of space.* Boston, MA: Beacon Press.

Bacigalupe, G. (1998). Cross-cultural systemic therapy training and consultation: A post-colonial view. *Journal of Systemic Therapies*, 17(1), 31–44.

Baker Miller, J. (1991). The development of a woman's sense of self. In J. Jordan, A. Kaplan, J. Baker Miller, I. Stiver and J. Surrey (Eds.), *Women's growth in connection.* London, UK: Guildford Press.

Banton, M. & Harwood, J. (1975). *The race concept.* London, UK: David and Charles.

Barker, P., Campbell, P. & Davidson, B. (Eds.) (1999). *From the ashes of experience: Reflections on madness, survival and growth.* London, UK: Whurr.

Başoğlu, M., Paker, M., Ozmen, E., Taşdemir, O. & Sahin, D. (1994). Factors related to long term traumatic stress in survivors of torture in Turkey. *Journal of the American Medical Association*, 27, 357–363.

Bateson, G. (1972). *Steps to an ecology of mind.* New York, NY: Ballantine.

Bateson, G. (1979). *Mind and nature.* New York, NY: Ballantine.

Bateson, M.C., Birdwhistell, R., Brockman, J., Lipset, D., May, R., Mead, M., *et al.* (1977). *About Bateson: Essays on Gregory Bateson.* Chicago, IL: N Fagin Books.

Bavelas, J.B. & Coates, L. (2001). Is it sex or assault? Erotic vs. violent language in sexual assault trial judgments. *Journal of Social Distress and Homelessness,* 10(1), 29–40.

Bayley, R. (1996). First person account: Schizophrenia. *Schizophrenia Bulletin,* 22, 727–729.

Beaudoin, M.N. (2005). Agency and choice in the face of trauma: A narrative therapy map. *Journal of Systemic Therapies,* 24(4), 32–51.

Beavan, V. (2006). *Angels at our tables: New Zealanders' experiences of hearing voices.* Psychology PhD thesis. Auckland, New Zealand: University of Auckland.

Behar, R. (1996). *The vulnerable observer: Anthropology that breaks your heart.* Boston, MA: Beacon Press.

Belle, D. (1990). Poverty and women's mental health. *American Psychologist,* 45(3), 385–389.

Bernstein, A.C. (2000). Straight therapists working with lesbian and gays in family therapy. *Journal of Marital and Family Therapy,* 26(4), 443–454.

Berry, D.B. (1998). *The domestic violence sourcebook: Everything you need to know.* Los Angeles, CA: Lowell House.

Bertrando, P. (2007). *The dialogical therapist: Dialogue in systemic practice.* London, UK: Karnac.

Beveridge, A. (1998). Psychology of compulsory detention. *Psychiatric Bulletin,* 22, 115–117.

Blake, D.D., Albano, A.M. & Keane, T.M. (1992). Twenty years of trauma: Psychological abstracts 1970 through 1989. *Journal of Traumatic Stress,* 5, 477–484.

Bourdillon, M. (1991) (3rd ed.). *The Shona people.* Gweru, Zimbabwe: Mambo Press.

Boyd-Franklin, N. & Hafer Bry, B. (2000). Reaching out in family therapy: Home-based, school and community interventions. New York, NY: Guilford Press.

Boyle, M. (1990). Schizophrenia – A scientific delusion? London, UK: Routledge.

BPS (2001). *Recent advances in understanding mental illness and psychotic experiences.* Leicester, UK: British Psychological Society.

Bracken, P. (2002). *Trauma: Culture, meaning and philosophy.* London, UK: Whurr.

Bracken, P.J. & Petty, C. (eds.) (1998). *Rethinking the trauma of war.* London, UK: Free Association Books.

Bradshaw, J., Finch, N., Kemp, P., Mayhew, E. & Williams J. (2003). *Gender and poverty in Britain,* Working Paper Series 6. Manchester, UK: Equal Opportunities Commission.

Breggin, P. (1983). *Psychiatric drugs: Hazards to the brain.* New York, NY: Springer.

Breggin, P. (1990). Brain damage, dementia and persistent cognitive dysfunction associated with neuroleptic drugs: Evidence, etiology, implications. *Journal of Mind and Behaviour,* 11, 425–464.

Breggin, P. (1991). *Toxic psychiatry.* New York, NY: St Martin's Press.

Breire, J. (1984). *The effects of childhood abuse on later psychological functioning:*

Defining post-sexual-abuse syndrome. Paper presented at the third national conference on sexual victimisation of children, Washington, DC.

Bridget, J. & Lucille, S. (1996). Lesbian Youth Support Information Service (LYSIS): Developing a distance support agency for young lesbians. *Journal of Community and Applied Social Psychology*, 6(5), 355–364.

Bringhurst, M.D.L., Watson, C.W., Miller, S.D. & Duncan, B.L. (2006). The reliability and validity of the Outcome Rating Scale: A replication study of a brief clinical measure. *Journal of Brief Therapy*, 5 (1), 23–9.

Bronfenbrenner, U. (1979). *The ecology of human development.* Cambridge, MA: Harvard University Press.

Brown, L.S. (1994). *Subversive dialogues: Theory in feminist therapy.* New York, NY: Basic Books.

Brown, L.S. & Ballou, M. (Eds.) (1992). *Personality and psychopathology: Feminist reappraisals.* New York, NY: Guilford Press.

Bryant-Davis, T. & Ocampo, C. (2005). Racist incident-based trauma. *Counselling Psychologist*, 33(4), 479–500.

Bulhan, H.A. (1985). *Frantz Fanon and the psychology of oppression.* New York, NY: Plenum Press.

Burgess, A. & Holmstrom, l. (1974). Rape trauma syndrome. *American Journal of Psychiatry*, 131, 981–986.

Burne, J. (1997, November 9). To the power of two. *The Guardian*, p. 13.

Burnham, J. (1992). Approach, method, technique: Making distinctions and creating connections. *Human Systems: Journal of Systemic Consultation and Management*, 3(1), 3–26.

Burnham, J. (2005). Relational reflexivity: A tool for socially constructing therapeutic relationships. In C. Flaskas, B. Mason and A. Perlesz (Eds.), *The space between: Experience, context and process in the therapeutic relationship.* London, UK: Karnac Books.

Burr, V. (2003). *Social constructionism* (2nd ed.). London, UK: Routledge.

Burton, M. & Kagan, C. (2005). Liberation social psychology: Learning from Latin America. *Journal of Community and Applied Social Psychology*, 15(1), 63–78.

Callicott, J.B. (1994). *Earth's insights: A multicultural survey of ecological ethics from the Mediterranean basin to the Australian outback.* Berkerley, CA: University of California.

Campbell, A. & Hemsley, S. (2009). Outcome Rating Scale and Session Rating Scale in psychological practice: Clinical utility of ultra-brief measures. *Clinical Psychologist*, 13(1), 1–9.

Cannon, W.B. (1932). *Wisdom of the body.* New York, NY: Norton.

Caplan, M. (2009). *Eyes wide open: Cultivating discernment on the spiritual parth.* Boulder, CO: Sounds True.

Carr, S.C. & Sloan, T.S. (2003). *Poverty and pychology: From global perspective to local practice.* London: Kluwer Academic/Plenum Publishers.

Cartwright, S.A. (1851). Report on the diseases and physical peculiarities of the negro race. *New Orleans Medical and Surgical Journal*, May, 691–715; repr. In A.C. Caplan, H.T., Engelhardt and J.J. McCartney (Eds.) (1981). *Concepts of health and disease.* Reading, MA: Addison-Wesley.

Cass, V.C. (1979). Homosexual identity formation: A theoretical model. *Journal of Homosexuality*, 4(3), 219–235.

Cass, V.C. (1984). Homosexual identity formation: Testing a theoretical model. *Journal of Sex Research*, 20(2), 143–167.

Cecchin, G., Lane, G. & Ray, W.A. (1994). *The cybernetics of prejudices in the practice of psychotherapy*. London, UK: Karnac Books.

Charles, K. (2008). Traveller disadvantage in education remains a significant challenge. In K. Morris (Ed.), *Spectrum – Journal of the National Consultative Committee on Racism and Interculturalism (NCCRI)*. Special issue on Education as part of the European Year of Intercultural Dialogue, 17, 14–16.

Chinen, A.B. (1996). The emergence of transpersonal psychiatry. In B.W. Scotton, A.B. Chinen and J.R. Battista (Eds.), *Textbook of transpersonal psychiatry and Psychology*. New York, NY: Basic Books.

Chodorow, N. (1978). *The reproduction of mothering: Psychoanalysis and the sociology of gender*. Berkeley, CA: University of California Press.

Chödrön, P. (2001). *Tonglen: The path of transformation*. Halifax, Canada: Vajradhatu Publications.

Chomsky, N. & Foucault, M. (2006). *The Chomsky–Foucault Debate: On human nature*. London, UK: The New Press.

Christensen, P. (1989). Cross-cultural awareness development: A conceptual model. *Counsellor Education and Supervision*, 28, 270–289.

Ciconello, A. (2007). *The challenge of eliminating racism in Brazil: The new institutional framework for fighting racial inequality*. Oxford, UK: Oxfam International.

Cienfuegos, A.J. & Monelli, C. (1983). The testimony of political repression as a therapeutic instrument. *American Journal of Orthopsychiatry*, 53(1), 41–53.

Clinks (2008). Less equal than others: Ethnic minorities and the criminal justice system. York, UK: Clinks.

Coates, L. (1997). Causal attributions in sexual assault trial judgments. *Journal of Language and Social Psychology*, 16(3), 278–296.

Coates, L. & Wade, A. (2004). Telling it like it isn't: Obscuring perpetrator responsibility for violent crime, *Discourse and Society*, 15(5), 499–526.

Coates, L. & Wade, A. (2007). Language and violence: Analysis of four discursive operations. *Journal of Family Violence*, 22(7), 511–522.

Coates, L., Todd, N. & Wade, A. (2000). *Four operations of language*. Paper Presented at Bridging the Gap Conference, Victoria, Canada.

Coleman, R. (1999) *Recovery an alien concept*. Gloucester, UK: Handsell Press.

Collins, P.H. (1995). Black women and motherhood. In V. Held (Ed.), *Justice and care: Essential readings in feminist ethics*. Boulder, CO: Westview Press.

Collins, P.H. (2000). The social construction of black feminist thought. *Signs: Journal of Wome in Culture and Society*, 14(4), 745–773.

Comas-Diaz, L., Brinton Lykes, M., & Alarcon, R. D. (1998). Ethnic conflict and the psychology of liberation in Guatemala, Peru, and Puerto Rico. *American Psychologist*, 53(1), 778–792.

Committee on the Elimination of Discrimination against Women (CEDAW) (1992). *CEDAW General Recommendations Nos. 19 and 20, adopted at the Eleventh Session, (contained in Document A/47/38)*, 1992, A/47/38. Geneva, Switzerland: UNHCR.

Copello, A., Orford, J., Hodgson, R. & Tober, G. (2009). *Social behaviour and network therapy for alcohol problems*. London, UK: Routledge.

Counts, A., Brown, J.K. & Campbell, J.C. (Eds.) (1999). *To have and to hit: Cultural perspectives on wife beating*. Chicago, IL: University of Illinois Press.

Cox, D.L., Stabb, S.D. & Bruckner, K.H. (1999). *Women's anger: Clinical and developmental perspectives*. Philadelphia, PA: Brunner-Routledge.

Craton, M. (1986). From Caribs to Black Caribs: The Amerindian roots of Serville resistance in the Caribbean. In G.Y. Okihiro (Ed.), *In resistance: Studies in African, Caribbean and Afro-American history*. Amherst, MA: University of Massachusetts Press.

Crenshaw, K. (1992). Whose story is it anyway? Feminist and anti-racist appropriations of Anita Hill. In T. Morrison (Ed.), *Race-ing justice, en-gendering power*. New York, NY: Pantheon Books.

Cromwell, R.E. & Olson, D.H. (1975). *Power in families*. New York, NY: Wiley.

Cronen, V.E. (1995). Coordinated management of meaning: The consequentiality of communication and the recapturing of experience. In S. Sigman (Ed.), *The consequentiality of communication*. Hillsdale, NJ: Lawrence Erlbaum Associates.

Cronen, V.E. & Pearce, W.B. (1980). *Communication, action and meaning: The creation of social realities*. New York, NY: Praeger.

Cronen, V.E. & Pearce, W.B. (1985). Towards an explanation of how the Milan method works: An invitation to a systemic epistemology and the evolution of family systems. In D. Campbell and R. Draper (Eds.), *Applications of systemic family therapy: The Milan approach*. London, UK: Grune and Stratton.

Cross, B. (1993). *It's not about a salary. Rap, race and resistance in Los Angeles*. London, UK: Verso.

Cross, J. (1994) Politics and family therapy: Power and politics in practice. *Dulwich Centre Newsletter*, 1, 7–10.

Cross, W.E. (1991). *Shades of black: Diversity in African American identity*. Philadelphia, PA: Temple University Press.

Cross, W.E. (1995). The psychology of nigrescence: Revising the Cross model. In J.G. Ponterotto and J.M. Casas (Eds.), *Handbook of multi-cultural counselling*. Thousand Oaks, CA: Sage.

Dallos, R. & Draper, R. (2005). *An introduction to Family Therapy: Systemic Theory and Practice* (2nd ed.). Maidenhead, UK: Open University Press.

Danto, E.A. (2005). *Freud's free clinics: Psychoanalysis and social justice, 1918–1938*. New York, NY: Columbia University Press.

Davidson, L. & Strauss, J.S. (1992). Sense of self in recovery from severe mental illness. *British Journal of Medical Psychology*, 65, 131–145.

Davis, A.Y. (1998). *Blues legacies and Black feminism: Gertude 'Ma' Rainey, Bessie Smith and Billie Holiday*. New York, NY: Pantheon Books.

Deegan, P. (1993). Recovering our sense of value after being labelled. *Journal of Psychosocial Nursing*, 31(1), 7–11.

DeGruy Leary, J. (2005). *Post traumatic slave syndrome: America's legacy of enduring injury and healing*. Milwaukie, OR: Uptone Press.

Derrida, J. (1994). *Spectres of Marx*, New York, NY: Routledge.

de Shazer, S. (1984). The death of resistance. *Family Process*, 23(1), 1–17.

Diprose, R. (2002). *Corporeal generosity*. Albany, NY: State University of New York Press.

Downing, N.E. & Roush, K.L. (1985). From passive acceptance to active commitment: A model of feminist identity development for women. *Counseling Psychologist*, 13(4), 695–709.

Du Bois, W.E.B. (1906/1994). *The souls of Black folks*. New York, NY: Dover.

Du Bois, W.E.B. (1996). *The Philadelphia negro: A social study*. Centennial edition. Philadelphia, PA: University of Pennsylvania Press.

Du Bois, W.E.B. (2007). *In battle for peace: The story of my 83rd birthday*. New York, NY: Oxford University Press.

Dutton, D.G. (2006). *Rethinking domestic violence*. Toronto, Canada: UBC Press.

Eaton, W.W., Romanoski, A., Anthony, J.C. & Nestadt, G. (1991). Screening for psychosis in the general population with a self-report interview. *Journal of Nervous and Mental Disease*, 179, 689–693.

Eisenbruch, M. (1990). Cultural bereavement and homesickness. In S. Fisher and C. Cooper (Eds.), *On the move: The psychology of change and transition*. Chichester, UK: Wiley.

Eisenbruch, M. (1991). From post-traumatic stress disorder to cultural bereavement: diagnosis of South Asian refugees. *Social Science and Medicine*, 30(6), 673–680.

Elkins, D., Hedstrom, J., Hughes, L., Leaf, A. & Saunders, C. (1988). Toward a humanistic–phenomenological spirituality. *Journal of Humanistic Psychology*, 28, 5–19.

Ellason, J.W. & Ross, C.A. (1997). Childhood trauma and psychiatric symptoms. *Psychological Reports*, 80, 447–450.

Epston, D. (1999). Co-research: The making of an alternative knowledge. *Narrative therapy and community work: A conference collection*. Adelaide, Australia: Dulwich Centre Publications.

Esteva, G. (1992). Development. In W. Sachs (Ed.), *The development dictionary: A guide to knowledge as power*. London: Zed Books.

Falzon, C. (1998). *Foucault and social dialogue*. New York, NY: Routledge.

Fanon, F. (1963). *The wretched of the earth*. New York, NY: Grove Press.

Fanon, F. (1967). *Black skin white masks*. New York, NY: Grove Press.

Fernando, S., Ndegwa, D. & Wilson, M. (1998). *Forensic psychiatry, race and culture*. London: Routledge.

First National People of Colour Environmental Leadership Summit (2005). Principles of environmental justice. In J.S. Dryzek and D. Schlosberg (Eds.). *Debating the earth: The environmental politics reader* (2nd ed.). Oxford, UK: Oxford University Press.

Fisher, A. (2005). Power and the promise of innocent places. *Narrative Network News*, 34, 12–14.

Fisher, S. & Greenberg, R.P. (1989). A second opinion: Rethinking the claims of biological psychiatry. In S. Fisher and R.P. Greenberg (Eds.), *The limits of biological treatments for psychological distress: Comparisons with psychotherapy and placebo*. Hillsdale, NJ: Lawrence Erlbaum Associates.

Foucault, M. (1976/2003). *Society must be defended: Lectures at the College de France, 1975–1976*. New York, NY: Picador.

Foucault, M. (1980). *Power/Knowledge: Selected interviews and other writings 1971–1977*. New York, NY: Harvester Wheatsheaf.

Foucault, M. (1982). The subject of power. In H. Dreyfus and P. Rabinow (Eds.),

Michael Foucault: Beyond structuralism and hermeneutics. New York, NY: Harvester Wheatsheaf.

Fourth World Conference on Women (1995). *Beijing declaration and platform of action*. Retrieved July 31, 2010, from www.un.org/womenwatch

Fox-Genovese, E. (1986). Strategies and forms of resistance: Focus on slave women in the United States. In G.Y. Okihiro (Ed.), *In resistance: Studies in African, Caribbean and Afro-American history*. Amherst, MA: University of Massachusetts Press.

Fredman, G. (2004). *Transforming emotion: Conversations in counselling and psychotherapy*. London, UK: Whurr.

Fredman, G. (2006). Working systemically with intellectual disability: Why not? In S. Baum and H. Lynggaard (Eds.), *Intellectual disabilities: A systemic approach*. London, UK: Karnac.

Freire, P. (1973). *Pedagogy of the oppressed*. New York, NY: Seabury Press.

Freire, P. (2006). *Education for critical consciousness*. London, UK: Continuum

Frith, S. (1995). The body electric. *Critical Quarterly*, 37(2), 2.

Fryer, P. (1988). *Staying power: Black people in the British Empire: An introduction*. London, UK: Pluto Press.

Gaita, R. (1991). *Good and evil*. London, UK: Routledge.

Game, A. & Metcalfe, A. (2001). Care and creativity. *Australian Psychologist*, 36(1), 70–74.

Gil, D.G. (1998). *Confronting injustice and oppression: Concepts and strategies for social workers*. New York, NY: Columbia University Press.

Gilbert, J. (2006). Cultural imperialism revisited: Counselling and globalisation. *International Journal of Critical Psychology*, 17, 10–28.

Goff, D.C., Brotman, A.W., Kindler, D. & Waites, M. (1991). Self-reports of childhood abuse in chronically psychotic patients. *Psychiatry Research*, 37, 73–80.

Golding, J. (1999). Intimate partner violence as a risk factor for mental disorders: A meta analysis. *Journal of Family Violence*, 14, 99–132.

Goldner, V. (1993). Power and hierarchy: Let's talk about it! *Family Process*, 32(2), 157–162.

Gombrich, R.F. (2006). *How Buddhism began: The conditioned genesis of the early teachings* (2nd edn.). London, UK: Routledge.

Gomm, R. (1996). Mental health and inequality. In T. Heller, J. Reynolds, R. Gomm, R. Muston and S. Pattison (Eds.) *Mental health matters: A reader*. London, UK: Macmillan in association with the Open University.

Goolishian, H. & Anderson, H. (1992). Strategy and intervention versus non-intervention: A matter of theory? *Journal of Marital and Family Therapy*, 18(1), 5–15.

Gould, S.J. (1997). *The mismeasure of man*. London, UK: Penguin.

Greeley, G. (1974). *Ecstasy: A way of knowing*. Englewood Cliffs, NJ: Prentice Hall.

Green, D. (2008). *From poverty to power: How active citizens and effective states can change the world*. Oxford, UK: Oxfam International.

Griffith, J.I. & Griffith, M.E. (1994). *The body speaks: Therapeutic dialogues for mind–body problems*. New York, NY: Basic Books.

Grof, C. & Grof, S. (1990). *The stormy search for the self: A guide to personal growth through transformational crisis*. New York, NY: Jeremy P Tarcher.

Grof, S. & Grof, C. (Eds.) (1989). *Spiritual emergency: When personal transformation becomes a crisis*. Los Angeles, CA: Jeremy P Tarcher.

Guilfoyle, M. (2003). Dialogue and power: A critical analysis of power in Dialogical therapy. *Family Process*, 42(3), 331–43.

Guilfoyle, M. (2005). From therapeutic power to resistance? Therapy and cultural hegemony. *Theory and Psychology*, 15(1), 101–124.

Gurman, A.S. (1982). *Questions and answers in the practice of family therapy* (Vol. 2). New York, NY: Brunner/Mazel.

Gutierrez, F.J. & Dworkin, S.H. (1992). Gay, lesbian and African American: Managing the integration of identities. In S.H. Dworkin and F.J. Gutierrez (Eds.), *Counseling gay men and lesbians: Journey to the end of the rainbow*. Alexandria, VA: American Counseling Association.

Gwaltney, J.L. (1980). *Drylongso: A self portrait of black America*. New York, NY: Vintage.

Hardy, K.V. (1993). War of the worlds. *Networker*, July/August, 50–54.

Hare-Mustin, R.T. (1994). Discourses in the mirrored room: A post-modern analysis of therapy. *Family Process*, 33(1), 19–35.

Harne, I. & Radford, J. (2008). *Tackling domestic violence: Theories, policies and practice*. Maidenhead, UK: Open University Press.

Harper, D., Mulvey, R.M. & Robinson, M. (2003). Beyond evidence-based practice: Rethinking the relationship between research, theory and practice. In R. Bayne and I. Horton (Eds.), *Applied psychology: Current issues and new directions*. London, UK: Sage.

Harrison, G. (2002). Ethnic minorities and the Mental Health Act. *British Journal of Psychiatry*, 180, 198–199.

Hayfield, A. (1995). Several faces of discrimination. In V. Mason-John (Ed.), *Talking Black: Lesbians of African and Asian descent speak out*. London, UK: Cassell.

Helms, J.E. (1984). Toward a theoretical explanation of the effects of race on counseling: A Black and White model. *Counseling Psychologist*, 12, 153–165.

Helms, J.E. (1995). An update of Helms's White and people of color racial identity models. In J.G. Ponterotto, J.M. Casas, L.A. Suzuki and C.M. Alexander (Eds.), *Handbook of multicultural counseling*. Thousand Oaks, CA: Sage.

Herman, J.L. (1994). *Trauma and recovery: From domestic abuse to political terror*. London, UK: Pandora.

Herman, J.L. (1997). *Trauma and recovery: The aftermath of violence: From domestic abuse to political terror* (rev. ed.). New York, NY: Basic Books.

Herman, J.L. (2001). *Trauma and recovery: From domestic abuse to political terror* (3rd ed.). London, UK: Pandora.

Hoffman, L. (1992). A reflexive stance for family therapy. In S. McNamee and K. Gergen (Eds.), *Therapy as social construction*. London, UK: Sage.

Hollander, N.C. (1997). *Love in a time of hate: Liberation psychology in Latin America*. New Brunswick, NJ: Rutgers University Press.

hooks, b. (1990). *Yearning: Race, gender and cultural politics*. Boston, MA: South End Press.

hooks, b. (1993). Sisters of the yam: Black women and self-recovery. Boston, MA: South End Press.

hooks, b. (1994). *Outlaw culture: Resisting representations.* New York, NY: Routledge.

Hopper, K. (1999). John Berger and Erick Holtzman. *Social Policy*, 30(2), 13–21.

House of Commons Home Affairs Select Committee, The (2007). *Young Black people and the criminal justice system, Second report of session 2006–07.* London, UK: The Stationery Office.

Hunt, R., & Jensen, J. (2007). *The experience of young gay people in Britain's schools.* London, UK: Schools Health Education Unit on behalf of Stonewall.

Ina, S. (2001). *Children of the camps: The documentary, teacher's guide.* Sacramento, CA: Children of the Camps Documentary and Educational Project.

Jay-Green, R. & Mitchell, V. (2008). Gay and Lesbian couples in therapy: Minority stress, relational ambiguity and families of choice. In A.S. Gurman (Ed.), *Clinical handbook of couple therapy* (4th ed.). New York, NY: Guilford Press.

Jenkins, A. (1994). Therapy for abuse or therapy as abuse? Power and politics in practice. *Dulwich Centre Newsletter*, 1, 11–19.

Jenkins, A. (2009). *Becoming ethical: A parallel, political journey with men who have abused.* Lyme Regis, UK: Russell House Publishing.

Jonstone, L. (1989). *Users and abusers of psychiatry.* London, UK: Routledge.

Juhu, D. (1994). *Patients as victims. Sexual abuse in psychotherapy and counselling.* London.UK: Wiley.

Kagawa-Singer, M. & Chung, R.C-Y. (1994). A paradigm for culturally based care in ethnic minority populations. *Journal of Community Psychology*, 22, 192–208.

Karumanchery, L. (2003). The colour of trauma: New perspectives on racism, politics, and resistance. *Dissertation Abstracts International Section A: Humanities and Social Sciences*, 64(4-A), 1391.

Kelly, J. G. (1987). An ecological paradigm: Defining mental health consultation as a preventative service. *Prevention in Human Services*, 4(3), 1–36.

Kempe, C.H., Silverman, F.N., Steele, B.F., Droegemueller, W & Silver, H.K. (1962). The battered child syndrome. *Journal of the American Medical Association*, 181, 17–24.

Kenny, M. (1997). *The routes of resistance: Traveller and second-level schooling.* Aldershot, UK: Ashgate.

Kessler, M. & Goldston, S.E. (Eds.) (1986). *A decade of progress in primary prevention.* Hanover, NH: University Press of New England.

Kimmel, M. (2006). Toward a pedagogy of the oppressor. In A.D. Mutua (Ed.), *Progressive black masculinities.* New York, NY: Routledge.

King, M., McKeown, E., Warner, J., Ramsay, A., Johnson, K., Cort, C., Wright, L., Blizzard, R. & Davidson, O. (2003). Mental health and quality of life of gay men and lesbians in England and Wales: Controlled, cross-sectional study, *British Journal of Psychiatry*, 183, 552–558.

King, M., Semlyen, J., Tai, S.S., Killaspy, H., Osborn, D., Popelyuk, D. & Nazareth, I. (2008). *A systematic review of mental disorder, suicide, and deliberate self harm in lesbian, gay and bisexual people.* London, UK: Care Services Improvement Partnership (CSIP).

Kingdon, D.G. & Turkington, D. (1999). Cognitive-behavioural therapy of schizo-phrenia. In T. Wykes, N. Tarrier and S. Lewis (Eds.), *Outcome and innovation in the psychological treatment of schizophrenia.* London, UK: Wiley.

Kitayama, S. & Markus, H. (Eds.) (1994). *Emotion and culture: Empirical studies of mutual influence*. Washington, DC: American Psychological Association.

Kleinman, A. (1987). Anthropology and psychiatry: The role of culture in cross-cultural research on illness. *British Journal of Psychiatry*, 151(4), 447–454.

Kosutic, I. & McDowell, T. (2008). Diversity and social justice issues in family therapy literature: A decade Review. *Journal of Feminist Family Therapy*, 20(2), 142–165.

Kubany, E.S. & Ralston, T.C. (2008). *Treating PTSD in battered women: A step-by-step manual for therapists and counsellors*. Oakland, CA: New Harbinger Publications.

Lago, C. (2006). *Race, culture and counselling* (2nd ed.). Maidenhead, UK: Open University Press.

Lajoie, D. & Shapiro, S. (1992). Definitions of transpersonal psychology: The first 23 years. *Journal of Transpersonal Psychology*, 24(1), 79–98.

Lanzmann, C. (1995). The obscenity of understanding: An evening with Claude Lanzmann. In C. Caruth (Ed.), *Trauma: Explorations in memory*. Baltimore, MD: Johns Hopkins University Press.

Larner, G. (1995). The real as Illusion: Deconstructing power in family therapy. *Journal of Family Therapy*, 17, 191–217.

Larner, G. (1999). Derrida and the deconstruction of power as context and topic in therapy. In I. Parker (Ed.), *Deconstructing psychotherapy*. London, UK: Sage.

Law, I. & Madigan, S. (1994). Introduction: Power and politics in practice. *Dulwich Centre Newsletter*, 1, 3–6.

Lee, L.J. (2005). Taking off the mask: Breaking the silence – The art of naming racism in the therapy room. In M. Rastogi and E. Wieling (Eds.), *Voices of color: First-person accounts of ethnic minority therapists*. London, UK: Sage.

Leppington, R. (1991). From constructivism to social constructionism and doing critical therapy. *Human Systems: The Journal of Systemic Consultation and Management*, 2, 79–103.

Lincoln, C.E. (1974). *The Black church since Frazier*. New York, NY: Schocken Books.

Lorde, A. (2010). I am your sister: Black women organising across sexualities. In C.R. McCann and S-K. Kim (Eds.), *Feminist theory reader: Local and global perspectives* (2nd ed.). New York, NY: Routledge.

Lovejoy, P.E. (1986). Fugitive slaves: Resistance to slavery in the Sokoto Caliphate. In G.Y. Okihiro (Ed.), *In resistance: Studies in African, Caribbean and Afro-American history*. Amherst, MA: University of Massachusetts Press.

Lowe, R. (1999). Between the 'no longer' and the 'not yet': Postmodernism as a context for critical therapeutic work. In I. Parker (Ed.), *Deconstructing psychotherapy*. London, UK: Sage.

Lowe, R. (2005). Structured methods and striking moments: Using question sequences in "living" ways. *Family Process*, 44(1), 65–76.

Lu, F.G., Lukoff, D. & Turner, R.P. (1997). Religious or spiritual problems. In T.A. Widiger, A. Frances, H. Pincus, M. First, R. Ross and W. Wakefield Davis (Eds.), *DSM-IV Sourcebook, Vol. 3*. Washington, DC: American Psychiatric Association.

Lukoff, D. (1998). From spiritual emergency to spiritual problem: The transpersonal roots of the new DSM-IV category. *Journal of Humanistic Psychology*, 38(2), 21–50.

Lukoff, D., Lu, F.G. & Turner, R.P. (1996). Diagnosis: A clinical approach to religious and spiritual problems. In B.W. Scotton, A.B. Chinen and J.R. Battista (Eds.), *Textbook of transpersonal psychiatry and psychology*. New York, NY: Basic Books.

Lundy, M.S. (1992). Psychosis-induced posttraumatic stress disorder. *American Journal of Psychotherapy*, XLVI, 485–491.

Madigan, S. (2007). Anticipating hope within written and naming domains of despair. In C. Flaskas, I. McCarthy and J. Sheehan (Eds.), *Hope and despair in narrative and family therapy: Adversity, forgiveness and reconciliation*. London, UK: Routledge.

Madigan, S. & Epston, D. (1995). From spy-chiatric gaze to communities of concern: From professional monologue to dialogue. In S. Freidman (Ed.), *The reflecting team in action*. New York, NY: Guilford Press.

Madsen, W.C. (1999). *Collaborative therapy with multi-stressed families: From old problems to new futures*. London, UK: Guilford Press.

Madsen, W.C. (2007). *Collaborative therapy with multi-stressed families* (2nd ed.). London: Guilford Press.

Markus, H. & Kitayama, S. (1994a). Introduction to cultural psychology and emotion research. In S. Kitayama and H.R. Markus (Eds.), *Emotion and culture: Empirical studies of mutual influence*. Washington, DC: American Psychological Association.

Markus, H. & Kitayama, S. (1994b). The cultural shaping of emotion: A conceptual framework. In S. Kitayama and H.R. Markus (Eds.), *Emotion and culture: Empirical studies of mutual influence*. Washington, DC: American Psychological Association.

Marston, G. & Watts, R. (2003). Tampering with the evidence: A critical appraisal of evidence-based policy making. *The Drawing Board: An Australian review of public affairs*, 3(3), 143–163.

Martín-Baró, I. (1988). The political psychology of Latin America. In G. Pacheco and B. Jiménez (Eds.), *Ignacio Martín-Baró (1942–1989): Liberation psychology for Latin America*. Guadalajara, Mexico: Universidad de Guadalajara–ITESO.

Martín-Baró, I. (1996). *Writings for a liberation psychology*. New York, NY: Harvard University Press.

Mason, B. & Sawyerr, A. (Eds.) (2003). Exploring the unsaid: Creativity, risks and dilemmas in working cross-culturally. London, UK: Karnac.

Masson, M.J. (1994) (rev. ed.). *Against therapy*. Monroe, ME: Common Courage Press.

Masters, K.J. (1995). Environmental trauma in psychosis. *Journal of the American Academy of Child and Adolescent Psychiatry*, 34, 1258.

May, R. (2000). Routes to recovery from psychosis: The roots of a clinical psychologist, *Clinical Psychology Forum*, 146, 6–10.

May, R. (2004). Making sense of psychotic experiences and working towards recovery. In J. Gleeson and P.D. McGorry (Eds.), *Psychological interventions in early psychosis services*. London: Wiley.

McDowell, T. (2005). Practicing a relational therapy with a critical multicultural lens: Introduction to a special section, *Journal of Systemic Therapies*, 24(1). 1–4.

McDowell, T., Fang, S-R., Gomez Young, C., Khanna, A., Brooke, S., & Brownlee, K. (2003). Making space for racial dialogue: Our experience in a marriage and family therapy training program. *Journal of Marital and Family Therapy*, 29(2), 179–194.

McDowell, T., Ingoglia, L., Serizawa, T., Holland, C., Dashiell, J.W., Jr., & Stevens, C. (2005). Raising multiracial awareness in family therapy through critical conversations. *Journal of Marital and Family Therapy*, 31(4), 399–411.

McGoldrick, M., Almeida, R., Preto, N.G., Bibb, A., Sutton, C. & Hudak, J. (1999). Efforts to incorporate social justice perspectives into a family training program. *Journal of Marital and Family Therapy*, 25(2), 191–209.

McGoldrick, M. & Hardy, K. (2008). *Re-visioning family therapy: Race, culture and gender in clinical practice* (2nd ed.) New York, NY: Guilford Press.

McGorry, P.D., Chanen, A., McCarthy, E., van Riel, R., McKenzie, D. & Singh, B.S. (1991). Posttraumatic stress disorder following recent-onset psychosis: An unrecognized postpsychotic syndrome. *Journal of Nervous and Mental Disease*, 179, 253–258.

McNamee, S. (2000). The social poetics of relationally engaged research: Research as conversation. In K.G. Deissler and S. McNamee (Eds.), *Philosophy in therapy: The social poetics of therapeutic conversation*. Heidelberg, Germany: Carl-Auer-Systeme Verlag.

McNamee, S. & Gergen, K.J. (Eds.) (1992). *Therapy as social construction*. London, UK: Sage.

Memmi, A. (1974). *The colonizer and the colonized* (Howard Greenfeld, trans.). London, UK: Earthscan Publications.

Mendez, C., Coddou, F. & Maturana, H. (1988). The bringing forth of pathology. *Irish Journal of Psychology*, 9(1), 144–172.

Menninger, K. (1966). *The crime of punishment*. New York, NY: Viking Press.

Meyer, H., Taiminen, T., Vuori, T., Aeijaelae, A. & Helenius, H. (1999). Post-traumatic stress disorder symptoms related to psychosis and acute involuntary hospitalisation in schizophrenic and delusional patients. *Journal of Nervous and Mental Disease*, 187, 343–352.

Miller, A. (1997). *The drama of the gifted child: The search for the true self*. New York, NY: Basic Books.

Moane, G. (1999). *Gender and colonialism: A psychological analysis of oppression and liberation*. London: Macmillan.

Moane, G. (2003). Bridging the personal and the political: Practices for a liberation psychology. *American Journal of Community Psychology*, 31(1), 151–169.

Montero, M. (2009). Methods for Liberation: Critical consciousness in action. In M. Montero and C.C. Sonn (Eds.), *Psychology of liberation: Theory and applications*. New York: Springer.

Montero, M. & Sonn, C.C. (Eds.) (2009). *Psychology of liberation: Theory and applications*. New York, NY: Springer.

Morales, E.S. (1992). Counseling Latino gays and Latina lesbians. In S.H. Dworkin and F.J. Gutierrez (Eds.), *Counseling gay men and lesbians: Journey to the end of the rainbow*. Alexandria, VA: American Counseling Association.

Moran, A., Brownlee, K., Gallant, P. & Meyers, L. (1995). The effectiveness of the reflecting team supervision: A client's experience of receiving feedback from a distance. *Family Therapy*, 22(1), 31–47.

Morgan, A. (2000). *What is narrative therapy? An easy to read introduction.* Adelaide, Australia: Dulwich Centre Publications.

Morrison, T. (1987). *Beloved.* London: Chatto & Windus.

Mueke, M. (1992). New paradigms for refugee health problems. *Social Science and Medicine,* 35(4), 515–523.

Mueser, K.T., Rosenberg, S.D., Goodman, L.A. & Trumbetta, S.L. (2002). Trauma, PTSD and the course of severe mental illness: An interactive model. *Schizophrenia Research,* 53, 123–143.

Mueser, K.T., Trumbetta, S.L., Rosenberg, S.D., Vivader R., Goodman, L.B., Osher, F.C., Anciello, A. & Foy, D.W. (1998). Trauma and post-traumatic stress disorder in severe mental illness. *Journal of Consulting and Clinical Psychology,* 66, 493–499.

Murphy, R.T., Rosen, C., Thompson, K., Murray, M. & Rainey, Q. (2004). A readiness to change approach to preventing PTSD treatment failure. In S. Taylor (Ed.), *Advances in the treatment of posttraumatic stress disorder: Cognitive-behavioural perspectives.* New York, NY: Springer.

Mutua, A.D. (Ed.) (2006). *Progressive black masculinities.* London, UK: Routledge.

Myerhoff, B. (1982). Life history among the elderly: Performance, visibility and re-membering. In J. Ruby (Ed.), *A crack in the mirror: Reflexive perspectives in anthropology.* Philadelphia, PA: University of Pennsylvania Press.

Myerhoff, B. (1986). Life not death in Venice: Its second life. In V. Turner and E. Bruner (Eds), *The anthropology of experience.* Chicago, IL: University of Illinios Press.

Ñāṇamoli, B. & Bodhi, B. (1995). *The middle length discourses of the Buddha. A translation of the Majjhima Nikāya. Translated from Pāli by B. Ñāṇamoli and B. Bodhi.* Oxford, UK: The Pāli Text Society and Wisdom Publications.

Nhất Hạnh, T. (2001). *Anger: Buddhist wisdom for cooling the flames.* London, UK: Rider.

Nhất Hạnh, T. (2003). *Creating true peace: Ending conflict in yourself, your family, your community and the world.* London, UK: Rider.

Nichols, M. (1984). *Family therapy: Concepts and methods.* Boston, MA: Allyn & Bacon.

Nutley, S.M., Davies, H.T.O. & Walter, I. (2002). *Evidence based policy and practice: Cross sector lessons from the UK.* Working Paper 9. Glasgow: ESRC UK Centre for Evidence Based Policy and Practice.

Nutley, S.M., Davies, H.T.O. & Walter, I. (2003). Evidence based policy and practice: cross sector lessons from the UK. *Social Policy Journal of New Zealand,* 20(1), 29–48.

Nylund, D. & Nylund, D.A. (2003). Narrative therapy as a counter-hegemonic practice. *Men and Masculinities,* 5(4), 386–394.

O'Hagan, M. (1996). Two accounts of mental distress. In J. Read and J. Reynolds (Eds), *Speaking our minds: An anthology of personal experiences of mental distress and its consequences.* London, UK: Macmillan.

O'Neill, D. & Morgan, M. (2001). Pragmatic post-structuralism (I): Participant observation and discourse in evaluating violence intervention. *Journal of Community and Applied Social Psychology,* 11(4), 263–275.

Offen, L., Waller, G. & Thomas, G. (2003). Is reported child sexual abuse associated with the psychopathological characteristics of patients who experience auditory hallucinations? *Child Abuse & Neglect*, 27(8), 919–927.

Office for National Statistics (2004a). *Social inequalities: Education: exam results differ by social status.* Youth Cohort Study (Department for Education and Skills) and Labour Force Survey (Office for National Statistics 2004). Retrieved December 5, 2008, from www.statistics.gov.uk

Office for National Statistics (2004b). *Social inequalities – Health: Manual workers die earlier than others.* Longitudinal Study, Office for National Statisticsand Census 2001. Retrieved December 5, 2008, from www.statistics.gov.uk

Palazzoli, M.S., Boscolo, L., Cecchin, G. & Prata G. (1980). Hypothesizing–circularity–neutrality: Three guidelines for the conductor of the session. *Family Process*, 19, 3–12.

Papadopoulos, R. (1987). *Adolescents and homecoming.* London, UK: Guild of Pastoral Psychology.

Papadopoulos, R.K. (2000). A matter of shades: Trauma and psychosocial work in Kosovo. In N. Losi (Ed.), *Psychosocial and trauma response in war-torn societies; the case of Kosovo.* Geneva, Switzerland: International Organisation for Migration.

Papadopoulos, R.K. (2001). Refugees, therapists and trauma: Systemic reflections. *Context*, 54 (April), 5–8.

Papadopoulos, R. K. (Ed.) (2002). *Therapeutic care for refugees: No place like home.* London, UK: Karnac Books.

Papadopoulos, R.K. & Hilderbrand, J. (1998). Is home where the heart is? Narratives of oppositional discourses in refugee families. In R. K. Papadopoulos and J. Byng-Hall (Eds.), *Multiple voices: Narratives in systemic family psycho-therapy.* London, UK: Duckworth.

Parker, I. (Ed.) (1999). *Deconstructing psychotherapy.* London, UK: Sage.

Parsons, R. (2006). Troubling language: Re-reading a narrative of trauma from political violence in contemporary Zimbabwe. *International Journal of Critical Psychology*, 17, 29–46.

Patel, N. (2003). Clinical psychology: Reinforcing inequalities or facilitating empowerment? *International Journal of Human Rights*, 7(1), 16–39.

Patel, N. (2008). Rape as torture. *Clinical Psychology Forum*, 192, 12–16.

Patel, N. & Fatimilehin, I. (1999). Racism and mental health. In C. Newnes, G. Holmes and C. Dunn (Eds.), *This is madness: A critical look at psychiatry and the future of mental health services.* Ross-on-Wye, UK: PCCS Books.

Pearce, W.B. (1989). *Communication and the human condition.* Chicago, IL: Chicago University Press.

Pearce, W.B. (1994). *Interpersonal communication: Making social worlds.* New York, NY: HarperCollins.

Pearce, W.B. (2007). *Making social worlds: A communication perspective.* Oxford, UK: Blackwell.

Pearce, W.B. & Cronen, V.E. (1980). *Communication, action and meaning: The creation of social realities.* New York, NY: Praeger.

Pearce, W.B. & Pearce, K.A. (1998). Transcendent storytelling: Abilities for systemic practitioners and their clients. *Human Systems*, 9(3–4), 167–185.

Pearsall, J. (Ed.) (1998). *New Oxford dictionary of English.* Oxford, UK: Oxford University Press.

Peterson, A.L. (2001). Being human: Ethics, environment and our place in the world. London, UK: University of California.

Poston, W. (1990). The biracial identity development model: A needed addition. *Journal of Counseling and Development*, 69, 152–5.

Poulton, R., Caspi, A., Moffitt, T.E., Cannon, M., Murray, R. & Harrington, H. (2000). Children's self-reported psychotic symptoms and adult schizophreniform disorder: A 15-year longitudinal study. *Archives of General Psychiatry*, 57, 1053–1058.

Presley, C.A. (1986). Kikuyu women in the 'Mau Mau' rebellion. In G.Y. Okihiro (Ed.), *In resistance: Studies in African, Caribbean and Afro-American history*. Amherst, MA: University of Massachusetts Press.

Preston, J. (2009). *Whiteness and class in education*. Dordrecht, The Netherlands: Springer.

Prevatt, J. & Park, R. (1989). The Spiritual Emergence Network (SEN). In S. Grof and C. Grof (Eds.), *Spiritual emergency: When personal transformation becomes a crisis*. Los Angeles, CA: Jeremy P Tarcher.

Prevention of Professional Abuse Network (POPAN) (2004). Ten years is too long: proposals for interim public protection measures in the talking therapies. London: POPAN.

Prilleltensky, I. & Nelson, G. (2002). *Doing psychology critically: Making a difference in diverse settings*. London: Palgrave Macmillan.

Prilleltensky, I. (2003). Understanding, resisting, and overcoming oppression: Toward psychopolitical validity. *American Journal of Community Psychology*, 31 (1–2), 195–201.

Prilleltensky, I., Dokecki, P., Frieden, G. & Ota Wang, V. (2007). Counseling for wellness and justice: Foundations and ethical dilemmas. In E. Aldarondo (Ed.), *Advancing social justice through clinical practice*. London: Lawrence Erlbaum associates/publishers.

Proctor, G. (2002). *The dynamics of power in counselling and psychotherapy: Ethics, politics and practice*. Ross-on-Wye, UK: PCCS Books.

Ranger, T. (1986). Resistance in Africa: From nationalist revolt to agrarian protest. In G.Y. Okihiro (Ed.), *In resistance: Studies in African, Caribbean and Afro-American history*. Amherst, MA: University of Massachusetts Press.

Rasheed Ali, S., Flojo, J.R., Chronister, K.M., Hayashino, D., Smiling, Q.R., Torres, D. & McWinto, E. (2005). When racism is reversed: Therapists of colour speak about their experiences with racism from clients, supervisees and supervisors. In M. Rastogi and E. Wieling (Eds.), *Voices of color: First-person accounts of ethnic minority therapists*. London, UK: Sage.

Read, J. & Wallcraft, J. (1992). *Guidelines for empowering users of mental health services*. London, UK: MIND publications and COHSE (Conference of Health Service Employees).

Read, J. (1997). Child abuse and psychosis: a literature review and implications for professional practice. *Professional Psychology: Research and Practice*, 28(5), 448–456.

Read, J. (Ed.) (2001). *Something inside so strong: Strategies for surviving mental distress*. London, UK: Mental Health Foundation.

Read, J., Agar, K., Argyle, N. & Aderhold, V. (2003). Sexual and physical abuse during childhood and adulthood as predictors of hallucinations, delusions and thought disorder. *Psychology and Psychotherapy: Theory, Research and Practice*, 76(1), 1–22.

Read, J., Perry, B.D., Moskowitz, A. & Connolly, J. (2001). The contribution of early traumatic events to schizophrenia in some patients: A traumagenic neurodevelopmental model. *Psychiatry: Interpersonal and Biological Processes*, 64(4), 319–345.

Read, J., van Os, J., Morrison, A.P. & Ross, C.A. (2005). Childhood trauma, psychosis and schizophrenia: A literature review with theoretical and clinical implications. *Acta Psychiatric Scandinavica*, 112(5), 330–350.

Reed, J. & Baker, S. (1996). *Not just sticks and stones: A survey of the stigma, taboos and discrimination experienced by people with mental health problems*. London, UK: MIND Publications.

Reiber, R.W. (Ed.) (1989). *The individual, communication and society: Essays in memory of Gregory Bateson*. New York, NY: Cambridge University Press.

Reinharz, S. (1994). Toward an ethnography of 'voice' and 'silence'. In E.J. Trickett, R.J. Watts and D. Birman (Eds.), *Human diversity: Perspectives on people in context*. San Francisco, CA: Jossey-Bass.

Renoux, M. & Wade, A. (2008). Resistance to violence: A key symptom of chronic mental wellness. *Context*, 97, 2–4.

Repper, J. & Perkins, R. (2003). *Social inclusion and recovery: A model for mental health practice*. London, UK: Baillière Tindall.

Richeport-Haley, M. (1998). Ethnicity in family therapy: A comparison of brief strategic therapy and culture-focused therapy. *American Journal of Family Therapy*, 26(1), 77–90.

Rivett, M. & Street, E. (2003). *Family therapy in focus*. London, UK: Sage.

Roberts, J. (1999). *Tales and transformations: Stories in families and Family Therapy*. New York/London: Norton.

Romme, M.A.J. & Escher, S.D.M. (1989). Hearing voices. *Schizophrenia Bulletin*, 15(2), 209–216.

Romme, M.A.J. & Escher, S.D. M. (1993). *Accepting voices*. London, UK: MIND Publications.

Romme, M.A.J. & Escher, S.D.M. (2000). *Making sense of voices: A guide for professionals working with voice hearers*. London, UK: MIND.

Romme, M.A.J. & Escher, S.D.M. (2006). Trauma and hearing voices. In W. Larkin and A.P. Morrison (Eds.), *Trauma and psychosis: New directions for theory and therapy*. London, UK: Routledge.

Romme, M.A.J., Escher, S.D.M., Dillon, J., Corstens, D. & Morris, M. (2009). *Living with voices*. Ross-on-Wye, UK: PCCS Books in association with Birmingham City University.

Romme, M.A.J., Honig, A., Noorthoorn, O. & Escher, A.D.M.A.C. (1992). Coping with voices: An emancipatory approach. *British Journal of Psychiatry*, 161, 99–103.

Root, M.P.P. (2002). Five mixed race identities: From relic to revolution. In L. Winters and H. DeBose (eds.), *New faces in a changing America: Multiracial identity in the 21st century*. Thousand Oaks, CA: Sage.

Roper-Hall, A. (1998). Working systemically with older people and their families who have 'come to grief'. In P. Sutcliffe, G. Tufnell and U. Cornish (Eds.),

Working with the dying and bereaved: Systemic approaches to therapeutic work. London, UK: Macmillan.

Rose, N. (1985). *The psychological complex.* London, UK: Routledge & Kegan Paul.

Rose, N. (2003). Power and psychological techniques. In Y. Bates and R. House (Eds.), *Ethically challenged professions: Enabling innovation and diversity in psychotherapy and counselling.* Ross-on-Wye, UK: PCCS Books.

Rose, S., Kamin, L. & Lewontin, R.C. (1990). *Not in our genes: Biology, ideology and human nature* (2nd ed.). Harmondsworth, UK: Penguin.

Ross, C.A. & Joshi, S. (1992). Schneiderian symptoms and childhood trauma in the general population. *Comprehensive Psychiatry, 33,* 269–273.

Ruiz, A.S. (1990). Ethnic identity: Crisis and resolution. *Journal of Multicultural Counseling and Development, 18*(1), 29–40.

Russell, G. (2007). Internalised homophobia: Lessons from the Mobius strip. In C. Brown and T. Augusta-Scott (Eds.), *Narrative therapy: Making meaning, making lives.* London, UK: Sage.

Russo, J. (2001). Reclaiming madness. In J. Read (Ed.), *Something inside so strong: Strategies for surviving mental distress.* London, UK: Mental Health Foundation.

Rutter, P. (1989). *Sex in the forbidden zone: When men in power – therapists, doctors, clergy, and others – betray women's trust.* London, UK: Fawcett Balantine.

Rycroft, C. (1995). *A critical dictionary of psychotherapy* (2nd ed.). London, UK: Penguin.

Said, E.W. (1986). *Orientalism reconsidered.* In F. Barker, P. Hulme, M. Iversen and D. Loxley (Eds.), *Literature, politics and theory: Papers from the Essex Conference 1976–84.* London, UK: Methuen.

Sandoval, C. (2000). *Methodology of the oppressed.* London, UK: University of Minnesota Press.

Sands, A. (2003). Seeking professional help. In Y. Bates and R. House (Eds.), *Ethically challenged professions: Enabling innovation and diversity in psychotherapy and counselling.* Ross-on-Wye, UK: PCCS Books.

Sarbin, T.R. (1990). Towards the obsolescence of the schizophrenia hypothesis. *Journal of Mind and Behaviour, 11*(3/4), 259–283.

Sarbin, T.R. (1991). The social construction of schizophrenia. In W. Flack, D. Miller and M. Weiner (Eds.), *What is schizophrenia?* New York, NY: Springer.

Schneider, C.D. (1992). *Shame, exposure and privacy.* New York, NY: Norton.

Scott, J.C. (1985). *Weapons of the weak: Everyday forms of peasant resistance.* New Haven, CT: Yale University Press.

Scott, J.C. (1990). *Domination and the arts of resistance: Hidden transcripts.* New Haven, CT: Yale University Press.

Seikkula, J. (2002). Open dialogues with good and poor outcomes for psychotic crises: Examples from families with violence. *Journal of Marital and Family Therapy, 28,* 263–274.

Selvini, M. & Selvini Palazzoli, M. (1991). Team consultation: An indispensable tool for the progress of knowledge. *Journal of Family Therapy, 13,* 31–52.

Sen, A.K. (1999a). *Commodities and capabilities.* Oxford, UK: Oxford University Press.

Sen, A.K. (1999b). *Development as freedom.* Oxford, UK: Oxford University Press.

Shaner, A. & Eth, S. (1989). Can schizophrenia cause posttraumatic stress disorder? *American Journal of Psychotherapy*, 4, 588–597.

Shaw, K., McFarlane, A. & Bookless, C. (1997). The phenomenology of traumatic reactions to psychotic illness. *Journal of Nervous and Mental Disease*, 185, 434–441.

Shotter, J. (1980). Action, joint action and intentionality. In M. Brenner (Ed.), *The structure of action*. Oxford, UK: Blackwell.

Shotter, J. & Katz, A.M. (1999). Creating relational realities: Responsible responding to poetic 'movements' and 'moments'. In S. McNamee and K. Gergen (Eds.), *Relational responsibility: Resources for sustainable dialogue*. London, UK: Sage.

Sivaraksa, S. (1992). *Seeds of peace: A Buddhist vision for renewing society*. Berkeley, CA: Parallax Press.

Smail, D. (1998). *Taking care: An alternative to therapy*. London, UK: Routledge.

Smail, D. (2005). *Power, interest and psychology. Elements of a social materialist understanding of distress*. Ross-on-Wye, UK: PCCS Books.

Smith, W.A. (1976). *The meaning of conscientizacao: The goal of Paulo Freire's pedagogy*. Amherst, MA: Centre for International Education, University of Massachusetts.

Sorenson, J. (1991). Mass media and discourse on famine in the horn of Africa. *Discourse and Society*, 2, 223–242.

Special Eurobarometer (2008). *Attitudes of European Citizens towards the environment*. Brussels, Belgium: European Commission.

Spinelli, E.D. (1994). *Demystifying therapy*. London, UK: Constable.

Stanton-Salazar, R.D. (2001). *Manufacturing hope and despair*. New York, NY: Teachers College Press.

Steindl-Rast, D. (1984). *Gratefulness. The heart of prayer*. New York, NY: Paulist Press.

Stoltenberg, J. (2000). *Refusing to be a man*. London, UK: Routledge.

Summerfield, D. (1998). The social experience of war and some issues for the humanitarian field. In P.J. Bracken and C. Petty (Eds.), *Rethinking the trauma of war*. London, UK: Free Association Books.

Summerfield, D. (1999a). Sociocultural dimensions of war, conflict, and displacement. In A. Ager (Ed.), *Refugees: Perspectives on the experience of forced migration*. London, UK: Cassell.

Summerfield, D. (1999b). A critique of the seven assumptions behind psychological trauma programmes in war-affected areas. *Social Science and Medicine*, 48, 1449–1462.

Summerfield, D. (2001). The invention of post traumatic stress disorder and the social usefulness of a psychiatric category. *British Medical Journal*, 322, 95–98.

Summerfield, D. (2004). Cross-cultural perspectives on the medicalisation of human suffering. In G. Rosen (Ed.), *Posttraumatic stress disorder: Issues and controversies*. London: Wiley.

Summit, R. (1983). The child abuse accommodation syndrome. *Child Abuse and Neglect*, 7, 177–193.

Taiwo, O. (1999). Reading the colonizer's mind: Lord Lugard and the philosophical foundations of British colonialism. In S.E. Babbitt and S. Campbell (Eds.), *Racism and philosophy*. Ithaca, NY: Cornell University Press.

Taylor, S. (2004). Current directions and challenges in the treatment of post-traumatic stress disorder. In S. Taylor (Ed.), *Advances in the treatment of posttraumatic stress disorder: Cognitive-behavioural perspectives.* New York, NY: Springer.

Taylor, S.E., Klein, L.C., Lewis, B.P., Gruenewald, T.L., Gurung, R.A.R. & Updegraff, J.A. (2000). Biobehavioral responses to stress in females: Tend-and-befriend, not fight-or-flight. *Psychological Review*, 107, 411–429.

Terr, L.C. (1991). Childhood traumas: An outline and overview. *American Journal of Psychiatry*, 148, 10–20.

Thompson, C.E. & Neville, H.A. (1999). Racism, mental health and mental health practice. *Counselling Psychologist*, 27, 155–223.

Tien, A.Y. (1991). Distributions of hallucinations in the population. *Social Psychiatry & Psychiatric Epidemiology*, 26, 287–292.

Todd, N. & Wade, A. (2003). Coming to terms with violence and resistance: From a language of effects to a language of responses. In T. Strong and D. Pare (Eds.), *Furthering talk: Advances in the discursive therapies.* New York, NY: Kluwer Academic Plenum.

Totton, N. (2006). Power in the therapeutic relationship. In N. Totton (Ed.), *The politics of psychotherapy: New perspectives.* Maidenhead, UK: Open University Press.

Trade Union Congress (2001). Labour Force Survey ILO unemployment rates by ethnicity Winter 2000/1. In *27 April 2001 – Black workers deserve better. A TUC Report.* London, UK: Trade Union Congress.

Trade Union Congress (2008). *Closing the gender pay gap: An update report for TUC Women's Conference 2008.* London, UK: Trade Union Congress.

Trickett, E.J. (1996). A future for community psychology: The contexts of diversity and the diversity of contexts. *American Journal of Community Psychology*, 24, 209–229.

Trinder, L. (2000). Introduction: The context of evidence-based practice. In L. Trinder and S. Reynolds (Eds.), *Evidence-based practice: A critical appraisal.* London, UK: Blackwell Science.

Troiden, R.R. (1989). The formation of homosexual identities. *Journal of Homosexuality*, 17(1/2), 43–73.

Tseng, W.-S. & Hsu, J. (1991). *Culture and family: Problems and therapy.* New York, NY: Haworth Press.

Turner, R.P., Lukoff, D., Barnhouse, R.T. & Lu, F.G. (1995). Religious or spiritual problem: A culturally sensitive diagnostic category in the DSM-IV. *Journal of Nervous and Mental Disease*, 183(7), 435–444.

UNDP (2005) *Human Development Report 2005.* New York, NY: UNDP.

Valaskakis, G.G. (1993). Parallel voices: Indians and others – narratives of cultural struggle. *Canadian Journal of Communication*, 18(3), 283–298.

van der Kolk, B.A. (2002). Assessment and treatment of complex PTSD. In R. Yehuda (Ed.), *Treating trauma survivors with PTSD.* Washington, DC: American Psychiatric Publishing.

van der Kolk, B.A., Pelcovitz, D., Roth, S., Mandel, F., McFarlane, A. & Herman, J.L. (1996). Dissociation, somatisation and affect dysregulation: The complexity of adaptation to trauma. *American Journal of Psychiatry*, 153(7), 83–93.

Van Dijk, T.A. (1992). Discourse and the denial of racism. *Discourse and Society*, 3(1), 87–118.

van Wormer, K.S. (2004). *Confronting oppression, restoring justice: From policy analysis to social action.* Alexandria, VA: Council on Social Work Education.

Vera, E.M. & Speight, S.L. (2003). Multicultural competence, social justice, and counseling psychology: Expanding our roles. *The Counseling Psychologist,* 31(3), 253–272.

Vessantara (2006). *The art of meditation: The heart.* Birmingham, UK: Windhorse Publications.

Wade, A. (1997). Small acts of living: Everyday resistance to violence and other forms of oppression. *Contemporary Family Therapy,* 19(1), 23–40.

Wade, A. (2005). *Honouring resistance: A response-based approach to counselling.* Vancouver, Canada: Viewers Guide Stepping Stone Productions.

Wade, A. (2007). Despair, resistance, hope: Response-based therapy with victims of violence. In C. Flaskas, I. McCarthy and J. Sheehan (Eds.), *Hope and despair in narrative and family therapy: Adversity, forgiveness and reconciliation.* London, UK: Routledge.

Wake, I., Wilmot, I., Fairweather, P. & Birkett, J. (1999). *Breaking the chain of hate.* Manchester, UK: National Advisory Group Publications.

Waldegrave, C. (1990). Just therapy. *Dulwich Centre Newsletter,* 1, 5–46.

Waldegrave, C. (2005). 'Just therapy' with families on low income. *Child Welfare,* 84(2), 265–276.

Waldegrave, C. (2009). Cultural, gender and socio-economic contexts in therapeutic and social policy work. *Family Process,* 48(1), 85–101.

Waldegrave, C., Tamasese, K., Tuhaka, F. & Campbell, W. (2003). *Just therapy – A journey: A collection of papers from the just therapy team, New Zealand.* Adelaide, Australia: Dulwich Centre Publications.

Walker, A. (Ed.) (1991). *Thesaurus of psychological terms* (2nd edn.). Arlington, VA: American Psychological Association.

Walker, L.E.A. (1984). *The battered women's syndrome.* New York: Springer.

Walker, L.E.A. (1986). Diagnosis and politics: Abuse disorders. In R. Garfinkel (chair), *The politics of diagnosis: Feminist psychology and the DSM-III-R.* Symposium presented at the conference of the American Psychological Association, Washington, DC.

Watkins, M. & Shulman, H. (2008). *Towards psychologies of liberation.* New York, NY: Palgrave Macmillan.

Watts, R.J., Griffith, D.M. & Abdul-Adil, J. (1999). Sociopolitical development as an antidote for oppression: Theory and action. *American Journal of Community Psychology,* 27(2), 255–272.

Watts, R.J., Williams, N.C. & Jagers, R.J. (2003). Sociopolitical development. *American Journal of Community Psychology,* 31 (1–2), 185–194.

Weinberg, G. (1972). *Society and the healthy homosexual.* New York, NY: St Martin's Press.

Welch, S. (1999). *Sweet dreams in America: Making ethics and spirituality work.* New York, NY: Routledge.

West, C. (1999). Cornel West on heterosexism and transformation. In E. Brandt (Ed.), *Dangerous liaisons: Blacks, gays, and the struggle for equality.* New York, NY: New Press.

Weston, K. (1991). *Families we choose: Lesbians, gays and kinship.* New York: Columbia University Press.

Wexler, P. (1992). *Becoming somebody: Toward a social psychology of school*. Bristol: Falmer Press.

White, M. (1995). *Reauthorising lives: Interviews and essays*. Adelaide, Australia: Dulwich Centre Publications.

White, M. (1997). *Narratives of therapists' lives*. Adelaide, Australia: Dulwich Centre Publications.

White, M. (2004a). *Narrative practice and exotic lives: Resurrecting diversity in everyday life*. Adelaide, Australia: Dulwich Centre Publications.

White, M. (2004b). Working with people who are suffering the consequences of multiple trauma: A narrative perspective. *International Journal of Narrative Therapy and Community Work*, 1, 45–76.

White, M. (2005a). *Workshop notes: Attending to the consequences of trauma* (pp. 19–23). Adelaide, Australia: Dulwich Centre Publications.

White, M. (2005b). *Narrative practice and exotic lives: Resurrecting diversity in everyday life*. Adelaide, Australia: Dulwich Centre Publications.

White, M. & Epston, D. (1990). *Narrative means to therapeutic ends*. New York, NY: W.W. Norton.

Wilkinson, M. (1992). How do we understand empathy systemically? *Journal of Family Therapy*, 14(2), 193–205.

Williams, J. & Watson, G. (1994). Mental health services that empower women: The challenge to clinical psychology. *Clinical Psychology Forum*, 64, 11–17.

Williams-Keeler, L., Milliken, H. & Jones, B. (1994). Psychosis as a precipitating trauma for PTSD: A treatment strategy. *American Journal of Orthopsychiatry*, 64(3), 493–498.

Wilson, J.P., Friedman, M.J. & Lindy, J.D. (Eds.) (2001). *Treating psychological trauma and PTSD*. London, UK: Guilford Press.

World Health Organisation (2004). *International Classification of Diseases* (ICD-10, 2nd ed.). Geneva, Switzerland: WHO.

Wright, L. (1997). *Twins: Genes, environment and the mystery of human identity*. London, UK: Routledge.

Wright, L.M. (1990). Research as a family therapy intervention technique. *Contemporary Family Therapy*, 12, 477–484.

Yehuda, R. (Ed.) (2002). *Treating trauma survivors with PTSD*. Washington, DC: American Psychiatric Publishing.

Index